CW00724268

CRUISING:
COASTWISE
AND BEYOND

CRUISING:
COASTWISE
AND BEYOND
Colin Jarman

NAUTICAL

Copyright © Colin Jarman 1985

All rights reserved. No part of this publication
may be reproduced or transmitted, in any form
or by any means, without permission.

First published 1985 by
NAUTICAL BOOKS
an imprint of Conway Maritime Press Ltd
24 Bride Lane London EC4Y 8DR

ISBN 0 85177 349 4

Typeset by Wyvern Typesetting Ltd, Bristol

Printed in the United Kingdom

By the same author:
Buying a Boat
Deck Seamanship
Knots in Use
Modern Rope Seamanship
Sailing and Boating

Note

Parts of this book are a revision of material that originally appeared in *Coastal Cruising* by
Colin Jarman, published by A. & C. Black.

To Mary, Annie and Barry

All photographs are by Colin Jarman except for those on pages 30, 31, 46, 49, 51, 117, 193 and 216 which are by Jonathan Eastland, and those on pages 264 and 265 which are reproduced by courtesy of *Yachting Monthly*.

Contents

Introduction

Cruising boats and their equipment are evolving all the time and new high standards being set in gear and equipment, particularly electronics, but the basic skills and problems remain pretty much the same and common to all who go to sea in small boats for pleasure. Seamanship is a continuous learning process where every experience can contribute towards your ability as a seaman, making you better able to cope with each successive new or strange situation.

These days great emphasis is rightly placed on safety at sea, both in the design of boats and the provision of the best possible safety equipment – lifejackets, safety harnesses, liferafts, emergency position indicating beacons, and so on – but essentially the safety of a crew is very much down to the skipper's attention to maintaining his craft in a sound, seaworthy condition and instilling in his crew a sense of the need to take care when performing all tasks about the boat. Whatever precautions are taken, however, it is still possible to come unstuck by being caught out in foul weather or having a person go over the side. At such times the skills and techniques that have, hopefully, been practised and learned in better times will see you safely through. A part of that learning, though not the practice, can come from reading such books as this.

It has been my intention throughout the book to offer advice, but in the main to try to promote thought and consideration. You may have found a different and better way of doing something – so be it, I simply offer an alternative. You may disagree with the advice I give; fine, but think about it. Everything here is based on my experience. Not everything is right in every situation, but it is the best I have found.

Good luck and happy cruising, may your skills and enjoyment carry you ever onward, coastwise and beyond.

1

Choosing a cruiser

In recent years, there has been an enormous upsurge in participation in sailing with family cruising very much to the fore. The rapid growth in the number of cruisers requiring moorings and marina berths has put a great strain on those facilities and indeed in some of the more popular boating areas it is extremely difficult to obtain a mooring exactly where one wants it without spending a long time on a lengthy waiting list.

The effect of all this has been to make it essential for prospective boat owners to investigate mooring facilities and the availability of berths in the area where they would like to base their cruiser well before selecting and buying any particular boat. The point here is that it may well be necessary either to accept a mooring that is not your ideal (for example a half-tide mooring rather than a marina berth) or to change your boating base to another harbour that is possibly less conveniently situated for your home. Either of these changes of plan may also mean an alteration in the type of boat you should buy. To take the extreme, it would be daft to buy a boat with a 6 ft (1.83 m) draft if she will only be afloat for an hour either side of high water on a mooring that a bilge-keeler could reach or leave for an extra hour either side of the top of the tide. Whatever anyone may say about the improved performance of a deep-keeled boat over a shoal-draft one, it is not such an improvement that it can compensate for the loss of two hours' sailing each weekend.

Once the mooring possibilities have been investigated, you are in a far better position to decide on the type of boat that is going to suit the kind of sailing you want to do and the waters in which it will be done. For instance, anyone planning to cruise mainly in an area of shoal water, such as the Thames Estuary, may deny himself and his family considerable pleasure if he rushes out and buys a deep-draft boat without first considering a centreboarder, lifting-keel design or bilge-keel boat, any one of which would open up a whole host of delightful and secluded anchorages tucked away at the heads of narrow creeks. On the other hand, if circumstances dictate that you sail the boat on a rugged or exposed coastline, a little estuary cruiser with a drop keel and most of her ballast inside the hull may be the last thing you should be looking for. In such waters a sturdy fin-keeler able to stand up to a blow and claw her way round a rocky headland is much more the order of the day.

If you have plans to do the occasional bit of club racing in between family cruises then you must take a look at what classes are raced in the area you will be keeping the boat and this may be a strong influence on your final choice. It is much easier to join an established fleet than to start a new one. Thus, if a particular design class is the predominant one, you would be well advised to give it serious consideration even if the boat does not meet exactly all your other criteria.

Crew numbers

A very basic point to consider is how many people you expect to have on board at the same time and the numbers of adults and children. After all, it would be very embarrassing to set off for your first weekend and find you have one more crew member than there are berths. Conversely, there is little point in buying an eight-berth boat when the usual crew will be just yourself and one or two others. The question of crew-to-berths ratio will reappear in Chapter 3 when we look at the problems faced by a group of people living together in a rather confined space for any length of time. Let it just be noted now, however, that young children do like to have their own bunks and know that they are theirs to retreat to at any time.

Moorings

There are two types of mooring: those that dry out (often called half-tide moorings) and those that do not; marinas come into the latter category.

In many areas half-tide moorings are the norm and boats using them are only able to get on or off for a few hours either side of high water as they dry out completely at low tide. This is a situation quite alien to yachtsmen based in other areas where moorings are mostly deep-water ones. In these regions of drying moorings it is usually bilge-keelers, centreboarders and lifting-keel boats that predominate as they are able to sit upright (or nearly so) while they patiently wait for each rising tide to lift them off the ground. This is in marked contrast to single-keeled, deeper-draft boats that heel over at most uncomfortable angles when the tide leaves them. Life aboard such craft at low water is virtually intolerable, whereas with the shoal-draft boats it is usually quite acceptable, making a night aboard on your own mooring something to be looked forward to rather than dreaded.

Deep-water moorings are, of course, nice to have, as you are then independent of tide and can come and go as and when you please. If they are single-buoy moorings around which the boat is free to swing, you should also be saved the worry of either another boat chafing alongside, as will happen on 'trot' or 'pile' moorings, or of your own boat rubbing against the pontoon of a marina berth. However many fenders are put out and however well the topsides are protected, a boat does eventually show signs of wear and tear under such mooring conditions.

Trot and pile moorings came into being as the creeks and rivers traditionally dotted with swinging moorings filled up and could take no more boats. In trot moorings boats are moored fore and aft to buoys laid in lines or 'trots', often with two boats alongside each other between the same pair of buoys. Pile moorings are similar, but the buoys are replaced with tall, rigid piles sunk into the riverbed. In both cases the boats must lie with their bows either up- or downstream; they cannot swing to the tide.

These trot and pile moorings made it possible to offer more berths in the popular sailing areas, but as the sport continued to grow it was necessary to devise another way of providing moorings and so the marina was born. Many of these have been dug out of riverside land, but others have been built out from the shore. In both cases boats are provided with a berth alongside or end on to a pontoon or staging so that they always lie heading in one direction. The arrangement, besides packing more boats into a given space, does have the practical advantage that crews can step aboard and load their gear easily without recourse to a dinghy to ferry people and gear out to the boat. One drawback, however, is that the wash of passing craft or the surge set up by a strong blow may set the moored boats rubbing and chafing against their pontoons to the detriment of topsides, fenders and warps. This problem is sometimes even more acute with trot or pile moorings where boats actually lie alongside each other offering the possibilities of rigging and/or guardrails getting tangled up and of fenders jumping out of place leaving the bare hulls to rub together. For these reasons such moorings must be quite well sheltered and owners must take a lot of care when securing their boats.

Trailer sailers

Having just stated that boats have to have moorings, let me now contradict myself and talk about a kind of boat that has been pushed very hard in recent times as being the answer to the problem of lack of moorings: the trailer sailer. One might more accurately term these 'trailerable yachts' and you can forget all visions of ketch-rigged trailers beating in against the ebb to turn into land yachts as the tide recedes. What we are talking about is a breed of light-weight cruising boat with lifting keel that can readily be loaded on to a trailer and towed by an average family car from one spot to another.

The sales pitch for these boats is that the owner does not need a mooring and thus saves a considerable expense. In reality, however, there are very few people in Britain, where good launching sites are few and far between, who are prepared to go through all the struggles and strains of towing to the waterside, launching, sailing, recovering and trailing home again each weekend. In America and Australia it seems that more people are prepared to do this, but in Britain trailer sailers are far more likely to be trailed to the waterside in spring, launched and kept on drying moorings during the season (to make use of their reducible draft to cut mooring costs) and then trailed home for laying up in the winter to cut storage costs. There is nothing wrong with this at all, but it is not what the sales literature often indicates.

Another interesting way of using trailer sailers is to keep them in a dry-land marina. In such establishments boats are kept ashore on individual cradles and when the owner wants to use the boat he telephones the yard and they launch her while he is travelling down from home. After use the boat is brought ashore and returned to her 'berth'. With the extremely high cost of developing conventional marinas this kind of set-up could well become more popular in the future.

Having said all that, some owners do indeed make wider use of the 'trailerability' of their trailer sailers and at least take the boat off to some distant cruising ground, that would otherwise be quite unattainable in the time available to them, for their summer holiday. For example, one could trail from England to the south of France, have a week or so sailing and trail back again, all within a fortnight's holiday period. That would be quite impossible if the boat had to go by sea. Indeed, the combination of the ability to lay up at home (cheaper, easier to work on her and no time wasted in travelling or running home for forgotten tools), a cheaper half-tide mooring and the feasibility of exploring completely new, remote cruising grounds for annual holidays, make trailer sailers extremely attractive craft for many families.

New? Secondhand? DIY?

When you start to think seriously about buying a cruiser, the old question of whether to buy a new or secondhand one soon crops up and on many occasions there is a third option – to build the boat yourself. Almost everyone you ask will give you a different answer, so we will look here at the pros and cons.

Taking new boats first, I would suggest that there are three main points in their favour:

1 Assuming a well-built boat from a respectable company, it is unlikely that there will be any serious trouble with either the structure or the fittings of a new boat in the short term.
2 It may be possible to incorporate some of your own ideas at the building stage. For example, slight alterations to internal layout or rearrangement of control lines or deck gear.
3 You can choose all the gear and equipment to suit your own requirements and pocket.

Set against these points are four disadvantages:

1 The other side of the last 'plus' point, i.e. the extra cost involved in equipping the boat right down to the last fender and sail tier and the knowledge required to do so adequately.
2 A new boat is generally more expensive (when fully equipped) than a comparable secondhand one.

15

3 However high the specification of a new boat, it still takes several seasons to adapt and adjust her for practical cruising – extra lockers to be fitted, cleats moved, extra stowage space for charts and so on.

4 You may not be able to buy a new boat 'off the shelf' and may have to wait a considerable time while she is built, especially if you require small alterations to the standard specification.

Turning to secondhand boats, I think there are five points in their favour and three against them. The good are:

1 You can often get more boat for your money than you would be able to if buying new.

2 The boat should already be fairly well equipped and outfitted.

3 Everything should have been tried and tested in one way or another and more than likely will have been altered if found wanting.

4 The novice has the benefit of someone else's experience in terms of gear, equipment and gadgetry.

5 The boat is available immediately.

The three points against secondhand boats are:

1 You have only the owner's account of the boat's history: how he has handled her, where he has taken her and what sands she has bounced on.

2 You will need to pay for a condition survey of the boat.

3 On an old boat there may well be quite a lot of repair work and replacing of old gear to be done to bring her up to a good seagoing standard, although this should be reflected in a lower price.

Trying to draw any sort of conclusion about this matter is an entirely personal thing, so I will refrain from commenting further. Of course, there is an alternative to buying either new or secondhand and that is to build, though here again you have a choice to make – build from a kit, from scratch or from a bare hull.

A very large number of people choose the do-it-yourself route to owning a cruiser but it is hard work and does take a considerable amount of time. The carrot, of course, is the money saved, but in reality this may not prove to be as much as was first supposed.

Building your own boat, besides being highly satisfying, does leave you fairly free to make modifications as you go, but great care must be taken that any modifications do not affect the structural integrity or ultimate sailing ability of the boat.

With glass fibre the most popular hull material for stock production boats, it is no surprise that most DIY people opt for a GRP hull for home completion. Many builders offer bare mouldings of their boats and various stages of 'kit' in which structural work has been done (hull and deck bonded, main bulkheads in, ballast in and so on) but there is still plenty left for the buyer to do. For this work he can either buy the parts from the builder, usually exactly what is used on the production line, or he can modify and buy elsewhere as he chooses. Good builders, who are sympathetic to the home completer, offer a back-up service for advice and help when problems are met. People do buy sets of plans and start right from scratch to build a cruiser but it is a long and arduous task requiring great confidence in one's own abilities plus a determination to see the job through.

When costing a home completion job it is impossible to account for one's time as this is the main area of saving over buying a completed boat. After all, a production builder may pay a substantially lower price for (say) a mast than the private individual would because the builder is buying several at a time against the one for the DIY man. Thus the actual expenditure on a home building project may not be very much less than the cost of a complete boat. What you have done though is to spread the cost over a period of time and avoided labour charges. It is up to you to decide if this is worthwhile and is what you want to do.

Chartering and crewing

As a newcomer to cruising you may feel (very sensibly) that you would like to get some experience before jumping in with both feet and buying a cruiser. Two courses are open to you – chartering and/ or crewing. Both are excellent ways of putting in some sea time and may also provide the opportunity of trying out one of the boats you are thinking of buying. This last point, coupled with being able to charter in the cruising area you think you would like to keep your boat in, makes chartering a very useful way of gaining experience.

Some yacht clubs maintain a list of people who want to be put in touch with skippers and of skippers who want to find a crew. Those that do not will certainly have a members' noticeboard where you can pin up a card stating that you are available to crew. Do not be put off by the fact that you do not know too much about cruising, but be honest about it. Sailing people are generally a pretty friendly breed and most are only too pleased to help others to learn.

With regard to chartering, you can either look for a firm offering skippered charters, that is one whose boats have a permanent skipper aboard to instruct and look after charterers, which is probably the safest bet if you have little or no cruising experience, or else you can go to a bareboat firm, that is one whose boats are skippered by the charterers themselves and look after yourself. In this case you will probably be required by the charter company to supply some evidence of experience. A very popular charter system, particularly in the Mediterranean, is the flotilla, where a group of boats sail in company with each other led by an escort vessel. This arrangement allows inexperienced families to look after themselves and gain experience in so doing, but at the same time remain under the watchful eye of an experienced flotilla leader who can guide them and sort out problems as they arise.

A proven successful combination of crewing and chartering is offered by the Island Cruising Club of The Island, Salcombe, South Devon, which owns several boats and whose members form their crews under permanent club skippers. The boats range from the schooner *Hoshi* and the beautiful old Brixham trawler *Provident* down through some medium-sized cruisers to dinghies, keel-boats and sailboards of various types. The club can also offer a range of courses leading to RYA qualifications as all their instructors and skippers are RYA approved.

The search begins

Earlier, I tried to point out the relative merits of buying a new or secondhand boat, leaving the final decision to you. Once that choice has been made you can get down to the real business of sorting out what is available. Even if you have decided to build from a bare hull or kit you have to begin by looking for a suitable new, complete boat. Indeed all boats start life as new ones so let us begin there. I suggest that the first thing to do is look through the advertisements in yachting magazines and pick out a handful of possibles. The next move is to write to the builders or distributors (or phone them) for a full specification and price list for each boat. When you receive all the relevant literature, study it carefully and you will probably find that a number of the boats will automatically cross themselves off your list for one reason or another. Having thus reduced the list of likely contenders to say three or four boats, go through the specifications carefully and list all the extra equipment that each will need to put them on a sound seagoing footing. The prices quoted may then look quite different and you may also find your order of preference altered.

If you are intending ultimately to do a home completion job you must also study the literature to see which companies offer the boats in part-built form and what stages are available. Consider, too, what they say about supplying all the bits and pieces for home building.

The list you started off with should now be down to a couple of real possibles and for these you should get in touch with the builders (or distributors) and try to arrange a trial sail. It is very important to try to have a sail on a boat before you buy her, for no matter how glossy the brochure, how attractive the boat looks in some showroom or boat show or how profuse has been the praise of yachting journalists in their magazine reviews, it is a boat in commission that you are interested in and it is only you who can decide whether or not a particular one will ultimately suit you. This is arguably most important if you are going to complete from a bare hull as you have the golden opportunity of rearranging small things that you do not like and it would indeed be heartbreaking to do all that work and then find that you do not really like the boat. Also boats represent a large investment of capital for most of us (or an expensive loan) and as such it would be foolish to sign a cheque, take delivery of the boat and then discover that she is not suitable for you after all.

Incidentally, having mentioned boat reviews in magazines, I think these are useful, despite their inevitable limitations, if only to compare your own judgement with that of someone who is in constant touch with a wide variety of craft.

Going back to secondhand boats, the process is similar in its stages, but somewhat wider ranging. Starting in the same way as for a new boat, a look at the advertisements in magazines may well send you off in search of a particular class of boat. Whether it does or not, the next stage is in fact three steps in one. Assuming that you sail (or hunt for boats) at weekends, you can spend a weekday evening browsing through the classified ads in the backs of one or two yachting magazines to see if there is anything there that sounds at all possible. If so then write off to (or call) the owner and ask him for a full specification and inventory of the boat. At the same time look in the magazine at the brokers' ads and find some in your area who are handling the general type of boat you want. Either send a letter to them stating as precisely as possible the kind of boat you are after, the approximate price you have in mind to pay and so on or, if you prefer, call in and talk to them, leaving the same information.

Besides visiting brokers' offices, the other practical part of the search is a wearying trek round one boatyard after another. The danger is that you will either become totally disillusioned or addicted to poking around under winter covers and peering into engine spaces so that you lose sight of your objective – to *buy* a boat. Beware.

Boat shows too offer an excellent chance to compare different boats. You can examine one and quickly hop on to the next with the first still fresh in your mind and you can also ask questions of the builder directly. There are often price reductions available as well, but as already mentioned, beware of buying a boat without having sailed her. Conditions in shows are quite different from those at sea.

Construction certificates

All boat buyers want to have some sort of reassurance that they are investing their money in a sound and seaworthy boat. A first-class indicator of her original construction is one of the certificates or notes issued by Lloyd's Register, of which the ultimate accolade is the +100A1 classification.

Any boat carrying that classification has been supervised by a Lloyd's surveyor throughout. The plans were approved first, then the materials, workmanship and working conditions were all accepted and the entire construction and fitting out was carried on under supervision. One of the requirements made by Lloyd's is that yachts given the +100A1 classification must be surveyed periodically by Lloyd's surveyors to ensure that they are being maintained to the highest standard. Thus a secondhand boat still 'in class' is one that you can be pretty happy about buying.

When it is not intended to submit the boat to these regular surveys, the highest classification available is the Lloyd's Register Building Certificate (LRBC). This certificate still covers the construction of the hull, deck and superstructure, rudder and stern gear, installation of engine and its associated gear, fuel, pumping and fire protection systems, electrical circuits and battery arrangements. The certificate is also only issued after satisfactory running trials.

A more common certificate among series production boats is the Hull Construction Certificate (HCC) for which, after approval of the plans, a Lloyd's surveyor watches over the construction of the hull, deck and superstructure, any integral tanks, the rudder and steering gear, fitting of the ballast, attachment of chainplates, installation of windows, engine bearers and bulkheads. Several builders obtain this certificate as standard for their boats and offer buyers the option (at an extra charge) of obtaining for them the LRBC for which the HCC is a prelude.

Finally Lloyd's Register offer the Hull Moulding Note (HMN), which is not actually a certificate but is a valuable document covering an unfinished hull passing from a moulding contractor to a finishing yard or from a hull moulder to a do-it-yourself home builder. It is the first stage in any of Lloyd's Register's other certificates and generally covers the hull and deck mouldings together with their related stiffening and supporting structures such as bulkheads. It provides a basic assurance about the structure and gives the moulder the chance to advise whoever is finishing the construction of any items to be fitted before the craft can be considered structurally complete. For the home boat builder this is just as valuable a document as the full ⊦ 100A1 or LRBC for anyone buying a complete boat.

A similar certificate, called the Minimum Structural Kit Acceptance Certificate, is issued by the Ship and Boat Builders National Federation (SBBNF). Designed to ensure that the customer buying a kit or bare mouldings for home completion gets a sound structure to begin with, the Certificate is split into two sections, A and B. A deals with the strength and integrity of the mouldings, covering structural items that should be completed by the manufacturer before the kit leaves his factory and B warns the home builder what further items must be completed in the manner intended by the designer to ensure the intended strength and integrity of the whole boat. The SBBNF strongly recommends buyers to have as many items in section B as possible done by the manufacturer. This, like the HMN, is a valuable document for the home builder.

All of these certificates apply to the *building* of the boat. Just because the boat was built to a high standard it unfortunately does not necessarily follow that she will still be in good condition when she is put on the secondhand market (unless she was built to

Sandblasting the bottom of an osmosis-riddled glass-fibre cruiser. This process strips off the affected material allowing the surface to be rebuilt with epoxy fillers and painted over to be, in many cases, better than new.

Osmosis has become one of the great worries for owners of glass-fibre boats. This is a severe case where the blisters have been burst and are being sandblasted so that repairs can be made. In virtually all cases repairs can be made, but it is obviously easier the earlier trouble is caught.

+100A1 and has been maintained in class), so it is always wise to get an up-to-date condition survey report before buying.

Surveys

Though the seller of a secondhand boat may tell you in all good faith that his boat is sweet and sound, he may be completely ignorant of some small, but serious, defect. It is, therefore, in your best interest to call upon the services of a professional yacht surveyor to inspect your chosen boat and to report on her condition before you actually buy her. The usual practice is for the potential buyer to make an offer for the boat 'subject to survey' and if this is accepted, he agrees to pay the cost of having the boat slipped, opened up, surveyed and returned to her original condition in the event of his deciding not to buy. On receipt of the surveyor's report, the buyer can present a list of defects and necessary work to the owner and they can try again to reach agreement on the price. This usually means a lowering of the price so that the buyer can have the faults put right without spending too much over the previously agreed figure. Of course, anything already used as a bargaining point is excluded from these subsequent hagglings.

The kinds of problem the surveyor will be looking for are structural damage, osmotic blistering on glass-fibre hulls, rot in wooden ones, excessive rust and electrolysis in steel or aluminium ones, inadequate or unsound fittings and equipment and poor repair work of any kind. He will also give a general assessment of the condition of all the sails, spars, rigging and so forth if they are available for his inspection. If so instructed or authorized he may request the removal of some keelbolts in an older boat to see what their condition is. He may, of course, be unable to examine certain things – for example, the masthead fittings if the mast is still stepped – but these should be specified in his report. He will also not report on engines and machinery unless specifically requested to do so and unless he is able to give them a proper trial, which is often impossible, particularly with the boat laid up ashore. A good surveyor will also stop his survey and contact the prospective buyer for new instructions if he comes across some unsuspected but major defect that would make the boat unsafe.

Naturally a surveyor's expertise and sheer hard work do not come particularly cheaply, but when weighed against the overall cost of the boat his fees are not exorbitant. Think how many thousands of pounds he could be saving you if he discovers something serious.

A lot of surveyors advertise for business in the classified ads sections of yachting magazines. Many of them are members of the Yacht Brokers, Designers and Surveyors Association (YBDSA) of Wheel House, 5 Station Road, Liphook, Hampshire GU30 7DW (Tel. 0428 722322), an organization which sets high professional standards for its members and lays down scales of charges. Non-membership does not mean a surveyor is no good, but membership does give an assurance of his professional standing. A list of members is available from the Association's offices or they can give you the names of members in the area you need and, incidentally, it does make sense to find one who lives reasonably close to where the boat is lying as the travelling costs (at least) will be lower.

Finance

Many people do pay for their boats out of savings, but even more people have to obtain a loan of some sort. For these people there are three main types of loan scheme: marine mortgage, hire-purchase and personal loan.

To obtain a marine mortgage (usually for up to 75 or 80 per cent of the purchase price) the boat to be mortgaged must be registered as a British ship through the Registrar of British Ships. The mortgage will not be recorded on her Certificate of Registry, but is noted by the Registrar and is consequently a loan method favoured by finance houses as it gives them precedence over other creditors should the owner of the boat fall into debt and be declared bankrupt.

Most mortgages are for five years, but periods of seven or ten years may also be available, usually depending upon the size of the loan. Interest may be calculated and paid in one of two ways: either capital is repaid in equal monthly instalments with interest paid quarterly in arrears, the interest being calculated on the outstanding capital balance at the rate of interest in force at the time, or the capital and interest are paid together in predetermined equal monthly instalments.

The former system can give the boat buyer a few nasty shocks as he will never know exactly how much the bill for the last quarter's interest will be since it is calculated according to a variable rate known as the Finance House Base Rate (FHBR). The finance houses determine this rate each month and if it goes up, so will your interest bill. With the second scheme the likely average rate is guessed at by the finance house and you know exactly how much you will have to pay monthly but not exactly how many months you will have to pay it for. If the rate fell dramatically during the mortgage period you would pay everything off in a shorter time than expected, but if it rose sharply it would take longer to pay off. Both methods leave an element of doubt, but for those with a tight budget the second system makes life much easier.

Hire-purchase is not particularly common on boats and is only available on quite small craft. The hire-purchase company actually owns the boat throughout the term of the agreement, the user only hiring her from them until he pays a nominal amount at the end of the agreement to buy the boat from them. The hirer can, of course, sell the boat before the end of the agreement, paying the finance company a settlement figure that they determine.

Finally there is the personal loan, which is also for relatively small sums of money. On these loans the interest is calculated at a flat rate for the whole period of the loan and is added to the amount borrowed then divided into monthly payments. Thus the borrower knows exactly how much he will have to pay each month and for how many months he will have to pay it. If interest rates fall much during the loan period this system works against you, but if they rise significantly then you win. It is something of a gamble but it does help budgeting.

Above all, do not try to get a loan that is larger than you are going to be able to pay comfortably. It will be a constant headache and will leave you short of funds for actually running and using the boat. It will reduce your enjoyment of sailing enormously.

Deposits and receipts

When the purchase of a boat is agreed subject to a satisfactory survey, the buyer gives the vendor or the broker a deposit (say 10 per cent) and for this he must receive a clear receipt stating that it is a refundable deposit that will be returned (minus any costs of restoring the boat after the survey) in the event of the sale falling through. The YBDSA can supply suitable forms or they may be had from the broker. Do get one properly completed and signed as it can save a lot of nastiness later.

Bills of Sale

These too are trouble savers. The exchange of Bills of Sale is compulsory for a registered boat but is advisable as proof of change of ownership on all boats. Bills of Sale are available from HM Customs and Excise, Forms Office, Kings Beam House, Mark Lane, London EC3, or from the local registrar of ships.

If the boat you are buying is registered, you will have to re-register her in your own name. To do this, you have to get a Bill of Sale from the registered owner, who also completes a declaration of ownership for the Registrar of his home port. On receipt of the boat's British registry papers, the Bill of Sale and the declaration of ownership (together with the current fee), the Registrar will re-register the boat in your name. When buying the boat with a marine mortgage it is likely that the finance house will do much of the paperwork for you and that makes life a lot easier.

Class owners' associations

As a source of information and friendly advice about a particular class of boat you can not do better than to contact other owners by way of the class owners' association, if one exists. The members of these associations are, after all, the people who own and use the class of boat and know far more about them than can ever be learned by a brief visit to the builder or a demonstration sail. Both of these are very valuable when choosing a boat, but prolonged contact, gained through ownership, must inevitably help one to discover a boat's true character and features – and faults.

The boat's builder or designer will usually be able to put you in touch with the secretary of the owners' association.

2

Types of cruiser

There are roughly seven separate categories of sailing cruiser, namely estuary cruisers (the smallest), coastal cruisers, trailer sailers, multihulls, motorsailers, cruiser/racers and offshore cruisers. Each of these types is planned with particular conditions of use in mind, although these may overlap to a considerable extent in some cases. Provided that the owner limits his use accordingly, his boat should fulfil her role satisfactorily.

Estuary cruisers

These boats are intended for pottering round the relatively sheltered waters of river estuaries. Their shallow draft, normally provided by a centreplate or small bilge keels, makes them ideal for working right up to the head of a creek and lying there in comfortable seclusion, while their accommodation is somewhat spartan and suitable only for overnighting. Being relatively small and cheap, they are the starting point for many people and can form the transition from dinghy sailing to cruising.

To call estuary cruisers overgrown dinghies or dinghies with lids on is in no way derogatory for this is more or less what they are. In many cases much of the ballast is internal and the crew has to sit to windward when the boat is closehauled or hard pressed. Unlike a dinghy, however, they are self-righting (or certainly should be, particularly if designed to Micro Cup rules) though a knockdown in an estuary is very rare.

The small size and light displacement of an estuary cruiser or Micro Cupper makes her ideal for trailer sailing. They are easy to load on to a trailer, they require only a small family car to tow them and launching is no great physical problem and may even be managed singlehanded with practice.

While an estuary cruiser is better equipped to sail in choppy conditions than a dinghy, she is still in no way suitable for long open water passages. True, a few such craft have made spectacular long-distance voyages, but these have usually been made after much preparation by highly experienced sailors. They definitely should not be emulated lightly.

Trailer sailers

While many of the small estuary cruisers are well suited to trailer sailing, most of the modern boats sold as trailer sailers are somewhat bigger, designed with more open water coastal cruising in mind. They generally have lifting keels as opposed to unballasted centreplates and many have purpose-designed road-cum-launching trailers. They need a rather larger family car to tow them and launching and recovery is made much easier by the presence of more than one able person.

The majority of trailer sailers are taken away from the water only for winter storage and summer holidays, spending the main part of the season on drying moorings. This system can be very satisfactory as the cost of winter storage is reduced if not entirely eliminated, mooring expenses are kept to a minimum and there is the opportunity of holiday sailing in waters beyond the normal cruising range.

Coastal cruisers

Coastal cruisers are somewhat larger than estuary cruisers and are designed to give the crew a little more space and comfort as well as being capable of more extended passage-making. The cabin is big enough to include a proper galley and sink and the toilet is usually installed in a separate compartment, though it may sometimes be screened off simply by a curtain if it is installed between the forward berths. The extra few feet in overall length make a surprising difference to the amount of accommodation space available. Whereas a 16-footer (4.75 m) can really only be used overnight, an 18- or 19-footer (5.5 m) is tolerable for a week or more and 20–22 ft (6–6.75 m) of overall length gives the crew very reasonable living space.

Apart from the larger types of trailer sailer, coastal cruisers usually have fixed keels in the form of either a single fin or a pair of bilge keels. Older craft may have a full keel with the rudder hung on

An example of the Wharram range of catamarans designed for home construction, mainly using plywood for the hulls and decks with timber cross beams. Accommodation is strictly limited and is in each hull with a platform providing the connection with the other hull. Wharram cats have made many remarkable cruises all over the world and have gained a reputation as safe seagoing cruising boats *if properly and strongly constructed.* Unfortunately there have been a number of disasters involving inadequately built boats.

its after end. In all cases the major part of the boat's ballast is carried outside the hull in whatever keel is fitted. A greater spread of sail is carried than on an estuary cruiser and the overall sailing and seakeeping performance is greatly improved. The weather must still be carefully considered, but open water on a coastal passage should not be a problem.

Small multihulls

Perhaps the greatest attraction of a multihull is her speed off the wind and consequent potential for longer passages in a given time, followed a close second by the often palatial accommodation achieved in many catamarans. Although the cruising multihull is considerably heavier than a racing one, they do still have this ability to bear away and go tearing off on a reach, much to the consternation of some monohull sailors.

In comparison with a monohull the multi also heels very little, making her attractive for sailing with youngsters or unsure spouses. It is a strange sensation for anyone used to monohull sailing, because as the wind gusts, instead of laying over to it, the boat just accelerates.

One drawback with multihulls is the fact that they are just as stable upsidedown as the right way up. In other words, in the thankfully remote possibility of a cruising multihull capsizing, she will remain inverted, unlike the knocked down monohull that will right herself. The answer is, of course, not to capsize and indeed it is extremely rare for a *cruising* multihull to be turned over, particularly on coastal or short sea passages of the type we are interested in in this book. The possibility is there, however, and the prudent owner will temper his assessment of wind and sea state accordingly when deciding if it is time to reef or stay in port.

One further problem is that many harbour and port authorities

A fin keel may have the performance edge over bilge keels, but when it comes to drying out for a scrub the fin keeler needs a post to lean against while the bilge keeler can stand on her own. However, cleaning and painting between the bilge keels is not a nice job. Special care not to upset the balance must be taken if you have to board a dried-out fin keeler. A bilge keeler usually allows movement all round her decks.

make higher berthing charges for multihulls than they do for equivalent length monohulls on the grounds that they take up twice as much room athwartships.

Motorsailers

As their name implies, motorsailers are boats with performance under either sail or power and indeed sail and power together. They have found favour with two entirely different groups of people. The first is the couple whose children have grown up and left home and who feel that they want to be able to start the motor knowing that it has the power to take them into both wind and tide without too much effort on their part. At the other end of the scale there are the young couples whose children are too small to be of much help in working the boat and who take up rather a lot of their mother's time and attention, leaving father on his own.

Motorsailers have frequently been referred to as 50/50s when describing their motoring and sailing roles, but it is not really a description of what is wanted from them. It would be better to call them (and design them to be) 100/100s, that is, with full capabilities under sail and the same under power. Too often in the past they have been either motor cruisers with a little steadying sail or else sailing cruisers with a big engine. Nowadays things are often more happily arranged and there are some very good motorsailers about that offer good performance while also protecting the crew with sheltered steering positions.

Cruiser/racers

In much the same way as motorsailers are a combination of the conflicting requirements of a sailing cruiser and a motor boat, so the boats described as cruiser/racers are a compromise between out and out racing design requirements and strictures and the needs of a cruising boat. A successful racing boat has to be designed to meet the relevant rating or measurement rule and to be sailed as fast and hard as her crew is able. To this end accommodation is spartan with more attention being paid to how well the crew can work on deck than how comfortable they are below. They often also have rigs that need much adjusting and careful attention. On the other hand, a cruiser is intended to take her crew from port to port quickly, but without overtiring or straining them and at the same time provide them with comfortable living quarters. Her rig should not need such expert control and she should be easily worked by only part of the full crew. Thus the requirements are largely conflicting and the successful racing design given a different keel and better accommodation and called a cruiser/racer is not always a very good cruising boat. It is a very fine balance that can be achieved but is not always.

Offshore cruisers

Trying to define an offshore cruiser as opposed to a coastal cruiser is not easy. The majority of larger coastal cruisers are suitable for offshore work provided that they have good, strong rigging and all their gear and equipment is up to scratch. These boats need to be capable of staying at sea in bad weather and even of clawing their way to windward against a rising gale in order to put some sea room between themselves and the land. It takes courage to bash *away* from a harbour knowing that you are in for a real buster and any boat intended for cruising in deep waters has to inspire sufficient confidence in her crew to allow them to do just that.

3

Cruiser design

The design of a small cruiser is like a three-dimensional jigsaw puzzle where all the pieces have variable shapes. From the hull inwards, the designer is faced with an incredible number of variables including such vital decisions as how many berths and what facilities to provide. Should he go for four berths and a tiny galley, or three berths and more living room, or even three berths, a galley and a fully enclosed toilet compartment? Designers now seem to be veering away from the idea of cramming in as many berths as possible and tending towards the reality that those on board have to be able to live in reasonable comfort – a trend that must be welcomed.

Fortunately the mathematics of yacht design is not our concern here as we are only interested in the end product, but the main features should be studied with an eye to how they affect our choice of boat.

Liveability

Since we sail for fun, it is only reasonable to expect a comfortable, if basic, standard of living on board our boats. I do not mean that every 18-footer (5.5 m) should have reclining armchairs and deep pile carpets throughout, but there should be a full length bunk for each member of the crew and adequate cooking and toilet facilities.

Bunks present quite a problem for the designer because they have to fulfil two roles: they have to be right for sleeping in comfortably and securely, while also usually having to be comfortable for sitting on. The two requirements are not quite mutually exclusive, but to combine them effectively is by no means an easy task for the designer.

The first requirement for a good seagoing berth is for it to be narrow enough not to allow the occupant to slide about as the boat moves in a seaway. At the head the bunk need not be much more than the width of a man's shoulders, while at the foot it can be half that. This means that the occupant must sleep more or less straight out (i.e. not curled up), but a berth that is too wide, allowing the person to roll about in it as the boat rides each wave, is a sure way to insomnia. The other requirement is that each berth should be fitted with some form of leeboard or cloth (sometimes called bunkboards or bunkcloths) to hold the sleeper in place if his is an 'uphill' bunk or the boat is moving violently. Opinions vary as to whether boards or cloths are better and it boils down to personal preference. Both stow conveniently out of the way under the berth cushions when not in use.

The problem with bunks as described above is that they are too narrow for use as comfortable seats and it is for this reason that most yacht bunks, where they are required to double as settees, are made wider than necessary for sleeping. It is an area of compromise for the designer who has to balance the two conflicting requirements. However, where the bunk does not have a dual function, the foregoing does provide a comfortable berth.

Generally speaking, bunks have either GRP (glass fibre) or plywood bases and between 2 in and 4 in (5–10 cm) thick foam rubber mattresses covered in either PVC or some easily cleaned fabric. Because this is the general pattern of things, it does not necessarily mean that it is the best idea. Much greater comfort can be achieved by having a canvas or rubber webbing base with a very thin mattress that is about $1\frac{1}{2}$ times the width of the bunk. This wide mattress can then be laid either up the ship's side (if that is to leeward) or up against the leecloth if that is on the downhill side. Such an arrangement allows you to sleep, whatever the boat's antics, in a protective trough, without having to lash yourself to the bookshelf or brace yourself against each and every lurch.

Although it seems daft in a way not to make use of all the available berths, life on board can often be greatly improved over the period of a one or two week cruise by reducing the crew-to-berths ratio. By taking, say, three people on a four-berth boat. This leaves more space for everyone and means that there is a choice of bunks for anyone coming off watch during a night passage. This principle applies to any boat in our size range and for anything more than a weekend cruise, often making a big difference to comfort and tempers, thus making a successful holiday out of what could

Quite a well-planned galley with a safety bar across the front of the cooker, which has adjustable pot clamps and is hung in lockable gimbals. There is pressurized hot and cold water to the sink, good work tops and storage space, but it would be difficult to clean crumbs and other debris from the work tops as the fiddles are not cut away in the corners. It would be nice also to see a belt for the cook or a bar across the entrance to the galley that he or she could lean back on when the boat's heeled to port. It is difficult to know what else to do with the space, but lockers outboard of the cooker are never a good idea as the cook has to reach over the hot stove and pans to reach them.

otherwise be a miserable disaster. This, of course, goes back to my earlier point about designers not cramming in more berths than the boat can really cope with.

On a very small cruiser undertaking a short sea passage, cooking may be little more than heating up the occasional can of soup or boiling a kettle, but for larger boats there are many excellent little stoves with a couple of burners, a grill and even an oven on more sophisticated models. These make shore-style cooking quite feasible, but even so there are plenty of ways to make the seagoing cook's life easier and safer. For example, the stove can be fitted with gimbals and surrounded by fiddle rails. The gimbals are a form of swinging bracket or mount that allows the stove to remain upright and level while the boat rolls or is heeled hard over. The fiddle rails consist of a metal 'fence' all round the stove to stop pots and pans sliding off. There may also be adjustable clamps running across the top of the stove to hold the saucepans exactly over the burner.

Fiddle rails are a definite asset on a gimballed stove, but on a fixed cooker they are essential if accidents are to be avoided. This is doubly true if there are young children on board who may reach for a saucepan handle to see what is cooking. Gimbals should have their pivots on a level with the burners, since if they are any distance above that the stove acts like a pendulum rather than a seesaw and whatever is on top is likely to be thrown off. It is also useful when moored in a quiet spot to have a method of fixing the stove so that it does not swing. This need only be a bolt or latch, but some are able to be lifted from their gimbals to stand on their bases.

Galley arrangements vary enormously and so too do their positions in the boat. In this cne the cooker can swing in its gimbals or be lowered to stand firm on the base when in a quiet harbour. There is provision for a cook's safety belt, but a 'crash bar' across the front of the cooker would be a good idea. On the right of the stove is a work top with a lid giving access to an icebox, while on the left are twin stainless steel sinks with a hinged cover that flaps outwards for extra standing area; a fiddle round this would help to stop things sliding off. A foot pump provides water at the sink faucet. In any galley using butane or propane gas it is sensible to arrange bottle stowage within easy reach of the galley or the main hatchway to encourage the cook to turn the gas off at the bottle when it is finished with. The cooker taps alone should not be relied on and the bottles must be kept in a locker that drains overboard not into the boat as gas is heavier than air.

In any case there should be a 'crash bar' across the front of the cooker space to prevent the cook being thrown on to the stove. Some people also provide their cooks with a hip-level canvas belt hooked across the galley providing a comfortable brace on either tack. On one tack the cook leans into the belt and on the other, with it across behind him, he leans back on it. In both cases he has his hands free to hold on or work.

The majority of cruisers are fitted with cooking stoves fuelled by propane or butane gas sold under the trade names Calor, Gaz, Butagas and so on. This has the convenience of domestic gas in that you simply turn the supply on and light it at the burner, but it has the drawback of being heavier than air so that any that is leaked will collect in the bilges and form a potentially dangerous gas/air explosive mixture. There have been many nasty accidents where a stray spark has ignited such an accumulation and it must be guarded against with utmost care. Piping for bottled gas must be installed with care using piping to British Standard and the locker where the bottles are held must be drained overboard above the waterline.

Some people do still prefer to cook on either paraffin or alcohol stoves because of the universal availability of paraffin, but pressurized paraffin stoves have to be preheated and flare-ups are not uncommon, although they are avoidable with care. Non-pressurized alcohol stoves tend to be rather slow in operation, but are usually much cheaper than other units.

Few small cruisers these days retain the 'bucket and chuck it' toilet arrangement, despite its being totally reliable, most having either a full-blown sea toilet or else one of the neat, modern chemical toilets. Although many people are rather touchy about the subject of toilets, in the confines of a small family cruiser they are a problem difficult to ignore. The widespread provision of enclosed toilet compartments has assisted in some respects, but good ventilation is essential and temporary deafness on the part of the crew is often desirable.

If treated correctly, in accordance with manufacturer's recommended procedures, the modern sea toilet is a good reliable product, but it is essential to impress upon crew members that there are certain non-effluent items they must not try to flush through. Chemical toilets too have come a long way in recent years and are clean and convenient, whether they are the open top variety or the water flush type. In either case they do have to be emptied regularly, but the chemicals used in them break down and deodorize matter most effectively, reducing the unpleasantness of the task greatly.

Keeping clothes, bedding and other gear dry, protecting them against damp and condensation, is no mean feat on a small boat. Very big plastic bags, such as those used for lining dustbins, will usually take all the clothes you want and they can be pushed down into lockers where they serve the dual purpose of keeping everything dry but also keeping it together. Similarly bedding can be stored in them during the day quite neatly, but in both cases whatever is put into the bag must be dry in the first place or it will grow mildew. These plastic bags are also very useful for hanging up in the companionway as splash flaps for the quarter berth, whose occupant may otherwise suffer a drenching with rain or spray each time the hatch is opened in poor weather.

Some manufacturers of sailing cloths produce special protective covers for jackets, dresses and other clothing, designed to go in hanging lockers. They keep the clothing dry and additionally take the chafe that the clothes might otherwise suffer as they swing to the roll of the boat.

The old adage of a place for everything and everything in its place is totally applicable on a small cruiser, but there is one deviation from this. It is a good thing, psychologically speaking, for each crew member to have one locker where he can dump his gear in any sort of a jumble he likes – a small area he can call his own and which no one else will touch. This used to be a man's bunk, where he could leave things and know they would not be disturbed, but on modern boats with bunks of necessity doubling as settees, this is rarely possible and so allocation of a private locker is a good idea.

Workability

Although there are several people on board, the family skipper is very often sailing his boat singlehanded. At sea, a husband and wife may have to sail watch and watch about if their children are too young or inexperienced to take their spells. Similarly, at times when a crew might be very useful, such as when getting underway or picking up a mooring, a mother may have to look after the children and keep them out of the skipper's way. Consequently the family cruiser needs to be set up carefully to make her convenient for singlehanding and the skipper must have thought out a plan of campaign.

A CQR anchor securely stowed in deck chocks. It is arranged to take up as little foredeck space as possible, but even so it would be far better to put it in a well-designed anchor well with a hatch over it to clear the deck entirely.

The deck and its associated hardware is a prime example of an area on a boat where thought can make working so much easier. Primarily it might be said that the deck is provided to give protection to offwatch crew members and to enclose the living accommodation, also in many cases to provide a step for the mast, but beyond that it is a platform from which to work the boat. Certain fittings have to clutter it up: the forehatch is desirable if only as a second means of escaping from the cabin and a certain number of cleats, fairleads and so on are needed, though these can be placed so as not to cause inconvenience. A samson post – a strong post passing through the deck and down to the keel – used to be stuck in the centre of the foredeck as a point for fastening the anchor cable or mooring lines, but this has generally been superseded by a big cleat through-bolted to a heavy back-up plate, often placed near the toerail (with perhaps a twin on the other side) to leave space centrally for the hatch of an anchor stowage well.

This removal of the stowed anchor from the deck into a covered well, large enough to accept both anchor and cable easily, at first seems a small development in yacht design but truly it can be said to have been of enormous significance. Sails no longer get ripped on the deck-stowed anchor, shins retain their skin and toes are left unbroken. The anchor must be lashed down in the well to stop it jumping about and causing structural damage in heavy seas, but certainly the anchor well is a splendid idea. It is unfortunate, therefore, that all too often the locker lid is poorly designed. In some cases the lid is completely free to fall overboard unless a retaining line is fitted by the owner (none having been provided by the builder), in others the lid can only be opened or closed once the anchor is set by hauling in some slack on the cable which passes directly over the lid from cleat to bow roller, and so the list goes on.

Care and attention to detail at the boat's design stage will circumvent most of these problems, leaving what is wanted: a deck area where you can stand, sit or kneel to work, depending on the prevailing conditions.

The majority of production boats require a crew member to go forward to the mast to hoist or lower sail as the halyards have their winches and cleats fitted to the lower part of the mast. If you look round at boats specially developed for singlehanded sailing, however, you will find that many lead their halyards aft to the cockpit with winches and cleats on the cabin top. This allows the work to be done from a much more secure position than the bucking deck of a small cruiser. Equally, it is only sensible on a small boat to place the sheet winches and cleats within reach of the helmsman so that he can trim them without leaving the tiller.

Sometimes it is necessary to leave the helm, whether to look at the chart, make a check on the lashings of some item up forward, stop something chafing, make a cup of tea or just to call the next watch. In any of these circumstances some way of keeping the boat on course

One of the better features of a modern cruiser can be the anchor well. This locker keeps the anchor and cable handy but separated from the accommodation and off the deck. The operative word though is 'can' as they can equally well be a real nuisance. This one is all right as there is a catch to hold the lid closed, hinges so that it can open without falling overboard, an exit moulding so that it can be shut with the cable led out and with the samson post sited ahead of the locker the lid can be opened without having to hold the cable aside. It would be improved with the fitting of anchor chocks or some way of securing the anchor within the locker.

Another useful feature of anchor wells. The sail has been bundled in it and the foredeck hand is sitting comfortably and safely preparing it for hoisting. Note the sensible use too of a lifeharness.

is required. Provided the boat can be balanced adequately it is usually enough to lash the tiller so that the boat sails herself, but the increased use of reasonably priced clip-on autopilots has made a world of difference. These powerful units that consume remarkably little in the way of battery power, can usually be rigged either to steer a course relative to the wind or a set compass course.

The advantage of these electronic units over wind-operated vane self-steering gears lies in their ability to steer the boat on a constant heading rather than on a course relative to the wind. This makes them suitable for use under power or when running up a very narrow channel. They do not relieve the person on watch of his watch-keeping duties, they are totally blind, deaf and dumb, but used sensibly they make the standing of a long watch much more tolerable and do give the watchkeeper the freedom he needs to work the ship, fetch a drink or whatever.

Wind vane gears can also give freedom from the helm, but are for use in more open waters where a sudden shift in wind direction and consequent change of course will not lead to a frantic dash for the helm to avoid trouble. Vane gears too are more cumbersome units than the clip-on pilots and are more complicated to install, besides being nearly permanent fixtures projecting over the stern. The small autopilots are simple to fit, sit neatly in the cockpit and can be removed and stowed in a trice. Unfortunately like all electronics they are operating in a hostile environment and if anything goes wrong it is a case of back to the factory, whereas a vane gear can often be repaired at sea.

Both types of self-steering gear are well worth considering if any shorthanded sailing is to be undertaken as they do provide useful relief from the helm and so conserve energies that may be needed at a later stage of the voyage. Even on quite short passages this is true and it becomes even more so when talking about going abroad or on longer overnight coastal passages.

A further requirement for practical family cruising is a simple and effective reefing system and much progress has been made in this area of sail handling during the last few years. So far as mainsails are concerned there has been a move away from roller reefing, where the mainsail rolls down round the boom, towards the slab or jiffy reefing systems. In these, a cringle in the luff is slipped over a hook on the gooseneck and a line through another cringle in the leech is used to haul it down to the boom and to apply outward tension to the new foot of the sail. Modern sailcloths have made it possible to apply this tension where in the olden days of points reefing the sailcloth could not handle it. Similarly, the strength of modern cloths obviates the need for any intermediate reef points other than to neaten up the loose bunt of the sail.

Round the boom roller reefing is still used, but it has lost favour because the set of the reefed mainsail is too often not as good as that produced by jiffy reefing the sail. This is generally because the boom droops at its outboard end as the sail is rolled down, occasionally going so far as to foul the cabin top. If the boom is correctly tapered (from outboard to inboard end) this can be avoided and an acceptable set achieved, but, as I say, it has lost favour.

What is showing a slow gain in popularity for mainsail reefing is the kind in which the sail rolls round its luff instead of the foot. In the Stoway system, produced by Hood Sailmakers, there is a luff spar inside the mast, which is of larger than normal section to house the spar and rolled sail, and the sail is loose footed on the boom (i.e. it does not slot into the boom nor is it attached by slides other than at the clew). Other systems go for a luff spar outside the mast, making it possible to adapt an existing rig, but the Hood system would appear to have the edge by being a complete, integrated design.

The traditional method of reducing sail forward of the mast is to change one headsail for another smaller one and this is still the most widely used method. Each sail should set to best effect and the weight of cloth should increase (to a limit) with the reduction in sail area to cope with the higher winds for which the sail is designed. There has been a move away from the use of hanks (metal spring hooks that attach round the forestay) for the luff of headsails, towards 'headfoils'. These are slotted aluminium extrusions that either replace the forestay or fit over it and into which the bolt rope along the luff of the sail slides. For racing purposes these are fine as they produce a good aerofoil leading edge, but for a family cruising crew they are hopeless since the sail is completely detached as soon as it is lowered and more often than not ends up in the water. Fortunately, the majority of non-racing owners can see this drawback and are sticking with hanks.

Much more sensibly, there has been a strong move recently towards roller reefing headsails. Unlike the old furling headsail system, these modern arrangements allow the sail to be set partially unrolled without damaging the sail; i.e. they can be used to reef the sail. Furling jibs are indeed useful in themselves, but it is so much more useful to have a reefing system. It allows the use of a single headsail in wind conditions from the lightest airs right up to very strong winds, simply by rolling more of the sail away as the wind increases or setting more by unrolling it as the wind decreases. It is still recommended to carry a storm jib – a separate, small jib made of extra heavy cloth with extra stitching at the seams – for use in gale force winds and many would advise the use of a true lightweather genoa in ghosting conditions.

The use of one sail over such a wide range of wind speeds has been made possible by the development that has taken place in sailcloth over the last few years plus the design of well engineered, strong roller gears. In general these involve the use of a luff spar, to which the sail is attached, with roller bearing swivels at head and tack. A large drum at the tack carries the reefing line, which may be of wire or rope, that leads aft to the cockpit. To unroll sail, the line is eased while the sheet is hardened in and to reduce sail the sheet is eased while the reefing line is hauled in. Careful sail cutting should mean that the sheet lead does not have to be changed as the sail area is reduced.

Headsail reefing of this type is a great boon to the shorthanded family sailor since it can all be handled from the cockpit, it does not require anyone to go on deck, the helm need hardly be left and the sail can be stowed quickly when entering an anchorage or harbour without having it lying on the deck. It is true that the set of the reefed sail is not quite as good as an individual sail of that area, but the slight loss in performance is outweighed by the ease and willingness with which the crew can (and do) set the right amount of sail for the prevailing conditions. Reefing and setting sail is no longer an unpleasant chore to be put off as long as possible. Thus, if the wind increases suddenly a few rolls can instantly be taken in, but then if the wind drops again five minutes later they can quickly be shaken out. The crew effort is minimized.

Sail plan

Modern production yachts are virtually all designed for Bermudian rig, with gaff rig the rare exception. However, sail plans have been changing with many people looking for easy sail-handling options

A Freedom 40, exhibiting the now widely used and popular Freedom rig of two wrap-around sails on unstayed masts. This 40 is reefed on both sails. The next reefing step being to lower the mainsail (the after sail).

In murky weather a Freedom 33 demonstrates the deep reef rig with the mainsail stowed and a reef in the foresail. The boat is still very handy under this rig and continues to perform well.

and these have polarized into choices between Chinese lugsails (junk rig) and what has become known as the Freedom rig or the cat-ketch rig.

Bermudian rig From the family man's point of view, the problem with Bermudian rig in the past has been that it has too often been a miniaturization of the rigs found on offshore racing boats where there are plenty of crewmen to handle large headsails and complex running rigging. Fortunately, at present, the trend has been away from masthead rigs with their large headsails and tiny mainsails towards fractional rigs with larger mainsails and headsails reaching up to a point several feet below the masthead. This redistribution of sail area means that the smaller crew has less area to handle in any one headsail and the job is that much easier, whether it is setting or handing the sail or sheeting it in in a stiff breeze.

Freedom or cat-ketch rig This modern innovation, on which much of the early work was done by American Gary Hoyt, involves the use

The Freedom 25 with designer Gary Hoyt at the helm. The larger Freedom yachts have ketch or schooner rig with unstayed masts, wishbone booms and wrap-around two-ply sails (see photo), but on this 25-footer there is a rotating wing mast, fully battened mainsail and the strange 'gun mount' arrangement on the pulpit for the spinnaker pole. The spinnaker itself is set from and recovered to the Terylene chute seen on deck. This has a glass-fibre bell mouth fixed in the pulpit. Like the rest of the Freedom range, the 25 is a fast, able cruiser, capable of easy single or shorthanded sailing.

of two unstayed masts, usually of equal height, on which are set triangular (Bermudian) shaped sails that wrap round the mast to form an aerofoil. The booms are two part wishbones with the sail lying between their arms. They are curved to accept the flow put into the sail by the wind. Some variants involve single ply sails running up a conventional mast track or groove with a conventional boom at their foot, but the masts remain unstayed and the principle of simplicity is retained.

The nice part about the Freedom rig with wishbone booms is that the heads of those in the cockpit are no longer in danger from a heavy boom as the boat is tacked or gybed. There is reduced windage aloft without the standing rigging and there are no flapping headsails to worry about. The aerofoil sections of the two sails appear to be very efficient and such boats have proved able, fast, easily handled cruisers. To some eyes they still look odd, but that is a matter of taste.

Jester, a 25 ft Folkboat hull with totally enclosed accommodation, central control position and Chinese lugsail rig. This is the boat developed by Colonel H. G. 'Blondie' Hasler, who reintroduced the Chinese lugsail to the West and developed it to its present level. He instigated the Singlehanded Transatlantic Race to promote the design and development of shorthanded cruising yachts and he (and subsequently Michael Richey, *Jester*'s present owner) sailed the boat in each race, so that *Jester* has now made some nine or ten Atlantic crossings ranging from the southern Trade Wind route right up to the far north route. Together with Hasler's development of the wind vane self-steering gear (shown on *Jester*'s stern), this boat has offered more to the cruising yacht designer than has been adopted. It's a shame as there is nothing like carpet slipper sailing to promote happy family cruising. A lot of people have adopted junk rig but few have taken the step of enclosing the control position to give their crew protection from the elements. We must be a mad lot to prefer to be out in all weather!

Chinese lugsails

This rig too is often criticized for its appearance, but again beauty is in the eye of the beholder. The idea of a fully battened balanced lugsail set on an unstayed mast is thousands of years old, having been used for that time on the junks of the Far East. It was not until Col. H. G. 'Blondie' Hasler was looking for a good singlehander's rig, however, that it was 'Westernized'. He, together with Jock McLeod, brought the rig to a high stage of development using modern materials and it is now a sophisticated, but extremely simple, rig to handle. A single halyard is used to hoist the sail and by lowering it the heavy battens concertina on each other, reefing the sail between retaining lines called lazyjacks. A multi-part sheet arrangement has leads from the outer end of each batten and so gives even control to the whole sail and remains effective when a portion is dropped down (reefed).

The handing or reefing process is so simple that a dozen sail changes in an hour (for example) would take less crew effort than one serious headsail change. It is also extremely quick, so a sudden squall can be coped with instantaneously and the boat need never be either over or under canvassed. There are drawbacks and these are mainly chafe in the long lengths of line and rope, the fact that in extremely light airs there is no extra sail that can be set and that at all times the sail is less efficient *to windward* than a conventional Bermudian arrangement. It is comparable to gaff rig on this point. Off the wind it is better than a Bermudian arrangement (unless a big spinnaker is set) as the whole sail area is exposed to the wind without blanketing. One further advantage is the very fact that there is a single sail, which remains permanently bent on. The point being that no space is required for sail stowage and thus more space is provided for the crew and their belongings.

The auxiliary

The power of engines installed as auxiliaries nowadays means that often a cruiser has pretty well equal performance under either sail or motor. You can not expect an auxiliary to drag you off a lee shore into the teeth of a gale, but you can expect it to power you through a prolonged calm or help you motorsail out of trouble. Manoeuvring in harbour, berthing in a marina or entering and leaving an anchorage are all operations usually carried out under engine and with the

The junk rigged schooner *Galway Blazer* was originally designed for a singlehanded circumnavigation of the world and has subsequently been used for many short- and singlehanded passages. With the turbulent southern oceans in mind she was designed without any superstructure, having a submarine or whale-like turtle deck and just the two circular, easily closeable hatches where the two crewmen are standing in the picture. All sail-handling running rigging is led to these hatches as are the self-steering gear control lines, thus the crew can sail the boat with only very occasional excursions on deck. *Galway Blazer* also carries a bipod jury mast permanently fitted on deck – the two poles can just be seen with their apex in the pulpit – and this has twice been used 'for real' off the pitch of the Cape of Good Hope on separate occasions. A truly remarkable cruising boat from which many lessons can be drawn.

An interesting and apparently very efficient development of the Chinese lugsail (junk) rig. The sails are fully battened and two ply, forming fairly rigid aerofoils around each mast. The sail plan retains the simplicity of handling that makes the junk rig so good for cruising.

modern auxiliary there is usually plenty of power. What must also be provided is manoeuvrability, both ahead and astern, and that is not always as good as it should be.

Where you have any say in the matter, choice of an auxiliary lies between outboard engines and inboard petrol or diesel ones. The outboard is generally mounted on a lifting bracket fitted to the transom where it takes up no space in the boat, but, being stuck out astern, it is vulnerable to damage and means that the propeller will often lift out of the water as the boat pitches to a sea. To get round this problem some boats are designed with a well for the outboard within the cockpit area. A moulded trunk with a hatch through the bottom of the boat allows the drive leg of the motor to protrude through the hull where it is deeper in the water, thus less likely to lift out on a swell, and the motor itself is protected against being swamped by a following sea as can happen with the unit fitted on the stern. The propeller, being deeper in the water, also means it has more bite and improves performance.

The power-to-weight ratio of an outboard is very good and they are much easier to remove and take to a service centre than an inboard. Many quite small units have a battery charging facility so that the boat can have electric lighting and even electric engine starting is feasible. The fuel for an outboard may either be a two-stroke petrol/oil mixture or it may be neat petrol. Most units are two-stroke, but the buyer does have a reasonable choice.

For inboard engines the choice between having a petrol or a diesel engine is difficult as there are numerous pros and cons for each. Taking petrol first, you have a motor that is comparatively cheap, but a fuel that needs lead-coated cheques to stop them bouncing! Petrol engines are fairly light but you have to carry large quantities of highly inflammable fuel. Looking at diesels, on the other hand, the initial cost of buying the motor is high, but the fuel bills are much lower. Where petrol engines need electrics, which are adversely affected by the salt atmosphere and general damp-ness of life at sea, a diesel needs none. Its correct description is a 'compression ignition' engine (a man called Diesel invented it), in which the fuel is ignited by compressing it. The extremely high pressures needed to do this account for the very heavy castings required for the engines and their consequent high weight com-pared with a petrol unit. One advantage of petrol engines is that they are just about the same as car engines and many owners therefore feel confident of their ability to maintain or repair them.

The governing factor in choice of auxiliary may well turn out to be space under the cockpit sole, for that is usually where the motor will have to be installed. It may not be an ideal place as the boat's stern will be weighed down and access for maintenance will be strictly limited, but not many people will accept the idea of having an engine installed in the middle of the saloon. It still means having the engine under the cockpit, but an arrangement now very popular on boats with fin keels and separate rudders, is the Saildrive. This consists of a drive leg, rather like that on an outboard, passing through a gland in the bottom of the boat and connecting to the inboard engine. It is a more compact arrangement than a conventional shaft and propeller and is considerably easier to install.

Keels

There are four types of keel arrangement in general use on small sailing cruisers: single-fin keels, twin-bilge keels (including 'triple' keels), centreplates and lifting keels or swinging keels.

Fin keels are single, centrally placed, deep ballast keels, usually aerofoil in cross section with the ballast weight evenly distributed throughout their length. A few have a torpedo-shaped ballast bulb at their foot, but this is not common. Fin keels are the modern equivalent of the older full-length keel. Some modern boats are still built with such full keels, but it is the fin keel that is the general form used today. It is widely accepted that a well-designed fin-keeled boat will have a better windward performance than an equivalent bilge-keeler, but off the wind there will be little or nothing in it. However, a properly designed twin-keeler will sail well enough to windward and other factors should determine your choice of keel form.

The general category of bilge keels can be sub-divided into two kinds: twin-ballasted keels attached to the hull below the turn of the bilges or a triple-keel arrangement with a central ballast stub and twin bilge plates or unballasted stubs on either side. The plates are usually simple sheets of steel bolted on, while the stubs are generally hollow or lightly ballasted glass-fibre mouldings. Twin-bilge keels proper are either bolted on cast iron with an aerofoil cross section or are glass-fibre mouldings filled with ballast and resin to keep it in place. It is easier to apply antifouling paint between twin keels than it is triple ones and the twin-keeler may sail marginally better, due to less drag, but there is not much in it.

Lifting or swinging keels have become popular with the emergence of trailer sailers. The whole ballasted keel can be either raised vertically into the boat or swung up into her after the fashion of a centreplate. Various kinds of hoist are used and occasionally hydraulics on larger yachts, but in each case the keel is lowered for sailing and not raised again until sailing is over and you are back on a mooring or about to take the ground. Sailing with the keel up would not be sensible as the centre of ballast would be dangerously high.

The centreplate is something of an attempt to achieve a combination of the advantages of a fin keel (its windward performance) with the shallow draft of a twin-keel boat. There are two forms of centreplate, one having the ballast in a shallow keel outside the bottom of the boat, the centreplate retracting into it, the other concentrating the ballast in the bilges of the boat with the centreplate housing in a box standing up in the centre of the cabin. This intrusion into the cabin space is one of the drawbacks to many centreboard cruisers and is a similar problem to that found in lifting-keel boats, although in those the case may go the full height up to the deckhead, but it is much shorter than a centreplate case fore and aft.

When talking about keels we are interested mainly in three things: their righting power, their ability to stop a boat making leeway and the draft they add to the hull. The keel(s) of any boat being considered for safe cruising *must* have sufficient righting power to bring the boat up from a 90-degree, mast on the water, knockdown. That is to say, if for the purposes of a test, the boat was hauled down so that her masthead touched the water – smooth water – and was then released, the boat should return to the upright position. This was a test first introduced by the Junior Offshore Group (JOG) who have done much to promote the designing of safe small cruisers.

What about the advantages and disadvantages of each of these keel types? Fin keels require plenty of depth of water, but make the boat close-winded and quick reacting to her helm. Bilge keels may not provide quite the same windward ability, but they stop the boat rolling so much downwind and they make shoal-draft cruising possible, with the bonus of letting the boat take the ground without recourse to legs (props fitted to the gunwales to stop her falling over). The centreplate also provides good windward performance and allows the boat to enter shallow waters safely, as do lifting and swinging keels, but old centreplate boxes have a tendency to leak and if there is an external ballast stub the boat will heel over when dried out. With lifting or swinging keel boats this will not happen as they sit on the bottoms of their hulls in the manner of internally ballasted centreplate boats.

Hull shape

Hull shape is to some extent determined by what the designer wants to put inside. For instance, if he wants to cram in extra berths, he is somehow going to have to increase the volume of the hull to take them. Hydrodynamics obviously have a lot to do with it and for a hull to have good windward ability it generally has to have a fine entry allowing the boat to slice through waves losing as little way as possible. This reduces the useable space inside the hull up forward and to overcome the loss of space the designer may have to spread the bow sections a bit, but if he overdoes it and the hull becomes bluff bowed, she will be stopped by waves and will tend to gripe when hard pressed. Just to complicate things, a boat wants to have fullness in her bow and stern sections to provide a degree of buoyancy. She also wants to have some beam to give stability, but not too much coupled with slack bilges or she will roll in a seaway. Going to the stern of the boat, the transom should never be allowed to drag in the water, but should be trimmed just clear to allow a clean flow past it. Modern design trends give fairly fine bows, maximum beam fairly well aft and broad, hard-shouldered sections aft for downwind stability. The designs are derived from racing boats and should not be extreme or the boat will be too lively for a family crew.

Depth of freeboard is also a difficult problem. Too much and the boat will be blown downwind, but she needs to have enough to provide headroom below and to keep the hull buoyant as it heels. Being so high out of the water that you can not dip a bucket of water from over the side is often annoying but more seriously, if the topsides are too high, recovering anyone who goes overboard can be very difficult indeed. When you choose a boat, obviously you cannot say that you want six inches chopped off the topsides, but it is a point worth sizing up when you first look the boat over.

Cockpits

Since a great deal of time is spent in the cockpit, either sailing the boat or relaxing at anchor, it is worthy of careful planning. Most production boats have a self-draining well with pipes running out through the hull – usually the bottom, but sometimes through the transom – to take water away. All too often these drains are so small in diameter that they hardly qualify even as rain drains let alone being expected to cope with a cockpit filled by a heavy, breaking sea. They must be at least $1\frac{1}{2}$ in (3.8 cm) in internal diameter and there should really be four of them. There should be seacocks where they pass out through the hull in case a pipe splits or comes adrift and they should be cleanable in case of blockage.

To make a cockpit self-draining the sole has to be at some height above the waterline, which in a small boat means that the well is somewhat shallow, making it less safe for the crew. The minimum depth for comfortable leg room is about 15 in (38 cm). For comfort the crew should be able to sit to windward when the boat is heeled and brace their feet against the opposite bench or locker top. When they lean back the coaming should be high enough to support them, but should slope slightly outboard to stop it digging into anyone's back. Another thing to be avoided is having cleats or winches that dig into you or catch and tear oilskins or trousers.

Building materials

Glass fibre is, without doubt, the most widely used boat-building material as it is ideally suited to series production with the same mould being used over and over again to produce identical hulls. Unfortunately for the buyer this repeat moulding means little or no say in such matters as internal layout, but it does offer great benefits in terms of reduced maintenance and leak-free hulls.

Other materials are used for small craft including cold-moulded wood, aluminium and, for amateur construction, plywood. Such materials as steel, ferro-cement and foam sandwich tend to be used for larger, one-off yachts, but there are plenty about.

Plywood is still an excellent material for small boats, particularly for home boatbuilders, since it is very easy to work with and is strong and light. What must be watched very carefully indeed is the quality of the plywood used. Ideally it should bear the British Standards Institute kite mark to show that it complies with BS1088 for marine grade plywoods.

Quite recently there was an upsurge in the use of cold moulding when an American boat-building company produced a new range of epoxy resins and created the Wood Epoxy Saturation Technique

(WEST system), in which the multiple layers of diagonally laid veneers are saturated and glued together with these special epoxy resins. The wood is then impervious to water and the whole structure is very light and extremely strong. It is highly suitable for one-off construction of either light, fast monohulls or fast multihulls, but is not a production building material.

Older wood building methods such as carvel and clinker are rare for new boats today, but many older boats are available on the secondhand market using these construction techniques. If a surveyor's report declares them sound there is no reason why they should not still prove quite satisfactory, provided that anyone buying such a boat is prepared to do the considerable amount of maintenance required.

Strip planking is another wooden building technique that has never been particularly widespread but is a good system. It normally involves building the boat upside down (as is the case with cold moulding and foam sandwich) over a frame. Very narrow strips of wood are laid in a carvel, edge to edge, fashion gluing and nailing them, each to the next. It is not a terribly easy process when compared with, say, plywood building, but it does produce a strong, tight hull.

Foam sandwich, where closed cell foam is sandwiched between two skins of glass fibre, steel, aluminium and ferro-cement (steel reinforced concrete essentially), are all good materials but they are mainly used for craft larger than the size range we are dealing with. There are small aluminium cruisers available, but not as many as might be expected.

Spars and rigging

New boats today are almost without exception fitted out with aluminium spars and stainless steel rigging. This does not mean that wooden spars and galvanized rigging are no good, it is simply that they require more maintenance for longevity. Wooden spars are also heavier than equivalent aluminium ones and put weight aloft where it is not wanted. The drawback to stainless steel rigging is that it can give little or no warning before breaking, whereas galvanized wire shows some signs of strain and wear well in advance of failure.

4

Gear and equipment

The range and variety of gear and equipment available to boat owners is quite staggering. Chandlers' catalogues are crammed with bits and pieces ranging from the highly practical, such as anchors and fenders, to the highly sophisticated electronic aids that have taken the fullest advantage of the microchip revolution. The difficulty is to sort out what is really needed, for most owners of small boats are on tight budgets and need to spend their money to best advantage and obtain the gear that will be of most practical value.

It is common when studying brochures on new boats to come across two separate lists, one headed 'standard inventory' and the other 'optional extras'. The former lists the gear and equipment included when you pay the basic price for the boat, while the latter lists other equipment that you may or may not decide to add. Exactly what is included in the standard inventory and therefore what will have to be added under the heading of optional extras, can make a very big difference to the boat's real price. Take two 22-footers (6.75 m) with the exciting names Boat A and Boat B. They are near enough the same and you are trying to decide which to buy. The main difference seems to be a matter of £1500 on their basic prices. Should you follow your natural inclination and go for the cheaper one?

If we look at the standard inventory list for Boat A we find that the basic price includes mainsail, No. 2 genoa, engine, cooker, sea toilet, anchor and cable, fenders, warps, pulpit, pushpit and guardrails. On Boat B, the apparent bargain, the list only includes mainsail, No. 2 genoa, cooker, chemical toilet, pulpit, anchor and cable. Neither has a full seagoing inventory, particularly the sail

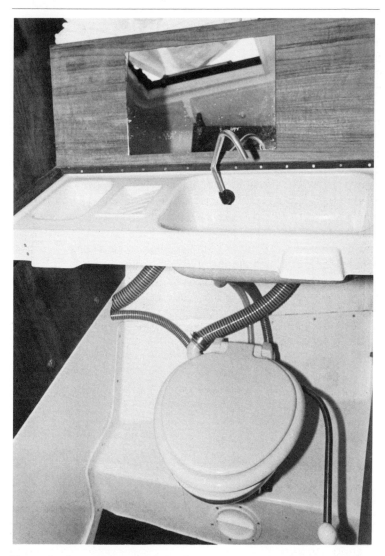

The confined space of a cruiser's heads compartment allows for little more than the toilet itself, but in this boat a clever arrangement of a foldaway basin is used. Water is pumped to the faucet with a foot pump and the basin drains into the toilet, which is used to pump the waste water overboard. Where a mirror is provided, as it is here, safety dictates that it should be a mirror tile or even polished metal, but not a true glass mirror.

wardrobe, but certainly Boat B is not the bargain she first appears and requires a fair bit of money just to bring her up to the level of Boat A. In fact it could turn out in the end that Boat B is actually more expensive than Boat A. The thing is to check very carefully what you are getting for your (or your money-lender's) money.

Basic essentials

Having warned that there are pitfalls when considering gear and equipment we can now look at what is essential to make a boat seaworthy, what is desirable to make seagoing more comfortable, what is needed on top of all this to make the boat cruiseworthy and finally some of the more practical luxuries. By seaworthy, in this context, I mean a boat suitably equipped to be taken to sea in safety and which is capable of withstanding bad weather commensurate with her design limitations. A cruiseworthy boat is a seaworthy one (within the meaning explained), but has also the additional bits and pieces for living aboard, such as a cooker, crockery, bedding and the rest – described as 'well found'. Most standard inventories take a midway position, but I hope you will see that we must first look at the basic items needed to make the boat *seaworthy*. These are:

Mast and spars
Standing rigging (if boat has stayed mast)
Running rigging
Mainsail
Working jib (No. 2 genoa)
Storm jib (No. 3 genoa)
Steering compass
Bower anchor
Cable (preferably chain, but frequently chain and warp – at
     least 3 fathoms of chain essential)
Kedge and 3 fathoms chain
Kedge warp
Echosounder (or leadline)
Odd spare lines, shackles, tape, seizing wire, hanks, slides,
     bulldog clips
2 springs $1\frac{1}{2}$ times length of boat
2 head lines twice length of boat
Navigation lights
Battery for nav. lights

Charts

Radio capable of receiving shipping forecasts (1500 m) and spare batteries

Watch or clock (with second hand) of known error

Pencils

Sharpener

Rubber

Parallel rulers/Douglas protractor/Hurst plotter or similar

Dividers

Nautical almanac (*Reed's* or *Macmillan and Silk Cut*)

Local pilots

Distance log

Log book

Notebooks

Engine and stern gear (or outboard) and fuel tanks

Fuel and spare can

Grease and lubrication oil

Fuel funnel (where needed, e.g. to fill outboard tank) with filter

Engine spares and manual – plugs, points, filters etc.

Tool kit – spanners, screwdrivers, hacksaw, screws, nails, hammer, pliers etc.

Tender

Painter

Oars and rowlocks

Dinghy bailer/sponge

Fire extinguishers

Pyrotechnics

First-aid kit

Fog horn

Lifejackets (one per crew member)

Lifebuoy

GRP repair kit

Odd bits of plywood and timber

Soft wood plugs for skin fittings

Spare reefing handle, if roller reefing fitted

Spare winch handles

Bilge pump with extension hose, spare washers, gaskets, diaphragms

Sail mending kit – needles, palm, thread, scissors, sailcloth

Knife

Marlin spike
Torch and spare batteries
Matches
Water tanks
Stemhead roller
Fairleads
Bitts, samson post or adequate foredeck mooring cleat
Fenders
Door lock
Black ball and cone (at anchor and motorsailing shapes)
Bucket on a line

Highly desirable

If you equip your boat with the 'essential' gear listed above and
assuming she is sound in wind and limb, she will be capable of
withstanding normal seagoing conditions, but the crew's existence
will be pretty spartan. There is only a very fine line drawn between
what is essential and what is desirable for comfortable seagoing, but
here goes:

Sheet winches (may well be standard equipment)
Halyard winches (may also be standard)
Oilskins
Lifeharnesses (one per crew member)
Sea boots
Dodgers/pram hood for companionway
Spare battens
Emergency tiller
Burgee/wind direction indicator
Barometer
Chart table
Handbearing compass
Tidal stream atlases
Binoculars
Pulpit, pushpit and lifelines (may be standard equipment)
Liferaft
Genoa (No. 1)
Shroud rollers/sail protectors on crosstree ends
Heaving line
Flag halyards

Ensign staff (essential if going abroad)
Code flags U, G, H, Q, N, C, V
Radar reflector
Interior lights and battery (probably standard equipment)
Lifebuoy lights

Cruising gear

Now that we have fitted the boat out for sea, what about putting her in a 'cruiseworthy' state? The list below contains several items that will not be found among the extras offered with the boat, but they are nonetheless necessary. Some you may already have available among your household goods.

Cooker and appropriate fuel
Gimbals and fiddle rails
Pots and pans
Washing-up bowl
Cutlery
Crockery
Thermos flask
Matches
Tea towels
Towels
Sleeping bags/bedding
Berth cushions
Bunk leeboards/leecloths
Riding light
Boathook
Toilet (possibly not the standard model)
Toilet paper
Ventilators (more than provided as standard)
Deck mop/brush
Boarding ladder

Luxuries

These are the kind of thing that can be added if and when wanted and if and when money allows:

Gas detector (if bottled gas used aboard)
Radio direction finder (RDF)

Cabin heater
Sextant
Self-steering or clip-on autopilot
Spreader lights
Outboard for dinghy
Electronic instruments and navigational aids including Satnav
    or Decca
Radar (on larger cruisers only)

I do not doubt for one moment that some people will disagree with the way I have categorized gear and equipment (or indeed that I have left many things out), but at least these lists will act as a guide and help you to sort out your own priorities. Exactly what gear you choose, and it will probably be an amalgam of all the lists, will depend to a very high degree on what size and type of boat you have and how you intend using her.

The three-year plan

What has to be kept in mind when choosing your boat is the fact that you are going to buy quite a lot of expensive gear over and above that included in the basic new boat price. In other words, if you have a total budget beyond which you simply cannot go, you must avoid buying a boat costing anywhere near that limit because you still have to buy extra gear, antifoul the bottom, insure her and pay for a mooring for the season – at least.

Once you have fitted the boat out with the basic equipment you can use the boat as she stands for a season, learning to handle her and planning what extra gear you want and looking at any modifications that would improve her. Then, at the end of the season you can re-examine your finances and buy some bits and make some modifications so that she is better for the second season. Again at the end of that season you can do more and buy more so that by the third year you have probably got the boat up to the standard you want.

Ropes and cordage

Very few people now use natural fibre ropes, everyone having been won over by the greater durability and strength of synthetic fibres. Of these, nylon is the strongest of the synthetics (ignoring

Bruce anchor hung in custom-made fittings on the pushpit of a Maxi 84. This arrangement leaves the anchor ready for immediate use, particularly when berthing bows on in a Mediterranean marina.

Kevlar and carbon fibre ropes whose use is somewhat less wide-spread in our kind of boat) with tremendous 'give' or elasticity. It is resistant to attack by alkalis but not acids. Because of its elasticity it is ideal for mooring and anchor warps where it will absorb much of the snatching and snubbing as the boat moves and surges in rough weather, although a boat anchored on a warp may not lie as quietly as one using chain and a much greater scope is always required. The stretchiness of nylon makes it hopeless for halyards as they need almost constant retensioning.

Polyester fibre ropes, which most people know under the trade names Terylene, Dacron or Tergal, are nearly as strong as nylon, but have very much lower stretch characteristics, especially in a form appropriately called 'pre-stretched'. Polyester fibres are resistant to attack by alkalis and to a lesser extent by acids.

Polypropylene and polythene (often called Courlene) are somewhat weaker than either nylon or polyester and are suscep-tible to abrasion, but have the advantage of being light, buoyant and relatively cheap. This last makes polypropylene popular for moor-ing lines, but this must be done with caution and great attention paid to anti-chafing gear. If considering the purchase of particularly cheap stocks of these ropes try to ensure that they incorporate inhibitors against degradation caused by ultraviolet radiation (sunlight). British standards insist on this, but some foreign makes are available that do not include any such inhibitors and these have a very short life. Polypropylene is resistant in some degree to attack by acids and alkalis, they all suffer under attack by solvents in paint or solvents for paint.

When we think of the general term 'rope', not worrying about what material it is made from or anything else, we tend to think of a three-strand hawser laid line. This consists of fibres or yarns twisted into strands with three such strands twisted (laid) together in a clockwise (right-handed) direction to form a rope. Left-hand laid ropes are now very rare but may be used for such things as log lines.

Three-strand ropes are good general-purpose lines for such jobs as mooring warps, dinghy painters or halyards (though plaited ropes are kinder on the hands in this application), but are not so good for such things as anchor warps, since the direction of twist imparted under load is critical. As suggested before, pre-stretched polyester should be used for halyards, not nylon, while the reverse applies to mooring warps.

Plaited ropes, which are softer to handle than laid ropes and often have lower stretch characteristics, take four main forms: all plaited, plaited core and sheath (e.g. Braidline), laid core with plaited sheath (a construction introduced by Marlow Ropes) and Marlow Multiplait (a cable laid anchor warp). The core and sheath ropes (whether the core is plaited or laid) are immensely strong and are kind to the hands, making them good for sheets and halyards. One of the advantages of these non-laid ropes is that they have no inherent twist and can accept it in either direction, making them ideal for things like lines on towing logs.

It is difficult to be dogmatic about what warps a small cruiser should carry, but apart from halyards and sheets, the following should act as a guide.

1 anchor warp (if all chain cable is not used) of at least 30 fathoms attached to at least three fathoms of chain. Suggest Multiplait about 12 mm diameter

1 kedge warp of 20 fathoms by 10 mm diameter with 3 fathoms chain

2 springs $1\frac{1}{2}$ times length of boat by 12 mm diameter nylon

2 head ropes twice length of boat by 12 mm diameter polypropylene

2–3 lengths of odd stuff about 5 fathoms each

1 heaving line 4–5 fathoms plaited 8 mm diameter, buoyant rope with weighted monkey's fist

1 hank lightweight 'cord' for lashings etc.

After a few seasons you will have had to replace perhaps a halyard and a pair of sheets and these can be put in the rope locker to see out their days in other employ.

While on the subject of choosing suitable gear, let me slip in a word about anchors and cables. Assuming that you plump for either a CQR or Danforth type of bower anchor, you should get one whose weight corresponds roughly to 1 lb (0.5 kilo) per 1 ft (0.3 m) of boat, with a tendency towards a heavier anchor than this formula gives. For boats under 20 ft (6 m) the cable, where it is to be all chain, should be $\frac{1}{4}$ in short link and at least 15 fathoms in length. Over 20ft (6 m) and up to 30 ft (9 m), 5/16 in chain is more suitable with 20–25 fathoms being carried. If you elect to carry an anchor warp instead, it must be attached to at least 3 fathoms of the relevant chain to avoid trouble with dragging anchors and the lengths might advantageously be $1\frac{1}{2}$–2 times the lengths suggested for an all-chain cable. Hanging a heavy weight some distance down the warp from the boat's bow helps to increase the catenary (sag) and so reduce surging and snatching, thus helping the anchor to hold, but watch out for chafe on the warp.

5

Trial sailing

Right from the start it should be made quite clear that you cannot *test* a boat when you take her out for a few hours. No matter what the weather and no matter how experienced you are, to test a boat you would need to live aboard for a time, take her out in fair weather and foul, sail her day and night and generally see how she goes in rough as well as smooth water. All of which takes a long time and in the end you would either love or hate the boat, but either way you would be past making an objective criticism of her. This, of course, is exactly the predicament that the yachting journals find themselves in when they try to review a boat.

Most of the magazines carry these reports, but the people who write them would, I am sure, be the first to admit that they can only express a personal opinion based on a few hours' sailing the boat and mentally comparing her with all the other boats they have been on of a similar type. Hence these reports are in no way a substitute for sailing the boat yourself, but they can act as a guide and useful adjunct for comparison with your own findings.

When you have reduced your list of possible boats to just two or three, then is the time to get in touch with the builders or local agents and ask for a demonstration sail. Most firms have or can make a demo boat available and will be pleased to take you out, but do not waste their time if you are not very seriously interested. If the firm does not have a boat available, or if you are buying secondhand and the boat you are after cannot be got into the water conveniently, you may be reduced to relying on any available magazine reports or, if she is a class boat, trying to get in touch with the Owners' Association (where there is one) and seeing if another owner will either give you an off-the-cuff opinion of the boat or, better, take you out for a sail.

Very useful services in this context are the Second Opinion and

Another Opinion schemes organized by the magazines *Yachting Monthly* in Britain and *Cruising World* in America. Under these set-ups willing owners of boats register their names and phone numbers with the magazines saying that they are prepared to talk about their particular type of boat, then a prospective owner can ring the magazine and be given a selection of names and numbers for the relevant classes he is interested in. A few phone calls later and he has the opinions and experiences of people who are already owners – satisfied and otherwise.

However you manage it, once out on the boat there are certain simple manoeuvres and exercises that you can carry out to gain an idea of how she handles and whether or not she is going to suit you. Before you even set sail you will look at the boat and that first impression is likely to be a lasting one. It can tell you a lot about the boat. There is an old maxim that if a boat looks right she probably is right and though there are bound to be exceptions it still stands as a reasonably sound rule of thumb.

A boat with a fine entry, not much freeboard and perhaps a deep keel will probably go well to windward, but the crew will be soaked. One with high topsides and a big cabin top has a lot of windage and will probably make considerable leeway in consequence. If a boat is of modern IOR form with a hard turn to the bilge, a shallow hull and considerable beam ending in a wide stern, she may fly downwind, but to windward the crew are likely to have to line the weather rail – not good cruising practice. If again she has too much beam on slack bilges, she will probably roll badly in a seaway. A nice clean run aft, where the water obviously flows easily away from the stern, points to a boat that will be easily driven and will not pull up a big quarter wave.

So much for first appearances, now let us get down to sailing the boat. There is no point in going out literally for a demonstration sail, you must be at the helm yourself and you must (in turn) work the boat yourself. Nor is there much point in simply sailing straight out and straight back; you will not learn a lot that way. The various manoeuvres described here are in no particular order, but each tells us something about the boat.

Under mainsail only

When entering an anchorage under sail, many people like to get the jib off and leave the foredeck clear for handling the anchor, but to do this safely the boat must remain totally controllable with just her mainsail set as it is not wise to rely entirely on the engine. She must be able still to beat, run, reach, tack and gybe. The same abilities will help when clearing away from an anchorage or mooring where, if the boat is lying head to wind, it is often more convenient to leave under mainsail, setting the headsail once in clear water instead of having it flapping about the foredeck crew's ears.

On a boat with a masthead rig, that is to say with the majority of the sail area forward of the mast, it is often the case that she will handle more easily under headsail alone than mainsail alone. This can only be determined by experiment, but is a vital piece of information.

When you have sailed out into clear water, drop the headsail and try making the boat run, reach, gybe and tack just to see how she goes. Do not expect her to be quite as responsive as with a jib set, or to point as high, or to tack as confidently, particularly in a sloppy sea, but she should still be able to make up to windward and, most important, you should still feel in control.

Foresail only

On many occasions it is not only easier, but pleasanter, to get underway with just a headsail set. For instance, if the wind is blowing from abeam or any freer you hoist the jib, or unroll it, let it flap while you clear the mooring, then sheet in and sail quietly off downriver. A boat designed with a big mainsail/small headsail rig (fractional rig) may not do more than run, reach or perhaps close reach under jib alone, but if the headsail is larger than the mainsail (masthead rig) you should be able to sail closehauled and make up to windward quite well.

Once again, ensure that you are in clear water, then drop the main and see what she will do under jib alone. Do not expect sparkling performance, but look warily on a boat that gets into irons every time you try to tack. See how close to the wind she will sail and whether the sheeting arrangement makes handling the jib fairly simple.

Heaving to

There is a tendency to associate heaving to with extreme weather conditions when progress is halted and the only thing to do is ride it out, but fortunately it is unusual for the weekend yachtsman to find

A 26 ft Stella hove to in rough weather. She rides buoyantly and makes little way, giving the crew time to eat, navigate or simply ponder shore lights or marks on a harbour approach.

himself in this predicament. Why he should be interested in how his boat heaves to is rather for stopping her while he has lunch, does some navigation, pulls down a reef or waits off a harbour bar for the tide to make. All quite legitimate occasions for heaving to but much less hairy and frightening.

The basic process for heaving to is to sail the boat closehauled then tack her, but instead of letting fly the jib and sheeting it home on the other side, you leave it alone so that as the ship's head comes through the wind, the jib is left aback. The mainsail tacks across normally and the helm is put right down (on some boats it may not need to go all the way down). To summarize, the jib is held aback, the mainsail is partially drawing and the helm is trying to turn the bows up into the wind. In this position the sails can be trimmed and the helm altered until the boat stops in the water and just makes a little leeway. Or that is how it should be. Try it and see, but if you have a full mainsail and big genoa set, do not be surprised if she still forereaches quite fast. Preferably change down the headsail and try again.

Lying athwart the wind

If you are sailing shorthanded and want to change the jib, often the easiest way to do it is to free the sheets right off and let the boat lie athwart the wind, just idling along, not going anywhere too quickly. When the boat is in that position, and usually the helm does not even need lashing, you can go forward and drop the headsail then hank on and hoist the new one. The same can be done if you want to reef without having a mainsail full of wind to contend with. Not all cruisers will sit quietly like this as they are often too delicately balanced, but if the one you are trying out is happy, so much the better.

Light airs manoeuvres

Obviously all the manoeuvres we are discussing can be performed in light airs, but most of them require a bit of a breeze to show the boat's real worth (or otherwise). When you do happen to go out in really light conditions, it is possible to get a feeling of how the boat will react in a stronger breeze by bringing her up on to the wind and trimming the sails so that she is sailing nicely, then when she has some way on, put the helm hard down and sit back. She should, if all is well, tack round and, with the jib aback, continue round until she gybes and comes up on the wind again, all without the sheets or helm having been touched.

While this operation might not mean a great deal in terms of normal boat handling, it does give an idea of her responsiveness. In a moderate breeze she should in fact tack and gybe round more or less continuously, but in really light weather she can only be expected to do it once or maybe twice.

It is illuminating to pick a fixed object and sail up to it then shoot up into the wind and see how far the boat carries her way. This is an essential piece of information when trying to come into an anchorage or trying to pick up a mooring where you want to stop the boat in exactly the right place. A very light displacement boat with a lot of tophamper will bring up quickly, whereas a heavier displacement boat will carry on for some distance, but in either case it is quite surprising how far the boat travels before stopping. It is lack of knowledge of this aspect of their boat's nature that makes so many owners overshoot their moorings or leave some poor crewman stretched between buoy and boat.

Reefing

When you are trying out a boat, even in light weather, it is important to try out the reefing system. Not only will you gain an idea of how well or otherwise the sail sets, but of how easy the process is to carry out. Are slab reefing lines led aft or are they at the mast while the halyard is led aft? This latter arrangement, for example, would make singlehanded mainsail reefing a tedious business as you would have to keep moving from mast to cockpit and forward again. If roller reefing is employed, does the boom droop when a reef is rolled in?

Some cruising yachts are now being equipped with headsail roller reefing as standard and while a good system makes headsail reefing wonderfully easy, the positioning of the reefing line winch must be right. It must be in a convenient place for turning the handle, but if possible it should also be within reach of the sheet winches to allow sail control by the person doing the reefing.

Setting and changing sails

When setting out on a trial sail, it is probably best to keep clear and let the builder's representative hoist sail and work the boat out of her berth (unless he asks for specific help), but once in clear water it is

Tucking in a reef on a breezy day. The man working at the mast needs one hand to steady himself as he stands up. He would be safer kneeling down when the job would still be within reach. The helmsman has turned the boat down wind to ease her motion, but still needs to watch what's happening in case the person on deck slips or a particularly awkward sea comes along.

not a bad thing to drop the sails and start from scratch yourself – wind, tide and other traffic allowing. By going through the process yourself you will find out whether the cleats and any winches on the mast are laid out for easy use and, if there is a bit of a lop on the water, you will soon discover whether her foredeck is an easy platform to work on or if she needs to have some more non-slip put on in way of the mast or on the forward slope of the cabin top. All too often the non-slip provided, particularly moulded into glass fibre, leaves a lot to be desired and on things like polycarbonate deck hatches it needs to be put on in strips or they become lethal when wet.

Headsail halyards should be long enough to be shackled or clipped on to the head of the sail while it is still on the deck. Also, while the sail is actually being changed, it is useful to be able to clip the halyard to the pulpit (usually to the eye carrying the lifelines) to stop it flying free. Try to imagine yourself changing headsails or reefing the main on a dark night and see if the halyards and so on would come readily to hand.

Weather helm

When a boat is said to carry weather helm it means that the tiller has to be held up towards the windward side (a-weather) to stop her luffing up into the wind. It is good for a boat to carry a little weather helm as it not only gives a bit of 'feel' to the tiller, but it also acts as a safety device, in that should the holmsman let go of the tiller or wheel (say in the extreme situation that he fell overboard) then the boat would luff up head to wind and stop. However, for easy shorthanded sailing she should only luff up slowly, otherwise it will be impossible to leave the helm even to tend the sheets and everything will have to be done with one hand permanently on the tiller – unless a clip-on autopilot or self-steering gear is latched in.

While a little weather helm is desirable, too much is certainly not and a strong tendency to gripe up when heeled by a strong gust can be a nuisance. Sailing through crowded moorings or in a very narrow creek would soon turn you grey if every puff made the boat luff frantically.

Handling under power

Much has been written over the years (and even more argued) about an effect called paddlewheeling. Let me now stick my oar in. The idea is that a righthanded propeller (one that revolves clockwise when looked at from astern) will tend to move the stern to starboard when driving ahead and a lefthanded prop will tend to move it to port going ahead. In some boats this effect is quite pronounced, while in others it is negligible and one can only find out by trying and seeing. This can be done by putting the engine up to moderate revs ahead and then letting go of the tiller. If the boat continues in a straight line the effect is clearly of no significance, but if the tiller swings over and the boat sheers off course then you can immediately tell which way the prop is 'handed'.

Further experiments can be done by turning the boat on full helm in first one direction then the other and noting the approximate diameter of the turning circle. If this is much less one way than the other, then again you can identify the direction of handing and whether it will have much effect on manoeuvring. Sometimes the effect is more pronounced with the boat going astern and on a few boats with big spade rudders the tiller can be swung over very hard and very quickly if the engine revs are too high.

To discover something of the boat's characteristics going astern, first try steering her in a straight line and then in a figure of eight pattern. Both *should* be quite easy, but this can often be a revealing manoeuvre. Next, try laying the boat across the wind and then attempt to bring either her stern or head up into the wind. Too much windage at either bow or stern will make this difficult and again you will be that much wiser about handling in confined spaces.

Going back to turning the boat, in the light of what you have just discovered about her handling both ahead and astern, see how she will come round by backing and filling in a kind of three-point turn. By using strong but judicious bursts of alternate ahead and astern power like this it should be possible to pivot the boat almost on her own axis without movement ahead or astern. The ability makes getting into and out of marina berths a lot easier.

Engine access

Boat engines almost always get far too little maintenance during the season and consequently when something goes wrong they are unfamiliar objects on which one has trouble working. However, assuming that you promise yourself you are going to be the exception and look after your engine properly, easy access will be of prime importance for routine regular maintenance.

Regrettably, many marine engines are installed in such a way that it is either impossible to get at them without taking half the boat apart or else you have to be a contortionist. The commonest place for an inboard engine is under the cockpit sole with, perhaps, a part of it sticking out into the cabin. This means that there must be removable panels to allow access to all parts of the engine and these must be removable without disrupting the whole boat. Check and see that this is so and that you can reach at least the main parts like the sparking plugs, fuel lines and filters, carburettor, oil filters, dipstick and oil filler, stern gland greaser, water pump, alternator and, on diesels, the fuel pump and injectors.

Outboards are a bit easier, but if the one you are looking at is transom mounted, make sure that it is possible to bring it inboard to work on it. Leaving it trailing when sailing is not ideal and trying to work on it when leaning out over the stern is just asking for trouble – spanners do not float.

Fuel tanks must have fillers arranged so that they can be topped up from on deck and without pouring fuel all over the decks. Dirt and water traps must also be accessible. Some means of determining the fuel level is required: gauge, sight glass or dipstick. What is provided? Even though many engines have electric starting fitted, they should still have a back-up hand starting system and this must be easy to operate. Too often it is fitted on the engine but, for example, there is no room to swing the handle. Check.

Further points

Not a lot here, but study the interior layout and try to imagine living on board when the boat is heeled over. Will locker doors fly open? Indeed are there sufficient lockers? Are there fiddle rails on the cooker? Is it gimballed? Are leecloths provided on the bunks or will you have to add them? Can the toilet be used without turfing anyone

Moving about on deck in any weather is a time of high risk. This man is keeping fairly low and has a tight hold on the guardwire while reaching for his handhold on the side of the main hatchway. Notice though that even with quite a wide and clear sidedeck he has still got a poor foothold as his boot is half on a sheet block track.

out of their bunk? Are there enough cabin lights? What is provided in the way of a chart table and is it adequate? Is there enough sail stowage or will some of the bags have to be moved from place to place? Is there sufficient working space in the galley? Are there plenty of good grabrails?

Are the decks adequately covered with an effective non-slip? Is the working area on deck – especially in way of the mast – reasonable and is it fairly clear of toe stubbers? Are the chainplates, grabrails, cleats and so on properly braced with through bolting to back-up plates?

Does everything give you confidence in the boat?

6

Talking of tenders

No matter where you keep your boat, whether it is in a marina, on a deep-water mooring or on a drying one, you must have a dinghy for use as a tender. Dinghies come in all shapes and sizes but are indispensable. Not only do they transport you and your crew between yacht and shore, together with shopping or bags of gear, but in dire emergency they can be used as lifeboats if a liferaft is not available. With such a complex role to play a dinghy has to be carefully designed and equipped.

Choosing a tender – rigid or inflatable

When choosing what dinghy to use as a tender your first decision must be whether to have a rigid dinghy or an inflatable one. Both have their merits and there is no straightforward 'you should have' type of answer. By asking yourself which you want you provoke a second question: are you going to have one or two tenders? Most of us answer that we cannot possibly afford two, which is reasonable, but if you do have two (of different sizes and types) you can use a large, rigid, high capacity dinghy to take all your junk out to the boat in one go and have an inflatable stowed away on board for use while away cruising. The best of both worlds perhaps.

Assuming you plump for just one tender you must weigh up the pros and cons. First, a rigid dinghy is robust and size for size has a greater volume for carrying passengers and gear than does an inflatable of the same overall length. Unfortunately though, a rigid dinghy towed astern of a small cruiser will knock her speed down appreciably. An inflatable, on the other hand, may not have the same volume of space, but it can carry a great weight as it is almost 100 per cent buoyancy. It can also pack down into such a small space that almost any cruiser can find room for one on board. Again, a rigid dinghy is permanently ready for use whereas an inflatable has to be pumped up each time you want to use it – and in case you have thoughts of towing it inflated, be warned that it is nearly always impractical (see Dinghies on passage, pages 86–9).

Thought should be given to what you propose to do with the dinghy when it is ashore. Is there a space at your club where you can leave it (a proper dinghy park perhaps), or will you have to take it home each weekend (obviously an undesirable situation)? If you keep your boat in a marina, will you have to haul the dinghy on deck (if there is room) or is storage space provided either ashore or afloat?

Materials

Glass fibre For rigid tenders, glass fibre is one of the most commonly used building materials and seems to stand up to wear and tear remarkably well. Many such tenders look a bit tatty, but are still sound and can be tarted up with a coat of paint. Repairs are quite easy and little maintenance is needed for a long life, but the gelcoat (the outer surface) does scratch easily when dragged over rough beaches or landing places. To give the necessary strength and rigidity the moulding must be reasonably heavy, but need not be overly so. Buoyancy can be provided by building in tanks containing closed cell foam and these are far less prone to damage than, for example, inflated buoyancy bags. Hull forms for GRP dinghies vary enormously: round bilge, hard chine, clinker, semi-catamaran, tunnel, cathedral and probably others besides. Bow shapes can be spoon, stem, rounded stem, transom (pram) or square. Look for a reasonable amount of beam coupled with firmly turned bilges for stability and load carrying, but clean lines and a good run aft for easy rowing – plus a keel, skeg or deep-bilge runners to aid directional stability. If an outboard is to be used then a wooden transom pad must be fitted to take the clamps.

Plywood Still a very common material for tenders as it is easy to work with and, therefore, ideally suited to amateur building. It is light and durable but must be protected by a good covering of paint or varnish to prevent damage to the edges of the laminate or even delamination. The minimum standard for marine ply is laid down in British Standard BS1088. Plywood is probably best suited to hard-chine construction and gains a lot of its strength by panels being

One of the advantages of a rigid dinghy like this pram is that with two people and their kit, the oarsman can row from a forward position while the centre of the boat is left clear for carrying all the luggage. In this way the boat is properly trimmed and can be pulled easily.

Contrast this with the horrendous picture of the inflatable with three people aboard. There is only one rowing position, in the centre, so any luggage has to be carried forward and with three people, as shown here, unless the weights are evenly distributed, the boat hogs (as this one does) inviting waves to wash in over the bows. Everyone is wearing lifejackets but when they get away from the shore the man in the bows is going to get a very wet bottom without oilskins. One good idea incorporated on many inflatables and which could well be copied on rigid dinghies is the fitting of grablines along each side.

curved in two directions. Unless built with buoyancy tanks that will contain closed cell foam, plywood dinghies must be equipped with buoyancy bags held in place by webbing straps. Apart from hard-chine construction, plywood may be cold or hot moulded in a round-bilge hull form or used in narrow planks for simulated clinker construction. Plywood tenders are usually transom bowed (pram type), but can also be spoon or stem. Using WEST system epoxy resins and finishes in the dinghy's construction will produce a light, strong and very durable boat.

Conventional timber Usually clinker-built, these dinghies are a rarity now although they have not lost their worth. They are strong and robust, able to stand many years of hard use and abuse, but they are difficult and expensive to build. Their weight and design make them good to row, but honestly rather impractical for use as tenders to the modern yacht other than as second dinghies running just between shore and permanent mooring. Either air bags or expanded polystyrene blocks should be used as buoyancy. These dinghies may be either stem or pram types.

Inflatables These are very widely used and do make very safe tenders – if one compartment is punctured the occupants are still supported by the remaining ones. Light weight makes them easy to bring aboard and when deflated they will stow away in a cockpit locker or go in the boot of a car. They are essentially one big air-filled fender so they are unlikely to damage the parent vessel's topsides. Little maintenance is needed and they have a long life, but its exact extent seems to vary directly with the price you pay for them. They do, however, after all these laudable assets, have some disadvantages. They can be extremely awkward to inflate and, indeed, deflate aboard a small cruiser. Also, in strong winds rowing is very difficult as most have short oars, necessitating short stabbing strokes, and their directional stability is very poor. Under engine the quarters can easily be pushed underwater when turning and in this respect the horseshoe shaped dinghies with wooden transoms are better than the oval ones with demountable outboard brackets. Whatever the shape of the dinghy it must be inflated quite hard to attain rigidity as this is all that provides stiffness. Floorboards help, but it is often the case that you *will*, no matter what, end up with wet feet and probably a wet backside as the fabric sole/bottom depresses when you stand on it and so all the spray or accumulated rainwater runs down to where your feet are. Similarly if you sit on the side tanks, as often happens when motoring, a quick turn or a slopping wave will wash over the round side tank and soak you.

Folding Somewhat surprisingly, folding or collapsible tenders have never really caught on despite many advantages. The main one of these is that you can have a normal plywood pram (with the advantages of that type of rigid tender) coupled with ease of stowage by folding it flat either on the cabin top or along the guardrails. As with inflatables there is the problem of having to construct the dinghy before use in emergency situations, but with well-designed ones this can be quicker than blowing up an inflatable.

Polyethylene These boats are usually formed by either sucking or blowing a sheet of the material into a mould. They are impervious to weathering, but colours may fade with time. It is a light material, needing very little upkeep, but it does score readily if dragged over pebbles. Sandwich construction makes polyethylene boats buoyant in the event of holing or swamping.

Aluminium A light, strong and durable alloy, but it is essential to use marine grade and to avoid mixing metals, otherwise serious corrosion will take place in the form of electrolytic action. Little maintenance is needed and many aluminium boats have lived for years without ever being painted. Foam or air buoyancy should be used and an all round fender is needed to save damaging topsides.

Carrying capacity

Like all things to do with boats, tenders are a compromise between the feasible and the desirable. Certain limitations are imposed upon the size of a dinghy; it is pointless having one big enough to carry the whole crew plus gear, cat, dog and carrycot all at once, if it is going to create massive drag when towed (never mind getting it on board). On the other hand it is equally pointless having one so small that everyone has to wrap their knees round their ears before the oars can be used and the whole thing is dangerous in the slightest chop.

Ideally you want to have a dinghy that can carry the whole crew at once, so that in an emergency they can all pile into it and stay afloat and only one journey from the shore needs to be undertaken to get everyone aboard the cruiser. However, if you have a little 20-footer (6 m) with four or five berths, a tender able to carry everyone will be far too big for taking on passage. A very rough guide to size might be that the tender should marginally exceed one third of the overall length of the parent vessel. Thus a 20-footer (6 m) would have a tender of 7 ft 6 in or 8 ft (2.25–2.5 m), a 24-footer (7.5 m) might have one of 8 ft or 9 ft (2.5–2.75 m) and a 30-footer (9 m) a tender of about 10 ft or 11 ft (3–3.5 m).

Given a rigid dinghy and an inflatable of the same external measurements, their carrying capacities in terms of volume would differ greatly. The rigid dinghy has only very thin hull sides and so has almost the same dimensions inside as out, barring the room taken up by buoyancy tanks. The inflation tubes of an inflatable, on the other hand, are of large diameter and greatly reduce the internal space. In terms of weight of gear carried, there need not be a lot of difference, but the inflatable will probably carry more. Point to watch: when an inflatable is heavily laden water will tend to wash over the sides, particularly when turning under power. Always, in any dinghy, keep the weight as low down as possible.

Dinghies on passage

Towing a rigid dinghy is not really the best method of taking a tender on passage – even a short coastal hop. In rough weather it will surge about, crossing and recrossing your wake, it may well ride up and try to board you and it could even capsize. Then again it can part its tow and disappear into the murk. When the weather is calm and the breeze hardly enough to push the boat along, a dinghy towing astern may mean that the boat is not making *any* progress. Unfortunately though, for many small boats, the only thing to do with a dinghy at sea is to tow it. There is rarely enough room on the deck of a small cruiser for such a cumbersome object and it is not a good idea to go without it.

An inflatable goes some way towards solving these problems as it can be deflated and stowed in a locker or lashed down on the cabin top. Larger boats may be able to carry it with just the bow (or stern) section deflated so that it fits on the cabin abaft the mast without interfering with boom or kicking strap. In the first case it must be readily accessible and in the second it must be possible to unlash and launch it quickly – even with just one section inflated it will

Inflatables should not be towed, they should be deflated or partially deflated and carried on deck or in a locker, but if you do decide to tow on a short passage in confined waters, pull the stem right up to the transom. This one is slightly low and can still swing about or even flip over. Note the bow dodger for keeping spray at bay when using an outboard to go to or from the shore.

support the crew and in reasonable sea conditions it is possible to inflate the other half in the water.

Towing an inflatable is strictly to be avoided. The dinghy is very likely to flip over, fill and act like a drogue, possibly even breaking the painter and being lost. If you really must tow it then haul the bows up to deck level lashing them hard against the fairlead (but watch out for chafe) and never tow it with a long painter, this is simply asking for trouble.

Returning to rigid dinghies, there are various dodges for making them more docile under tow. The most obvious is to use two painters, which limits the possible weaving from side to side and means that, if one parts, the dinghy is still attached to the parent vessel. Keep the tension on the real painter rather than the auxiliary one as it is likely to be stronger and better secured. The towing ring should be positioned low down on the stem or bow transom to lift the bows out of the water slightly. In this way she rides on her after sections where a skeg or bilge runners will help to keep her straight on course. Both the skeg and the runners can usefully have slots cut through them to act as handholds in the event of the dinghy capsizing and depositing the crew in the water. A length of elastic shock cord lashed across a bight of the painter will absorb much of

Towing a rigid dinghy on two painters helps to stop it sheering from side to side across the wake and also provides a back-up if one of the painters should part.

the snatching, but even so the painter must have a fair lead from the cruiser's quarter cleat and in rough going it is as well to wrap some rags round it to stop any chafing. Oars and any other loose gear in the dinghy must be lashed securely before setting off.

If the dinghy does show signs of wanting to join you in the cockpit, try letting her off on a long painter with another warp trailing over the stern. Alternatively, a funnel can be lashed on to the painter to stop the dinghy running up on to the towing boat. Fit it to the painter with the open end towards the dinghy as it will then pull through the water easily when the dinghy is towing properly and will be reversed to act like a parachute drogue if the dinghy rushes up and over-rides it. When lying at anchor a bucket can be trailed over the dinghy's stern when it is bumping alongside at anchor (usually in a wind against tide situation) and really does work well, but you would be surprised the number of people who have got underway only to find the bucket still trailing astern – until you do it!

None of this advice about towing a dinghy sounds too cheerful, but it is not the best way of taking a dinghy to sea; it just happens to be the only way on many occasions. The only point in its favour is the fact that it is already afloat in an emergency.

Whenever possible, the best place for a dinghy at sea is securely lashed down on deck. An inflatable can have one end deflated so that it fits on the cabin top under the boom, leaving both kicking strap and main hatch unhampered. In this semi-inflated state it can be launched and will support the crew's weight while they complete its inflation. This is the best place too for any other dinghy (aside from the increase in windage), but you must make sure that there is no problem with the boom fouling it when the mainsail is reefed. The other thing to be aware of is how much the dinghy obscures the helmsman's view forward and off to one side. He must remember to take a look round the dinghy at frequent intervals. Needless to say, I hope, the lashings you put on the dinghy must be very tight and if at all possible should be from a number of eyebolts specifically intended for the job rather than from the grabrails and it is best if the dinghy sits in properly fitted chocks. The lashings must be quick and easy to untie.

An inflatable can, of course, be deflated entirely and stowed away in a locker when you put to sea, but make sure it remains quickly accessible without a pile of ropes and fenders on top of it. Oars too should be to hand.

One other alternative to towing a dinghy is to sling it in davits off the stern of larger craft. These are like a pair of little cranes overhanging the stern, which are used to lift the dinghy clear of the water either in slings or by strops fastened to strong points within the dinghy. Then by lashing the boat in against the davits it can be carried clear of both the water and the yacht. Davits are not really practical on a cruiser of less than about 30 ft (9 m), but they are convenient. They do, however, leave the dinghy somewhat vulnerable to attack by marauding seas rushing up from the quarter, also to damage in harbour. They prohibit the use of vane operated self-steering gears and in rough weather a lot of spray will collect in the dinghy and this may have to be bailed out at intervals.

Buoyancy

Any dinghy being used as a yacht tender should be provided with sufficient buoyancy to stay afloat and support the crew even when it has been swamped or capsized. This buoyancy may take the form of built-in compartments filled with closed cell foam, air bags or expanded foam blocks. The built-in chambers filled with foam are perhaps the best system if only because they provide seating. Air buoyancy bags are perfectly effective if strongly secured by webbing straps, but they can be punctured. Their straps must be well secured as the strain on them when they are called on to provide buoyancy is enormous. For the same reasons foam blocks must be well secured and it is easiest to place these (like the bags) under existing thwarts to save space. The foam used in the blocks must be of a closed cell type.

Fendering

An inflatable dinghy is, in effect, one big fender, so there is not much worry about their damaging anyone's topsides, but with a rigid dinghy it is necessary to fit a substantial all round fender to prevent damage. Traditionally, this fender is a tightly stretched length of coir (grass) rope and this remains one of the most effective types of

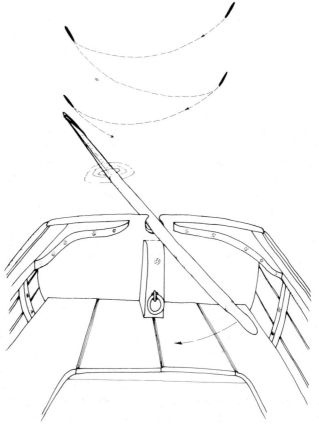

Sculling is a knack, but it *looks* like this.

fendering. More modern materials though are widely popular, usually D-section plastic tubing screwed on to the gunwale, but this is a fairly hard material and can still give a nasty knock to paintwork. One company recently introduced a large-diameter inflatable all-round fender for rigid dinghies that not only acts as a fender, but also gives additional buoyancy.

Painters

I said in the section on Dinghies on passage (page 85ff) that the painter should be led from a ring placed as low down on the bow as practicable. It should also be long and strong. I would suggest that a line of about 8–10 mm diameter and approximately 3 fathoms in length is about right. This gives plenty of scope for mooring the dinghy under most circumstances and allows for a fair amount of chafe before it needs replacing. A second painter is always a good idea and it is wise to carry a coil of warp and a small anchor in the dinghy just in case.

Sculling

Sculling over the stern with one oar is a very pleasant and efficient means of propelling a dinghy. But it is a knack. It comes from the wrist and is best practised with a second oar available in the boat should you get into difficulties. The diagram opposite should make the method clear, but it does need practice.

Dinghies and outboards

Where your mooring is a long way from the dinghy launching site it is undeniably easier not to have to row but to be able to start up an outboard and chug along under power. For a dinghy of about 8–10 ft (2.5–3 m) a 1½ h.p. motor is generally adequate and will push you along in most conditions, but a little more power for larger, heavier dinghies will be of benefit. If you choose a larger motor make sure it does not exceed the horsepower for which the transom was constructed. To reduce the damage to the transom caused by the outboard clamps, wooden pads should be fitted inside and out. They need not be very thick but should be replaceable and will, on glass-fibre dinghies, be essential to prevent the motor vibrating itself free.

Be careful when handling a laden dinghy under engine not to turn too sharply or water may lap in over the gunwales. You will find when alone in the dinghy that you have to move forward to trim her as the outboard tends to push the stern down into the water. To make this easier it is necessary to fit an extension tiller to the outboard. Finally, never stand up to steer; if you fell overboard there would be nothing between you and the propeller.

Rowing positions

When only one person is in the dinghy a rowing position from the centre thwart is fine, but as soon as you get a second person on board, or want to carry gear or equipment, the boat goes out of trim. The best place to carry gear is amidships where there is most space. This is also the best place for children and things like carrycots, where they can be watched. For it to be possible a second rowing position must be fitted at the bow thwart, then one person can sit aft, the oarsman forward and the centre of the dinghy is left free for whatever is to be carried.

Liferafts

On larger cruising yachts it is common practice to carry an inflatable liferaft on deck. This is an excellent idea but alas not a cheap one and for this reason some people prefer not to buy one, but to hire one for the duration of their longer summer cruise or any other decent offshore passage. In either case the liferaft must have the designed capacity to accommodate the full crew and it must be kept in a position from which it can quickly be released and launched. The bitter end of the painter, which is also the line used to trigger the inflation system, must be kept made fast to a strong point on the boat at all times. The liferaft should contain an emergency pack with water, flares, food, a torch, a knife, a small first-aid kit, a bailer and a small paddle. There should also be some means of topping up the inflation.

Liferafts must be serviced annually by a qualified service station and even if packed in a glass-fibre canister as opposed to the alternative soft valise, it must be treated with care: do not stand on it and try not to leave it exposed to boarding seas as the water may enter and corrode various essential parts. If hiring a raft make sure the certificate is in date.

A sailing tender like this inflatable can give all the family a lot of fun. Parents can enjoy sailing to and from the shore or another friendly boat and kids can both learn and undertake serious adventures exploring up strange creeks and inlets.

A simple conversion from rowing tender to sailing tender. A glass-fibre stem dinghy has a mast stepped through the forward thwart, a leeboard on a line dropped over the side and an oar used for steering. Much fun and no great problem to arrange.

Sailing tenders

We discussed a little earlier the question of outboards for dinghies. The alternative may be to have a tender that can be sailed. There is great fun to be had with such a dinghy, both by adults and children. It can be used for going ashore, visiting other yachts, or simply (and often most adventurously) to explore new creeks and harbours. The rig should be modest and simple, usually either a lugsail or a low Bermudian sail. A daggerboard or leeboard will help to give reasonable windward performance without the complexity of a centreboard. In fact, throughout, simplicity tends to increase enjoyment.

Servicing inflatables

Although inflatables require remarkably little upkeep they do need looking after to keep them in good order. Wash out sand and grit from between the buoyancy tubes and the bottom fabric as this will tend to chafe. Make sure the valves are clear of dirt otherwise they will leak. If the fabric does get cut or scuffed it can be painted with a proprietary refinishing material to restore it.

Have a care

Do not overload a dinghy – better to make more than one trip than to swim and lose all your gear.

Lifejackets should be worn at all times; they take up very little room in a car and may save your life when there is no one about to help you if you get into difficulties.

Oars and rowlocks should be tied into the dinghy, particularly on passage, as their loss can be very troublesome.

Take a look at the painter occasionally to see if it is chafed. If you are underway when chafe is noticed near the parent vessel (usually at a sharp-edged fairlead) and you cannot attend to it immediately, haul some of the line inboard, otherwise the dinghy will be lost should the line eventually break. This is another occasion when two painters are a comfort.

Fishing and rowing practice all at the same time. The dinghy, on a day like this in a quiet anchorage, is a paradise for small children, who can vent their energy learning useful boat skills and escape from their parents' immediate attention. Lifejackets are essential.

Make sure the painter has been made fast before you step out of the dinghy.

When stepping into a dinghy step into the centre and sit down straight away. Transfer your weight *slowly and smoothly* to or from a dinghy. Do not rush.

Have a couple of propeller sheer pins ready for the outboard; they could save you a long row.

7

Weekending

Inevitably people living in the confines of a small family cruiser have many more opportunities for getting on one another's nerves than they normally do at home. Tolerance is one thing you cannot buy in a shop: you have to take enough with you to last the whole weekend. As a parent you have a difficult job, you have to command instant obedience from your children to keep them out of danger in an emergency, yet you must not shout at them every five minutes to get out of the way or pull on that rope, or they will not recognize when some situation is a real emergency. Whether parents can really be joint skippers is something of a thorny problem as in general a small boat needs to be a dictatorship; a dictatorship tempered by love, thoughtfulness, consultation and a good insurance policy, but nonetheless a one-person command. Children, of course, suffer from their normal problems of keeping their parents under control with the additional factor that for once one of them really does know best – or most certainly should and must always appear to.

Catering

Many people used to the relative expanse of a kitchen in a modern house will find the confines of a small boat galley pretty restricting. Larger yachts do have quite good cookers with multiple burners, grills and ovens, but work space is limited, there is unlikely to be a fridge and water is in short supply. The galley on a small weekender may be a real shock with just a two-burner stove and a washing up bowl. In this case it is sensible to do as much preparation of meals as possible at home. Things like stews can be made up and cooked at home then placed in Tupperware sealed containers so that they only need heating up on the boat. Jellies with plenty of fruit in them can be taken straight from a fridge (again in a Tupperware

Sea·Pye

The cockpit can be a great playpen for children when the boat is anchored or on a mooring. All round lifelines help to make it a reasonably safe area, but lifejackets are still a good idea and if young children are to be allowed to move about on deck then they are essential. An adult too should be aware that children are playing and keep half an ear open in case of cries for help.

container) to the boat and if eaten the same evening will still be set. Camping-style cool bags and boxes are useful here as well.

One of the more convenient ways of producing slightly exotic meals is the use of specially packaged cook-in-the-bag meals produced by the firm of Stevens-Lefield. These foil-packed meals do not require any special storage and last indefinitely. They are cooked by immersion in boiling water and menus include coq au vin, goulash and chicken supreme.

For longer passages planned over a weekend a supply of sandwiches, chocolate, fruit, boiled sweets and other 'goodies' will go a long way towards keeping the crew alive without the need for any prolonged galley work when it may well be a bit bouncy and uncomfortable below.

This really is the crux of the whole business, to keep work in a small galley to the absolute minimum, with the possible exception of the Saturday night slap-up dinner. For this meal you are likely to be in harbour or tucked away in a sheltered anchorage and whatever the galley's facilities are they can be used to best effect. A wonderful piece of cooking equipment on a boat is a pressure cooker; not only is it a good, deep saucepan, in its proper role it can be filled and put on the stove (with the lid making sure its contents stay in place) while you clear up and sort the boat out, snugging down for the night and when you are ready so too is a piping hot meal. Soup makes a nourishing drink on passage and a Thermos flask of it made up before getting underway will only require pouring out when you want it.

Galley slave

I do not know if I should address this section to the ladies and tell them not to let themselves become galley slaves or to the men and tell them not to let the women spend their whole time cooking. True, some women are perfectly content to do nothing on a boat except cook, but it is not really a good thing. A woman should be competent to handle the boat in case of emergency and in any case it is to be

A child plays happily with some seaweed on the foreshore while dad struggles down the landing stage with all the family gear to load in the dinghy. And why not? Cruising is for family enjoyment and a piece of seaweed may well be more interesting than being allowed to help fetch and carry, particularly if every other step brings an exhortation to 'take care'.

A toddler can be easily secured in the cockpit by running a light line from one side to the other and then clipping the child's pram or pushchair harness onto it. This should be done behind the child's back, just in case they find out how to escape. This harness arrangement gives the toddler freedom to move about (even offer a half-eaten biscuit to her mother) and practise standing up without the parents having to worry about an uncomfortable lifejacket.

hoped that she can find other pleasures in sailing besides turning out three-course meals going to windward in a Force 6.

Men should make every effort to take some of the burden on themselves. A cold lunch, for example, does not take great culinary skill, but it is one less chore for their wives to do. Whoever cooks the evening meal should not have to wash up afterwards, even if she does at home. The 'slaving over a hot stove' cliché is rather apt on a boat where you may well have to hold a saucepan in place with one hand, hang on with the other and stir the pot with a spoon in your teeth. Even if you think you have done your bit with bringing the boat safely to anchor and feel you want to put your feet up and relax after a hard week at the office, remember that someone else has probably had just as hard a week tidying up after the kids and making sure there is a hot meal ready for you when you come home. So be fair and give her a break too. You both probably need a rest.

Point to remember: boiling liquids can scald. Do not work wearing just a swimming costume, always cover up, even if it is with a suit of oilskins and do not let little children near the stove in rough going.

Dunnage

Dunnage is the old seaman's name for his luggage and like anyone else he has to bring it aboard in something. Most of us were raised in the belief that you should never take a suitcase on a boat, but should pack everything in a soft bag that can be stowed away in a locker. Because this is such a widely accepted idea I would advise you to go along with it on other people's boats, but on your own you can do what you like and that may well be to use a suitcase. Although a case cannot be stowed easily in a locker, it is in effect a locker in itself, a portable one. During the day it can be stowed in a quarter berth and during the night at anchor it can stand on the cabin sole. You can sit on them and kick them about and they will still keep their contents intact. If you insist on taking tidy clothes with you then they usually stay tidier longer in a solid suitcase than they do in a hanging locker where they will probably spend much of their time rubbing shoulders with salty or muddy oilskins, besides swinging about chafing on a bulkhead.

Each person should aim to bring the minimum he or she needs in the way of gear. This may consist of an extra jersey and a change of clothes in case you get wet, but people manage to add a fantastic amount on top of that. It really depends what you keep permanently on board. For instance, there is no reason why you should have to cart washing and shaving gear on board each time you go or even a basic make-up bag, as these can quite well be kept on the boat for the season.

Small children, particularly babies, seem to require more bits and pieces than all the adults put together. Nappies, clothes, bedding, food, milk, nappy washing substances (or lots of plastic bags to carry used disposables), creams, oils, powder and so on. Try as you might there seems to be no way of cutting down much and the mountain always has to be carted back and forth.

One of the most useful things you can have is a ditty bag into which you drop loose change, car keys, house keys, wallet, etc. and know they will not get lost. A small pouch with a Velcro fastened flap to close it is a good arrangement.

A place for everything

Hackneyed as it may sound, it really is necessary to decide on a place for everything and then to keep it there, otherwise you will get in a real mess and not be able to find something vital in an emergency. It is no good then to have to rout round in a locker by torchlight (if you can find the torch) trying to locate a shackle spanner or just a clean nappy for the baby. Where a locker is not perfectly easy to see into it is as well to tape a list of the contents on the door. This, by the way, is not a bad job to get the children to do one day when you are at anchor waiting for the tide or a break in the weather. It is not a difficult task or too boring, but they will be making a real contribution to the running of the boat.

In very small cruisers it is useful to make up some netting which can be fastened either to the deckhead or hull sides to act as extra stowage for charts or clothing. Flares can be strapped to the bulkhead with shock cord, binoculars can be stowed in a specially made box (or a moulded plastic one bought from a chandler) also fastened to a bulkhead within reach of the cockpit.

Clothes that are to be stowed in lockers can well be wrapped in big polythene dustbin bags with a packet of silica gel included to stop them getting damp and mildewed. In fact there are a hundred and one uses for polybags on board, but *do not ever throw them over the side* as they do not decay and can foul propellers or block up cooling water intakes. They are the obvious thing to use for collecting used disposable nappies, which can then be taken ashore and thrown away in rubbish bins without causing anyone any problems.

The loo

Until a few years ago it was commonplace for small cruisers to have a lavatory bucket, which had the virtue of being utterly simple, but now it is the norm to have an enclosed toilet compartment fitted with a sea toilet or, possibly, a self-contained chemical one, either flushing or not. The modern boat toilet is a functional, clean and generally efficient piece of apparatus, but however tidily enclosed it may be it is still a central feature of the accommodation and for this reason it must be polished, powdered, ventilated and pampered with as much care as a prize poodle.

As the loo, even if it is enclosed, is such a central feature of life aboard a small cruiser the whole crew has to learn 'instant deafness' and develop the ability to ignore and carry on with their own business. The one crime that will always remain is blocking the loo up and so the distinction must be made between 'disposable' and 'flushable', the former items being best consigned to a plastic bag for disposal ashore. Even the flushable items are best dealt with in this way, leaving only organic waste to pass through the toilet system.

Destinations

When deciding where to go for a weekend or for that matter a week, a fortnight or any length of time, you have various factors to take into consideration.

1 First and foremost is the capability of the crew. Should you have very young children on board you can only hope to make passages of a few hours' duration. It is not much fun for them being told to sit still, even with the dubious promise of being allowed to 'help' with steering or sail trimming. A picnic on a beach somewhere and a chance to stretch their legs probably holds far more attraction for them and why not? This is supposed to be an enjoyable sport for all the family.

Carrycot-sized babies are in some ways less of a problem as they can be wedged securely where no-one is going to tread on them and then left to sleep until their next feed – and you had better make sure their mother is available to give them that feed when they want it or your eardrums will regret it! If you must make a long passage with children aboard it is often better to do it at night in the hope that they will stay asleep. With the aid of an anti-seasickness pill (which often causes drowsiness anyway) this is quite likely. In fact many children trot off to their bunks without being told when the wind pipes up and the sea gets a bit rough. An excellent thing for everyone.

Apart from the children, it is likely that there will only be two of you aboard and you must recognize your limitations and plan a weekend cruise accordingly. If the weather is rough you are obviously going to make a shorter passage than you might otherwise do and you will not choose to go to windward.

2 Whatever sort of cruising you do a careful watch must be kept on the weather and on weather forecasts, particularly the shipping forecasts. I will say more about them in Chapter 16, but for now let me say that if you are planning to head, say, northeast and the forecast is for a rising nor'easterly, you are probably going to have to go somewhere else; there is just no point in banging your head against a brick wall if you do not have to. This adapting of plans according to prevailing conditions is an integral part of cruising seamanship and certainly not something to be looked down on. After all, you are cruising, not competing in a race over a set course and there will be plenty of times when there is simply no soft option open to you.

3 Another major factor is the tide. If you keep your boat on a drying mooring then before you do any planning of where to go, you must consult a set of local tide tables and see when you will be able to get away. In a small cruiser there is very little to be gained by trying to buck a foul tide, particularly if wind and tide are together, even using the engine to motorsail. It is always better to plan your passage so that the tide is under you for as much of the time as possible and be prepared to change your plans if necessary.

Back home – on time

One further calculation affecting the question of where to go is the matter of the time at which you have to be back. As with time of departure, time of return to a mooring may be restricted by tide and you must be sure that you can get back when there is still sufficient water. Few of us can say 'To hell with it. I'll skip work on Monday and go in on Tuesday.'

In order to catch the right tide home it will more than likely be necessary to get up at some apparently ridiculous hour, but once you are up and doing you usually feel an odd sense of satisfaction. The modern cruiser has a more powerful and reliable engine than was once the case and getting back is less of a problem than it used to be, but the effort still has to be made. However, if there is a flat calm you can motor at least most of the way and if the wind fills in from dead ahead you can always help yourself along by motorsailing.

Keeping the log

Apart from its primary function of providing the navigator with all the information about courses, wind, speed and so forth that he needs to keep track of the ship's position and progress, the log book also acts like a diary. It forms a day-to-day record of where you have been and what you have done, making fascinating reading for a winter's evening when the summer seems so far away.

Perhaps it is as well to use separate books for navigational information and narrative (or opposite pages) but the inclusion of children's comments, drawings and activities add greatly to the log.

Even when you are not really navigating, only ticking off marks as they pass, it is still worthwhile keeping up the log. If you do so conscientiously and the weather suddenly closes in, you have a last *known* position from which to work up your DR rather than a 'Wasn't that the so and so buoy we passed last?' vague idea.

Yacht clubs – use and abuse

Many yacht clubs have showers and a drying room for the use of their members and they are usually generous enough to allow visiting members of other recognized yacht clubs to use them. The normal practice is either to make a visiting yachtsman a temporary member of the club, if he is to be staying for some time or else to charge him a nominal sum for the use of the facilities.

In either case visiting crews must treat the premises and members with respect and neither misbehave nor leave (for instance) the showers in a dirty or untidy state. You would not like visitors to

A pair of clove hitches well spaced on the burgee stick allow it to be hoisted to the masthead. By hardening down on both ends of the halyard the stick is kept straight with the burgee flying clear of the truck.

When using a strange anchorage the line of moored boats is usually a good guide as to safe places to drop the hook. As can be seen here anyone anchoring other than in line with the moored boats is in danger of lying on the mud-bank at low tide. Notice the normally submerged stakes, too.

Peace settles over the anchorage as everyone snugs down for the night. The perfect end to another perfect day's cruising.

your home club getting drunk and breaking the place up so do not do it in someone else's club. Be sociable but do not be a nuisance. Similarly, if a club disallows children in the bar room, respect the rule even if you disagree with it. Where they are allowed in, keep them under reasonable control.

Adding up weekends

We saw earlier that there are a lot of factors limiting how far you can take a small boat in a weekend bearing in mind the need to return to base on Sunday night. However, if you want to go further afield but can still only spare weekends to do it in, consider the possibilities of sailing as far as you can (or want to) on both Saturday and Sunday (instead of returning on the Sunday) and then leaving your boat in whatever port you fetch up at until the following weekend, using public transport back to your home. This is certainly a viable way of going abroad possibly prior to a family cruise. It saves taking part of the holiday period simply to get there and back.

It does mean leaving your boat in a strange harbour, putting her in someone else's charge and if it is a marina it could be expensive. That, coupled with the cost of public transport, certainly are matters to be weighed up, but it does solve a number of problems and by this system of 'adding up weekends' you can extend your cruising area enormously.

8

Seamanship

Seamanship is the practical art of working and handling a boat. Good seamanship is something to be proud of. It is not just sailing the boat from port to port without mishap, it is knowing your boat and how she will behave in every situation and applying that knowledge to advantage. We can never hope to be complete seamen, we are forever learning, but we can go a long way towards it and part of that journey is accomplished by watching other people and recognizing their seamanship.

Sail handling

Making and handing sail involves working around the foot of the mast and, on a small cruiser at sea, this is not a safe place to be. Great care must be exercised at all times as you are high up and probably working with both hands for most of the time, leaving nothing to hold on with. The safest way of working on the foredeck is to sit down, though many people opt for kneeling instead. In any case try to stand up as little as possible and when you have to, for instance to swig on a halyard before using the winch, first hang on and second put one foot behind you just in case something slips or carries away and you go flying backwards. The bitter ends of all halyards should be made fast either by passing the end through a hole in its cleat and tying a figure of eight or, better, by making them fast to swivel eyes specially located at the mast step.

    Doing up or undoing shackle pins can be a devil of a job when the boat's movement is at all lively or your hands are cold and it is as well to avoid their use on sheets and halyards as much as possible. Snap shackles with piston action pins are far better (although it is not completely unknown for them to come undone) and a better alternative to the screw pin shackle is the captive pin type where

On very small cruisers it is almost essential to sit down or kneel when working on deck. The motion of a small boat even in a calm sea is jerky and unpredictable; it can all too easily throw you off your feet.

the pin is secured by a half turn and cannot be taken right out of the shackle, thus preventing its loss.

Lightweight Terylene blows and billows about if given the chance and the only easy way to handle it is when it is in the bag, so as soon as you take a sail out, smother it and, when dropping a headsail, lash it down with shock cord or tiers quickly. Never get to leeward of a sail that is being set or handed as it can easily push you overboard and flogging cringles can cause nasty accidents. Be careful, too, that you do not stand on a lowered sail as the cloth is very slippery against either itself or the deck and your feet will probably shoot out from under you.

When you go to hoist a foresail that has to be hanked on to the forestay, clip on the tack first then run your hand up the luff clipping each hank on in turn until you reach the head. This ensures no foul-ups with hanks going on in the wrong order or twists in the sail. After you have attached the halyard (checking it is not twisted round the forestay), go back to the tack and run your hand along the foot till you reach the clew and attach the sheets. In the case of a headsail setting in a groove on a luff spar you clip on the tack, run your hand up the luff to make sure it is not twisted, clip on the halyard and feed a few inches through the guide and into the groove. Then run your hand along the foot and attach the sheets. The sail must then be hoisted quickly before it blows overboard or before it comes out of the groove.

All these procedures are intended to avoid any twists in the sail and if they are always carried out there will not be any trouble. Always watch the sail when hoisting it to spot any snags or problems and come time to take the headsail off, drop it, lash it down and as soon as you unfasten the halyard, clip it on to either the pulpit lifeline loop or a rope becket attached to the deck for this purpose. A knot can usefully be put in the fall of the halyard so that when it is against the entry sheave into the mast (assuming internal halyards) the halyard snapshackle can just be clipped on as described. In this way the halyard is secured and held reasonably tight without having to turn it up on the cleat, avoiding a trip back to the mast.

The question of when to reef looms larger in many people's minds than it really needs to. What you must remember is that she is *your* boat, they are *your* sails, mast and rigging and the crew is *your* responsibility. Always reef early and never be afraid of looking stupid with shortened sail when everyone else has full sail set. You may have heard the forecast they missed and anyway, your boat and crew are not their boat and crew. Also, consider reefing simply to reassure a nervous crew. There is no point in crashing along, leaping from wave to wave, however marvellous and exhilarating it may seem to you if you scare hell out of your crew and they refuse to go sailing again.

Small cruisers, in general, prefer being sailed upright to plugging along on their ears. If they are hard pressed their shape in the water is all wrong, the keel is less efficient in its prevention of leeway and there is a massive expanse of hull presented to the wind while the sails themselves spill air and lose their drive. In such conditions it definitely pays to tuck in a reef or two as soon as she seems hard pressed and let her sail more upright. She will make better progress and everyone will be more comfortable and happier.

If you have to reef at sea do not try to do it with the boat still crashing along, rather slow right down or even heave to so that she is making almost no way but still riding the waves easily. You can then take your time to tuck in a neat reef so that the sail sets and draws well. If you have the chance and see the need to reef before putting to sea so much the better and remember that it is easier to shake out a reef than it is to take one in. Generally it is better to reef the mainsail before changing the headsail for a smaller one (though obviously a light weather genoa should be changed for a heavier one) as this often lessens the increasing weather helm and, with a masthead rig, it keeps the driving sail area large.

Leaving moorings

Just to add a little extra spice to the sailing life, wind and tide always manage to combine in a new way each time you come to or leave your moorings and for that reason it is impossible to be dogmatic about how it should be done. The situation must be weighed up afresh on every occasion and due allowance made for the prevailing conditions.

Before you make any hasty moves to cast off, take time to look at what the wind and tide are doing and how the boat is lying in relation to them and to other boats in the anchorage. With the wind and tide there are three basic situations: wind with tide, wind against tide and wind across tide. Conspiring against you in conjunction with the wind and tide are the four possible types of mooring: a deep-water swinging mooring (the easiest of the lot), fore and aft buoy moorings, fore and aft pile moorings and marina berths. It all sounds a bit daunting, but there are rarely any problems that a little sound seamanship will not see you through.

Wind with tide: swinging mooring This is the easiest situation of all. First decide whether you want to beat up against the wind and tide after you have fallen clear of the buoy or whether you want to run off downstream. Assuming the former, choose the tack that gives you a slant clear of other craft and hoist sail with the sheets freed right off. Whon all is roady tho buoy can oithor bo chuckcd ovor, which allows you to drift astern and use a backed genoa to cast the boat's head round on to the desired tack, or the buoy can be walked aft and the tide turns the boat's head on to the right tack. If you want to run off down tide your best bet is to walk the buoy all the way aft, so that the boat turns end for end on the buoy, rather than making a rather large and sweeping turn close to other craft.

Wind against tide: swinging mooring This one is not quite so easy. The boat will probably lie across the tide at some angle determined by her hull and keel form and her above-water windage. In most cases the best bet will be to hoist a jib, cast off and get clear of the mooring by running or reaching into open water, then round up and hoist the mainsail.

Wind across tide: swinging mooring Here again the boat will more than likely lie at an angle to both wind and tide, but you will probably be able to hoist both main and jib without the boat careering about fouling the mooring. If you can set both sails then you can proceed as though the wind were blowing with the tide, but if you can only get the jib up then you are in for a wind against tide manoeuvre.

Wind with tide: buoys fore and aft In this situation the boat will be lying with all the strain on one mooring. If this is the bow mooring then all you need to do is bring the stern mooring forward outside everything and tie it to the bow mooring, casting the pair off together. Where the strain is on the stern mooring you can either make the bow one fast aft and run off under jib alone until you reach clear water and can round up to set the main, or you can turn the boat end for end. To do this one person takes the bow buoy aft outside everything while the other person leads the stern buoy forward. When she has settled down again you can take the slack mooring rope forward and cast the boat's head off on either tack with all sail set, taking care, of course, not to sail over the slack mooring line.

Wind against tide: buoys fore and aft Again, what you do depends on which way the boat is lying and whether the wind or tide is the stronger influence. Assuming that wind and tide are about equal you can usually bring the buoys together at either bow or stern and move off as you would from a swinging mooring. If they do not balance you are usually better off turning the boat's head into the stronger one.

Wind across tide: buoys fore and aft First make sure that the boat is downwind of the mooring warps or she will foul them when you cast off. The best bet is usually to bring the buoys together either at bow or stern depending on which way you want to leave the moorings. But do be careful not to sail over the ropes or you will get them wrapped round keel or rudder. Always bring buoys together on the windward side and if you plan to motor out, get well clear before engaging gear.

If you are moored fore and aft to mooring piles you do not have to worry about bringing the moorings together, you can moor the boat to one pile or turn her end for end, just as you please. There may, however, be another boat moored alongside, in which case you are virtually in the same position as being in a marina berth alongside a pontoon. In most cases it will make sense to prepare to leave under engine, turning the boat or moving her out using warps, springs and fenders. We will return to this in the section on Alongside berths (see page 122).

Unfortunately, much of what we have just said sounds complicated. In fact leaving your moorings need not be a difficult manoeuvre, but you must think out a plan with the crew before you make any move. Take things slowly. If you want to and have room, just drop the moorings and drift clear before making sail, but once sailing remember that a boat will turn more tightly (and slow up in the process) if you luff her up. If you are running into trouble and try to bear away you will speed up, swing round in a wide turn and probably end up in a far worse situation.

Picking up a mooring

It is scant comfort when it happens to you for the umpteenth time, but everyone misses their moorings sometimes, even people with years of experience. What the experienced person does though is to recognize the fact that he is not going to make it and go round for a second attempt while the boat still has way to manoeuvre. The whole aim with picking up a mooring is to bring the boat up to the buoy with as little way on as possible – ideally with none at all. Of course, you can only hope to do this by practising and learning how much way your boat carries under various conditions of wind and sea.

One way of experimenting to determine this is by using a plastic drink container as a marker buoy – moor it by a line attached to a brick or large stone out in clear water – and sail at it from all angles. Upwind, downwind, across the tide, with it and against it, trying always to stop the boat as close to the buoy as you can. The same can be done under engine, knocking it into neutral at what you judge to be the right place and gliding up to the buoy.

As with all mooring problems, the easiest to deal with is the deep-water swinging mooring, but when it comes to picking up a mooring, as opposed to laying her alongside a wall, a pontoon or another boat, they all have to be treated in much the same way.

Wind with tide This again is usually the easiest situation. Approach from downwind and either tack up to the buoy, luffing at the last moment to bring it under the bows or better, if space allows, reach across to it. By doing this you can control the boat's speed all through the approach by easing and hardening the sheets, using them like a throttle. You are in control all the way and can even decide to go by and make another approach. As you come up on the buoy, line it up with a mark on the shore beyond; if it stays in line you will hit the buoy all right, but if it moves you will miss and you must change your course accordingly.

Wind against tide Where a reaching approach (as described above) is not possible, get upwind of the buoy and drop the mainsail before running down under headsail only. As you approach the buoy take some of the way off by starting the jib sheets and letting the sail flog (or rolling part of it up on a headsail roller reefing gear); you can always harden in (or set more sail) if the boat falls short. If

A quiet entry to a quiet anchorage in a misty dawn. Manners dictate no shouting at such times and this approach under headsail alone (when conditions allow) is just right. Although not needed on this occasion, the foredeck hand is seen using a very long boathook to extend his reach considerably.

you have fore and aft moorings and have left the buoys tied together, you must take care not to let the boat swing over the slack line.

Wind across tide Approach from down tide controlling the boat's way by hauling in or freeing off the sheets. If you like, you can drop the headsail and approach under main alone, giving yourself a clear foredeck for the actual pick-up, but this depends on how the boat handles without a jib. With fore and aft moorings try to pick them up to windward so that the boat does not foul them as she swings round.

Relative strengths of wind and tide still have to be assessed even if you decide to motor on to a mooring (or into a marina berth). Use one or both to help control speed and ultimately to stop the boat, for in both cases, either sailing or motoring, the ideal is to bring the boat to a dead stop at the buoy or alongside the pontoon. That happens rarely, so aim to overshoot a buoy slightly and fall back, giving the foredeck hand time to make the pick-up and take a turn; falling short would mean reaching for the buoy and immediately having to combat a widening gap. It is arguably better to have an experienced person on the foredeck making the pick-up and the less experienced hand on the helm rather than the other way round, as the experienced one can call out or signal helm orders and can judge whether or not the 'shoot' is going to come off. Having said that, though, I must admit that my wife (who is less experienced with boats than I am) insists on my being at the helm while she makes the initial pick-up. At that point I move forward to secure the buoy while she shuts off the engine or hands sails. That is the way she likes it and it seems to work.

With a small cruiser where the freeboard forward is quite low it is usually possible to do without a boathook and just lean over to pick up the buoy by hand. Heretical as it may sound I strongly favour this procedure because it means that if the boat is making so much way that you can not hold on, all you have to do is let go, whereas with a boat hook you have to reach further away and struggle to unhook it, probably losing it altogether. Also you can bring the buoy on deck

Running a mooring line to a pile in a trot of such moorings at low tide. Secure your boat temporarily to one that is already berthed if need be and then run your own lines off in the dinghy.

and take a turn without having to hold on with one hand while you grope round trying to find a secure place to put the boathook down and know it will not roll overboard.

If you do not like the above method or if you are shorthanded, an excellent device to use is the Star mooring hook. A line is run from the hook to the samson post or mooring cleat, so that when the buoy is hooked the pole is pulled out, the spring snaps shut across the hook and you are made fast to the buoy and can get the sails off at leisure before hauling up and securing properly. A refinement of this technique is particularly useful for singlehanding. Run the line from the hook through a snatch block at the bows and from there aft outside all to the cockpit. The buoy is then picked up from the helm and hauled forward to the bows, which allows you to bring the boat right up to it without a mad dash from tiller to foredeck.

Anchoring

The main problem with anchoring is dropping it in the right place so that your vessel lies snug on the right scope of cable clear of any other anchored boats. If your proposed anchorage is fairly full when you arrive it is wise to sail (or motor) through it taking a good look round before deciding just where to lie. Note how other craft are lying and try to work out where their anchors are so that you do not drop yours on top of them. Also, as you pass through check the depth of water so that you can work out how much scope you will need. The *minimum* recommended is three times the depth of water at high water for all chain cable and five times the depth at HW for warp and chain combination.

Try to approach your anchoring site in the same direction as other boats are lying, which is normally with their bows into the tide, though if the wind is stronger they may be wind rode. Once you start your approach, using much the same techniques of motoring or sailing as for picking up a mooring, try to let go when the boat has come to a standstill and is just beginning to gather stern way. The boat's movement away from the anchor is important to lay the cable out and stop it all piling up on top of the anchor. Once about half the total scope has been veered take a turn and snub the anchor in firmly then pay the rest out slowly. To test if the anchor is biting, rest your hand on the cable beyond the stemhead roller and feel. If the anchor is dragging the cable vibrates and jumps; if it is holding all is quiet.

118

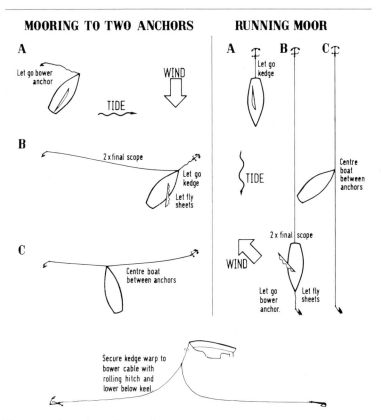

MOORING TO TWO ANCHORS

A

Let go bower anchor

WIND

TIDE

B

2 x final scope

Let go kedge

Let fly sheets

C

Centre boat between anchors

RUNNING MOOR

A   **B**   **C**

Let go kedge

TIDE

Centre boat between anchors

2 x final scope

WIND

Let go bower anchor.

Let fly sheets

Secure kedge warp to bower cable with rolling hitch and lower below keel

Two ways of mooring to two anchors.

Choosing the exact spot to let go is largely a matter of experience and a good deal of trial and error, but a useful guide is to let go at a distance ahead of where you want to lie equal to three times the depth at HW, measured in boat lengths, plus one boat length. For example if the depth of water at HW is 4 fathoms, you will need to lay out 12 fathoms of chain and if the boat is 24 ft (7.5 m) or 4 fathoms long, you should drop anchor $3 \times 4/4 + 1 = 4$ boat lengths ahead of where you want to lie. This is an approximation and refers to chain scope, but it does help. For rope and chain scope the multiplication factor is 5 rather than 3.

Where there is a foul bottom you may decide to bend a tripping line on to the crown of the anchor in the hope that if it fouls some obstruction you will still be able to retrieve it. For this purpose a line equal in length to *at least* the depth at HW should be used with a

119

float, such as an empty plastic bottle, on the free end. When you drop anchor, throw the buoy and line well clear so that they do not tangle with the cable.

If the sea in the anchorage is rough and the boat is snubbing at the cable, some of the snatching can be relieved by bending a nylon warp on to the cable at water level and taking the load on that rather than the chain. The stretchiness of the nylon absorbs much of the snatching. Alternatively, run a heavy weight down the chain to increase the catenary (curve) of the cable. This gives a better lead from the anchor and makes it necessary for the weight to be lifted each time the boat falls back, thus again reducing the snatching. Such anchor weights can be bought with a large saddle attached so that they slide down the cable easily. A line must be bent on for hauling it back up prior to weighing anchor. It is also true that in heavy weather any boat will lie more comfortably if the scope is increased well beyond the recommended minima of 3 or 5 times the depth and also chain always makes things steadier than rope.

When it is time to weigh anchor you are faced with two main situations, one where there is plenty of room to leeward or down tide of your position and the other where there is not. If there is plenty of room you need not worry too much, you can get sail on, preferably mainsail only, leaving the foredeck clear, haul up short, break out and as the boat gathers stern way, reverse the helm to bring her head round then correct it when the sail fills and sail away. On the other hand, if the next boat astern is a bit close you must either haul up short and just as the anchor breaks out cast her head off on one tack or else run up a jib and when the anchor breaks out back it, reverse the helm and spin round tight to run out of the anchorage. The trouble is that you cannot guarantee success with either of these manoeuvres and it may be more prudent to leave the anchorage under engine rather than sail, making sail once you are clear. Indeed it is sometimes sensible to have it running (in neutral) while sailing out. One final trick would be to turn the yacht at anchor and haul in the cable from the stern, so that she is already pointed downwind when the anchor breaks out.

Occasionally an anchor digs in too hard to be broken out by hand and you have to motor or sail it out. Motoring out requires less space, you put the engine just ahead so that the strain is kept off the cable and it can be brought aboard easily by the foredeck hand. This person must point frequently in the direction that the chain is leading to help the helmsman (who cannot see the cable) steer

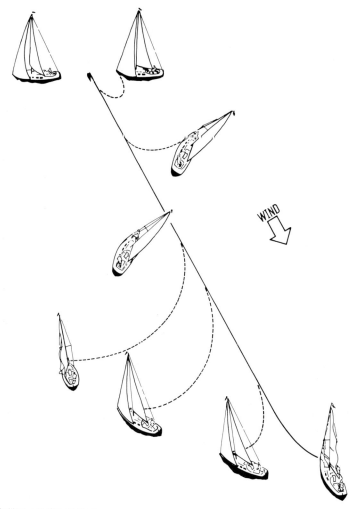

Sailing out the anchor.

straight up the line of it. When the cable comes up and down a couple of turns are taken on the mooring cleat *quickly,* keeping fingers well clear, to snub the anchor out as the boat passes over it. You may have to use higher revs to do this, but do not use more than you have to. Once the anchor is broken out, slow down again and bring the anchor aboard.

The process for sailing an anchor out is a bit more complicated.

121

Great care must be taken at all times to avoid trapping fingers in the cable. First get the boat sailing by backing the headsail to cast her head round and then letting draw as soon as possible. Keep her sailing full and bye, almost on a close reach, to maintain speed, and as she approaches the limit of the cable's scope, tack and have the foredeck crew haul in cable until it begins to go taut, at which point it should be secured, and tack at the further limit. Gather in more cable on the next leg and this or the next board should take the boat close to or over the anchor. As soon as the cable comes roughly up and down it must be snubbed so that the boat's way will break the anchor out. Once it has been broken out way must be taken off otherwise the cable and anchor will scrape the topsides as they are brought aboard.

Berthing alongside

Whether going alongside a wall or a marina pontoon, the two primary rules here are to come alongside *slowly* and to get a stern line ashore *quickly*. Probably the most frequent occasion for berthing alongside is when going into a marina and here, because of the layout of the marina, you will not have any choice as to the way you approach the berth and also very little room for error with other boats moored close by and another arm of the pontoon system there as well. Obviously in such a situation it would be foolhardy to try to sail into the berth if your engine is functional; much better either to motor in dead slow or even put lines ashore and warp the boat in.

Before trying to berth you must take a careful look at what the tide is doing – carrying you into the berth, holding you out of it or what? Then, with due allowance made for its effect, head into the berth at an angle with a man on the foredeck ready to take a *stern* line (led from the quarter forward outside everything) ashore as soon as he can. When he can safely step off on to the pontoon he should quickly take a turn on one of the mooring cleats on the pontoon towards the stern and after pulling in the slack be prepared to surge the line round the cleat and help stop the boat. Taking a turn like this is essential with even the smallest cruiser as without it he would be pulled off his feet.

Given a choice of alongside berths, it is easier to go port side to if you have a right-handed propeller. This is because the stern will be kicked to port, into the berth, when the engine is put astern to stop the boat. In any case the stern line will check way and tend to draw the stern in. Once alongside you can make up with bow line and springs as necessary. A spring, incidentally, is a line led from one quarter to a mooring point by the bows or from the bow to a mooring point by the stern. They stop the boat surging about in her berth, hold her close and parallel to the pontoon or quay and can be used eventually to turn the boat end for end or work the bows (or stern) out of the berth.

Before leaving your alongside berth another study of the tidal stream is required to see how best to make it help you in the manoeuvre. If it is directly off the pontoon you are in luck as you can more or less cast off and drift out from the berth, but it more usually runs along the berth in one direction or the other or at some angle to it. The wind must be assessed in the same way. If it is in any part off the berth it can be used to advantage, but if it is holding the boat in you have more of a problem. An extreme case of this might necessitate laying out an anchor to haul off to. Let me hasten to say that there is rarely much serious difficulty in leaving an alongside berth, particularly a marina berth. In this case there are plenty of handy places to lead warps to for hauling off on.

Where the tide or current is running along the berth, much use can be made of it to sheer the boat's bows or stern out and let you motor or sail off. If, for instance, the flow is from ahead, you can cast off all but the after spring (running from quarter to mooring point towards bows), give a kick astern with the engine and the boat will pivot on the spring with the bows easing out ready for you to move off ahead. A fender may be required to protect the quarter from being damaged on the wall or pontoon. A similar manoeuvre can be carried out without any current or stream and can just as well be done using the forward spring and drawing out stern first.

If the wind and/or water flow pushes you on to the berth you will probably not be able to push the boat off far enough to be able to motor out easily. Springing as described above may do the trick, but it is possible that you will have to warp out by running long lines to

Basic mooring lines when alongside a quay or another vessel.

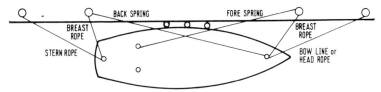

BACK SPRING   FORE SPRING
BREAST ROPE   BREAST ROPE
STERN ROPE   BOW LINE or HEAD ROPE

convenient mooring places to windward or upstream. It is probably best to control these lines from on board (using sheet winches if necessary), but leave someone to cast them off once you have cleared the berth.

Running, reaching and beating

To my mind, running wing and wing dead before the wind is not a happy way of sailing. One moment's missed concentration by the helmsman or the slightest wind shift and the boat is running by the lee in imminent danger of a gybe. Nor is it a very fast point of sailing as the apparent wind speed is greatly reduced. No, I would say that whenever possible (i.e. not when running up a narrow channel through crowded moorings, for instance) it is much better to luff up a little and sail on a very broad reach. The boat will move faster, be easier in her motion (roll less) and be more positive on the helm, making the helmsman's job that much easier.

Even when your destination does lie directly downwind it remains a better plan than running straight down on it to haul the wind slightly and then every so often gybe round and bring the wind on to the other quarter. In this way you progress downwind in a series of gybes along a zigzag course, the whole process being called, logically, tacking downwind. A broad reach is faster than a dead run and this increase in speed combined with the reduced strain on the helmsman more than makes up for the slight increase in distance actually sailed. After you have spent some time slogging to windward in a short head sea or rolling downwind it is quite remarkable the feeling of peace and steadiness gained when you come round on to a reach. Suddenly everything is quiet and the boat runs smoothly along, a compass course can be set with some hope of its being kept to and all is well with the world.

Reaching is probably the point of sailing on which a boat will be at her best or can be at her best, but careful sheet trimming is needed to get her going really well. Bone idle people like myself tend to adjust the sheets to a position where the boat is driving along reasonably well and then sit back to enjoy the view, while others will leap wildly round the deck muttering that the halyard's set up too hard or the jib's too flat. A halfway attitude is really what you want. Tend the sheets and other controls but do not let playing with them become a fetish.

Boats of modern design can make good progress to windward,

but the distance sailed through the water is always far in excess of the direct line over the ground and it tends to be a slow miserable business. The wind seems stronger and colder, the seas are always the wrong length and the boat slaps into each one, but we have to spend time beating to windward whether we like it or not and so it is worth looking at some of the techniques involved to try to make better progress and cut down the misery time.

Not surprisingly, the first thing to do is concentrate on getting the best out of the boat. The direction of the wind is changing slightly all the time and to take advantage of these variations your own course will alter continually, which in turn means approaching each sea at a slightly different angle. All these variables have to be kept weighed and balanced to give the best possible progress, driving the boat fast but making ground as quickly as possible. Never pinch the boat in rough or open water, rather let her sail a degree or two free. She will sail faster, drive through the waves better and ultimately reach wherever you are beating to sooner.

The aim must be to keep the boat moving the whole time, even if it means sailing her full and bye rather than hard up on the wind. Keep the sails full and drawing all the time. If the luff begins to lift, bear away before the boat slows. Keep an eye too on the approaching waves as even quite small ones can knock a light boat off course and can stop a small boat dead in the water, leaving her hobby horsing up and down in the same hole until the helmsman can get her to bear away and pick up speed again. The art is to anticipate more awkward waves and ensure that the boat has plenty of way on when she meets them, even if it means bearing away a bit just beforehand. The ground lost to leeward in so doing will be offset by her continuous movement through the water.

There is rarely any point in trying to insist that the helmsman steers a particular compass course to windward. Give him a course to act as a guide by all means, but leave him free to steer as best he can, provided that a note is kept of what the average heading is.

When sailing with your family as crew, remember that they are not muscle-bound gorillas and that even a fairly small headsail can take a fair bit of sheeting in, winches or no winches. Consequently, it is sensible to have a 'team tacking' system, where one of the crew lets fly the lee sheet as you put the helm down and the sail loses its drive and another takes up the slack and sheets in on the new tack. The first crew member then fits the winch handle and grinds in the last few feet while the second tails the sheet (that is, keeps tension on the tail after it leads off the winch barrel). Do not try to spin the boat round on her heel and have everyone leaping about tripping over their own feet, rather sail her round slowly giving everyone time to sort themselves out and perform their tasks without tangles. In heavier boats you can shoot up into the wind for some distance in smooth water and still come round on to the new tack, thus gaining bonus distance to windward, but many modern boats are too light for this and will end up in stays (stuck head to wind) if it is tried.

Boats with small cockpits and large crews benefit enormously if the tiller is made so that it can be lifted vertically while tacking and then dropped back again afterwards. Not all boats by any means have this arrangement and it is something that can be done in the winter, but it is worth it as it also helps when entering a tight berth under power or approaching a mooring buoy as the helmsman can stand up on a locker to get a better view over the cabin top yet still steer the boat.

No boat makes best progress to windward if she is laid over on her ear. It is uncomfortable and slow, so remember to drop a reef in or change down the headsail if the boat shows signs of being over pressed.

Man overboard

There are three main problems to be dealt with here. The first is the most basic and that is how to stop a person falling overboard in the first place. The second is how to locate someone in the water, possibly at night, and the third is how to recover the person from the water. It may seem trite to mutter about prevention being better than cure and to say that no one should go overboard in the first place, but it *is* infinitely better to take all possible precautions against its happening.

When working on the foredeck of a small cruiser it is always safer to sit or kneel rather than stand up. The helmsman should be attached to the boat with a harness at night or whenever alone on watch in rough weather. Also anyone going forward in rough weather should wear a lifeharness and *clip it on*. It may not actually stop you falling into the water, but you will still be attached to the boat and if she is kept moving you will surf alongside and can usually pull yourself back aboard over the lee rail with surprisingly little effort.

One of the problems with handling a lifeharness line is that the

Man overboard! At least he's attached by a harness to the boat.

clip has to be taken off the guardwire at each stanchion and reattached on the other side of it. Thus a better system is to have a jackstay (a slack wire rope) running between foredeck and cockpit along each side deck. This allows the hook to run free the whole way. Alternatively one of the new Latchway fittings can be used. These actually roll past the stanchions, remaining attached to the guardwire all the time, leaving you free to move fore and aft without unclipping and clipping on again. I have not had the opportunity to try one but they sound excellent.

Obvious advice includes avoiding standing (or kneeling) on lowered sails as they are extremely slippery. Also to be careful if you have to walk along narrow side decks. The list of advice is long, but assuming that someone does go overboard, what then?

The immediate problem is to find the person and get a buoyancy aid to them, whether it is a lifebuoy, a lifejacket or a floating cushion. You must have a *practised* plan both for finding and recovering a person from the water: different boats different ways. The old rule of chucking a lifebuoy in the water, gybing round and making a quick lunge with the boathook just does not work. The gybing part is all right as it is the beginning of a plan, but there is no point in throwing a lifebuoy from 50 yards away so that the person in the water has to make the effort of swimming for it. After all, what if they are injured?

127

Attached to the boat by his lifeharness the man in the water 'planes' beside the boat and can haul himself aboard unaided. On this exercise we actually found it easier for him to do this than to stop the boat and then try (with help) to clamber back over the rail. It must be on the leeward side though, so you may have to tack the boat.

It is much better to turn the boat round quickly, sail back on any point of sailing and drop a buoyancy aid close to them as you pass. *Then* you can think about picking them up, once you know that there will be something to pick up. One thing about lifebuoys: the majority of boats carry horseshoe-shaped ones in wire brackets on the pulpit, which is fine provided that they can be lifted out quickly. Many of these lifebuoys have a surrounding rope with ends that clip together and these, if done up, may prevent the buoy being lifted out at all. Check, because there certainly will not be time to fiddle about undoing them in an emergency.

Having said that there is no point in throwing a lifebuoy over if it is out of reach of the person in the water, let me now modify that statement. In heavy seas or at night, if the lifebuoy can be put over near the person and it has a light and/or Dan buoy attached, then it may help to get you back to a position close to the man overboard. From water level it probably will not be visible or will only be so at rare intervals, for even the slightest swell will hide it from a swimmer's view, but from the boat it *might* be seen and that is arguably sufficient reason for putting it in the water.

Finding a person in the water is tricky at the best of times, but in rough weather or at night it can be extremely difficult. Flashing a torch about destroys night vision so it must be used with discrimination. Assuming more than two people on the boat, one person must be given the job of watching and pointing to the man overboard right from the moment he goes in. If you are on your own or when no one can see the person in the water, you must follow a search pattern strictly. By following a careful pattern you stand a far better chance of finding a swimmer than you ever would by blundering around wherever instinct misleads you.

Assuming the boat to be on a dead run when someone falls in, the spinnaker, if one is set, must be handed quickly and the boat brought round to beat back along your track. Time each board so that you progress evenly along the old course with equal search areas on both sides. Try to estimate how far back the person in the water could be, tending towards the pessimistic to ensure that you sail past before turning back. Once you are sure you have passed his position, turn and retrace in a series of beam reaches as shown in the diagram opposite.

A broad reach situation can be tackled in much the same way by first gybing and then sailing close to the wind back parallel to the old course. A series of beam reaches, this time from a position to

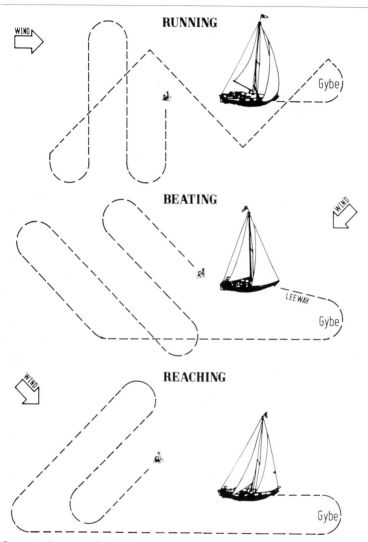

Suggested systems for picking up a man overboard.

windward of the person in the water, should bring you down to him.

What about the engine? A fair question, why not make your search under power? So far I have been lucky enough not to have to put all this theory to the true test, consequently I have no concrete evidence to offer on this matter. My feeling is that if you are under sail anyway, it is better to remain so, at least until the swimmer is

A softly inflated dinghy provides a good staging point for recovering anyone who has fallen overboard. In this case the person (the author) could haul himself into the dinghy (it was just an exercise, it wasn't for real) but another crew member could well enter the dinghy and help.

sighted. The suggested patterns are designed for convenience under sail and I think the noise of the engine might drown out the sound of a shout or whistle. If, however, you are under power when someone falls overboard then of course it is best to motor back on a reciprocal course. If you do not spot him then you must return again in a series of timed runs across the course as described before.

Once the person has been found, and it must be assumed that he is found, then you have the second major task – recovering him aboard. While one detailed person keeps watch on the man overboard, prepare to make a close pass and hand over a lifejacket, lifebuoy, floating cushion or something to help him stay afloat while you make preparations to recover him. Remember that from his low vantage point it only takes a 6-inch-high (15 cm) wave to hide anything floating, so it must be placed close to him.

Keep watching the man overboard and get ready to pick him up. A fitted boarding ladder over the stern with a section that folds down under water is a great asset when trying to pick someone up. Failing that though, the best recovery method is to launch a half-inflated rubber dinghy and get him into that. It buys time and at this stage it is very important to do just that. Someone may have to get into the part-inflated dinghy to help by pushing the fabric down under the swimmer and if so he must be kitted out with a lifejacket and lifeline – you do not want a second person in the water.

Catamarans and trimarans often have netting stretched between their hulls or the outriggers and the main hull. If this is of large open latticework rather than small mesh netting, it may help to unfasten three sides and lower it into the water for use as a scrambling net. It

Don't necessarily try to pick up a man overboard at the first attempt. You may do more to help him by making a close pass and getting a lifebuoy to him (rather than near him) and then going round again for an organized pick up.

Recovering a person from the water is always a difficult job but for the crew of a lightweight, modern multihull there is the added difficulty of the boat leaping and dancing on the smallest waves. The very lightness of the boat means that she is thrown about wildly and even if the crew manages to grab hold of the person swimming they may not be able to hold on long enough to rescue him. Following the tragic loss of the expert multihull sailor Rob James from his trimaran *Colt Cars GB*, the boat's new skipper, Jeff Houlgrave, devised a unique and apparently very effective rescue technique making use of the open weave netting normally spread between the outriggers and the hull. By unfastening three sides of the netting it drops down into the water becoming a useful scrambling net. If the person in the water is still fit they can climb up the net or, if need be, another crew member can climb down to give assistance. This photograph was taken during a demonstration of the technique.

Using the main halyard (and preferably a winch) to lift a waterlogged man aboard may be the only course open to a weak family crew.

should provide good hand and footholds (if the mesh is large enough) and could work well.

Before going alongside under power, put the engine into neutral and *stop it*. Even in neutral the propeller can creep and it could easily be kicked into gear accidentally, causing serious injury.

If you have to recover someone over the side of the boat, it may help to drop the guardrails and heel the boat to reduce freeboard. Do warn everyone though that the guardrails are no longer there, because as soon as they go, the handhold they offer goes. Once alongside get a line round or attached to the person in the water so that they will not be separated from the boat again.

Actually getting a person from the water can be the hardest part of the whole operation as he will be waterlogged and possibly weak and cold. Take care not to fall in yourself and if necessary use a halyard to haul him up, or attach a rope round him to a winch. Another way is to drop a sail into the water, work him into that and then haul the sail up, rolling him aboard with it.

Do not be fooled, getting someone aboard is hard. Try it on a warm day at anchor when everyone is swimming anyway and just see.

It may not be good for the sail, but anything goes if it helps to recover someone from the water. The difficulty may be in making the sail sink sufficiently to get the person into it. Lowering the guard rails at this point also might help.

Finally, once you have recovered the person overboard you must treat him for shock. Warm blankets and sleeping bags wrapped round him, a hot cup of tea or coffee, preferably with sugar, but *do not give him alcohol.*

I have rather laboured this subject as it worries many people and is ignored by others. It is a serious problem that should be discussed and practised as far as possible, remembering that it may very well be the skipper in the water.

Running aground

This seems almost a way of life for some people. You see them running from shoal patch to shoal patch with gay abandon and rarely getting into serious trouble. Most of us have done it enough times to think we have learnt to be more careful – but we have not. In a quiet backwater where the bottom is soft mud and the boat will not come to much harm it is no big deal, but if you ground on an offshore bank with a rising wind you could be in trouble. There are times when running aground intentionally can get you out of trouble since there is no surer way of stopping the boat. For instance, if you run into an anchorage and the halyard jams a quick luff on to a convenient mudbank could save the day.

Trying to get off in the direction you went on is a fairly basic plan, but if the bottom shelves gradually and the tide is ebbing you must work very quickly. If you grounded with a following wind, get sail off immediately to stop her driving even further on, then either try to motor off astern or pole her off with the spinnaker pole or oars taken from the dinghy. Laying out a kedge into deep water takes too much time if the tide is falling fast. Boats with a single keel can have their draft reduced by heeling them over, but this will not work for a bilge-keeler, which has least draft when upright. Indeed with a bilge-keel boat it may well be time to put the kettle on.

Despite the presence on board of an echosounder it is quite common to run aground when beating up a narrow channel, in which case you can often back the jib to turn her head then let draw and sail free. On the windward shore with a rising tide you do not have to worry as the tide will lift you and the wind will stop you going further up the bank. On a lee shore you must lay out a kedge to windward so that you do not go any further as the boat floats.

Do remember that an echosounder tells you the depth of water under you, not ahead of you. In other words it tells you when you *are* aground not when you are *going* aground.

Centreboarders and lifting-keel boats have a distinct advantage in grounding situations as they can quickly reduce their draft by winding the keel or plate up. This is definitely an asset in shoal waters.

Kedging

A kedge can be used in two main ways, one as an anchor to lie to, either by itself or more usually in conjunction with the bower anchor, and the other as a fixed point to haul off to, either from a berth alongside a wall or a mudbank on which the boat has grounded. Ideally the kedge should be of sufficient size to give good holding power, but of a different type from the bower anchor. In practice most people carry a fairly small kedge, which means that conditions must be light before you can lie safely to it with no other anchor down. On the other hand it does mean that it can be taken off in the dinghy and laid out easily in the event of (say) a grounding.

When you lay out a kedge using the dinghy, carry the anchor and its warp in the dinghy rather than trying to let the warp run out from the yacht. Make the bitter end fast on board then lower the anchor into the dinghy and flake the warp down in the stern. Do not try to coil it as it will then inevitably snarl up as you row off. Alternatively, if you want to take the bower anchor with its chain, or even a particularly heavy kedge, make a bowline round the crown of the anchor the same length in the bight as the depth of the water, then row out with this line flaked down in the dinghy. Anchor the dinghy and haul the anchor to you over the bottom, dragging the cable with it. This you will find infinitely easier than taking the anchor and chain in the dinghy. Once in position, untie the bowline and there you are.

If you use a warp on the kedge (as is usual) it will have to have at least 3 fathoms of chain between the anchor and warp to keep the angle of pull low and to ensure that the anchor stays well dug in.

Lying to two anchors is often a safeguard in a rough anchorage, provided you can be sure no-one will foul the second anchor. Drop the main anchor to one side of where you want to lie and, paying out twice as much chain as is required to lie to, sail or motor away at right angles to your desired berth until you reach the limit of the chain scope. Then, drop the kedge and pay out its warp as you haul in half the length of the chain. This is now your berth, centred between the two anchors. Secure the kedge warp to the main anchor cable with a tight rolling hitch (retaining the bitter end on deck) and lower it down to below the foot of the keel so that when the tide turns the boat can swing clear of it.

When you want to keep the boat lying in the middle of a creek (or some other narrow gap) it may be necessary to moor her fore and aft with an anchor over the bow and another out astern. As you run into the berth let go the kedge from the stern and run on, paying out twice as much cable as is needed with regard to the depth of water. Bring up hard on this anchor to make it bite deeply and then let go the bower anchor. Pay out cable on that and haul in on the kedge until the boat is centred between the two. Later, when you want to get underway again, reverse the process, paying out scope on one cable and hauling in on the other. Break out the anchor and you are conventionally anchored to a single anchor, from which you can get underway in the usual manner.

Manners for mariners

Anchorages are crowded places these days and it is often hard to obtain berths in marinas. It is usual to have to spend the night in close proximity to several other occupied craft and this means that consideration must always be shown to others. Not only in the way we moor (that is to say without fouling or lying too close to another boat and without making up mooring lines on top of others so that no-one can cast off) but also in what we do and how we behave.

Don't Have the volume turned right up on radios or cassette players when listening to music or the weather forecast.

Hog VHF Channel 16 for non-emergency transmissions. Wait for a break in traffic, make contact and immediately change to a working frequency.

Chuck litter, especially plastic materials, overboard.

Shout and swear, even when getting the anchor up.

Run generators in the middle of the night or let exhaust fumes blow across neighbouring boats.

Hold noisy parties late at night when children may be trying to sleep.

Let children play where they will annoy other crews.

Do Be friendly, pass the time of day with other people and if you make friends with other crews invite them aboard for a quiet drink or cup of tea.

Stop halyards slapping on metal masts. Few noises are more irritating.

Pass on (accurately) the latest weather forecast if asked for it.

Lend a hand if one is needed.

Think.

Competent wives

Aboard many small family cruisers the husband does the majority of the actual sailing while his wife cooks, looks after the children and occasionally takes the helm when instructed to 'head for that buoy'. But what happens if the husband hurts himself or, worse, if he falls overboard? Fair enough there are certain jobs aboard, like hauling up a recalcitrant anchor, with which a man may be better able to cope by virtue of greater physical strength, but it is foolish not to ensure that the woman (and older children) are competent at least in the basic handling of the boat in case of loss or damage to the skipper.

Wives should certainly be capable of making and taking in sail (the old hand, reef and steer), of sailing on all points, of *heaving to*, starting the motor and operating its controls, rounding up to a buoy and of dropping anchor. Knowledge of how to use the VHF radio if one is carried also makes sense for emergency situations. I emphasize heaving to, not only because it is a manoeuvre useful in emergencies, but because it gives you time to think. You can heave to to look at a chart, await a flood tide into port, radio for assistance, anything.

When practising any manoeuvre, be it mooring or man overboard, try to ensure that your wife can carry it out at least competently – and do not be disheartened if she is better than you are, that could save your life one day.

Rules of the road

More correctly these are the 'International Rules for Preventing Collisions at Sea', which are drawn up by an international committee. The rules must be learnt and understood by all who go to sea. The complete regulations are far too long to reproduce here, but they can be found in publications like *The Macmillan and Silk Cut Nautical Almanac* or *Reed's Nautical Almanac*. They govern navigation lights and sound signals in addition to their fundamental purpose of laying down rules for action when two vessels approach one another.

There are times when a sound knowledge of the rules of the road are a definite comfort. Naval ships on exercise often make unexpected course changes and it is generally as well to avoid them entirely, but in restricted waters you just have to obey the rules.

Points to remember: If you have to alter course do so *positively* and in *good time*. Also, something that many people forget or ignore, as soon as you start your engine, *even if you are motorsailing*, you become a *power-driven vessel* and are then governed by the rules for power vessels. Never dice with ships, particularly in narrow channels or separation zones and if in doubt get out.

9

Pilotage

Often without the proper chart table and working space found on larger craft, the navigator of a small family cruiser spends much of his time doing what is called 'coastal pilotage' rather than more formal navigation. He learns to look at a chart and see a three-dimensional picture of the shoreline and to look at the shore and see it as a two-dimensional chart. What he is really doing is nautical map reading. This is not to suggest that it is unnecessary to learn the more formal navigation methods. On the contrary, to cruise safely and successfully sound knowledge of coastal navigation principles is essential, but it is also essential to realize that while you may be able to keep up an accurate plot in fine and settled weather, as soon as a bit of sea gets up or the weather closes in, in fact just when you most need a good plot, you are likely to have your hands full coping with the boat and all you will be able to do is sail by eye.

Reading the chart

A chart is not just a pretty picture to look at, nor is it simply a jumble of confusing numerals and squiggly lines. It is a mine of information about both the sea and the coastline. All you have to do is learn to read it. Building up a picture in your mind from a chart is a bit like 'painting by numbers', the chart is the numbers on canvas and the land and sea the finished painting. Just as an Ordnance Survey map uses contour lines to show heights and gradients of land, so a chart uses contour lines on the land parts and sounding lines on the sea. The closer together the countour lines the steeper the land or the more quickly the seabed is shelving. From this information alone you can start to visualize the coastline: whether it consists of cliffs and steep hills with deep water close in or low, undulating land with shallows and shoal patches extending well offshore.

Of course, some parts of the coast are easier to navigate by eye than others. Where you have a rocky coastline with well defined bays, headlands and hills, even perhaps an off-lying island, it is fairly easy, but if the coastline is low with undulating features and shallow water to keep you well offshore, it is not easy. Such features as there are must be kept under close surveillance and good use must be made of buoys, beacons and depth readings.

On particularly hilly coasts the direction of sunlight can be tricky as it may, for instance, throw into prominence a hill that is perhaps some way inland and tone down a hill closer to the shore. Then again it can get behind a hill and shroud an otherwise prominent landmark in shadow. Sunlight on a low-lying coast can make it difficult to see where land becomes sea and a river mouth can be all but invisible quite close in. Here, in fact, the cruising man becomes a buoy-hopper, ticking off each one as he passes it, but he must steer an accurate course between them and must be sure to *identify* all marks. The danger is to assume that a buoy or mark is the one you are looking for without any positive identification. That way you can come badly unstuck.

Transits

Many of the more difficult creeks and harbours are provided with what we call leading marks to guide boats in. These marks usually take the form of two shore beacons, which are lit at night, one being kept directly in line with the other. That is to say they are kept 'in transit'. Such transits are common and of great value, but the coastal topography in any area provides many natural transits. For example, a headland may line up with a particular off-lying rock or a church with a hilltop or clump of trees.

The beauty of transits is that they give an incontrovertible position line. There is no possibility of compass error or misreading or anything else and if you can find two transits that form at the same time (come 'on' at the same time), then you have an absolute fix of your position. This of course is seldom possible, but when it does happen it is a great source of comfort. One thing to be taken into account in areas of great tidal range is that at low water (or thereabouts) a buoy may well be out of position, blown off station at the limit of its riding chain or carried away down tide. This will not make a great deal of difference to its position, but it could be enough to throw a transit slightly out.

When you are planning a passage look out for possible transits on the chart and make a note of them to use as one more check on your boat's position. You may not need them in the event, but if you are stuck at the helm for some reason and only have such a list at hand you will at least have something to go on.

Distance off by eye

Judging distance at sea can be extraordinarily difficult and is something that comes only with practice, but there are one or two tricks that help and hardly require any instruments. The real criterion for judging distance off is what you *cannot* see rather than what you *can* see. For instance, you can get a far better idea of how far off the coast you are by the fact that you cannot yet see the windows of a house than by the fact that you can see them though they are 'not too clear'.

The following table gives a rough idea of distance by observation rather than measurement.

Distance	Details visible
100 yards	Face of person on shore is seen as pale shape with dark lines for eyebrows and possibly line of mouth can be seen. Guardrails and rigging visible.
200 yards (approx 1 cable)	Face now just a pale blurr, tide seen to ripple round buoys, stagings, piles quite clearly.
400 yards	Person generally blurred, but leg movements visible. Just about see rigging.
500 yards	Person seen as dark splodge, crossbars on house windows just detectable, uprights plain to see.
1 mile	Large buoy shapes clear, small ones shapeless, windows recognizable, traffic clear people just dots if seen.
2 miles	Small buoys usually lost, large ones little shape, windows seen as dots, traffic visible, ship's sidelights first seen at night.
3 miles	Bow waves of ships seen from cockpit and waves breaking on shore.

4 miles	Hedges, individual trees, houses and wet roads, but little detail. Beach dipped below horizon and colours tending to assume uniform bluish grey.

You can get quite a good idea of distance off with a couple of very basic instruments, namely a pencil and a clear plastic ruler. Hold the pencil at arm's length and line the tip up on some object viewed through the right eye. Close the right eye and open the left. The pencil will jump to the right. Note this distance and, using it as a unit, measure off four such units to the left of dead in front of you and four to the right: the distance so covered is your distance off. In fact the number of units needed seems to vary from person to person

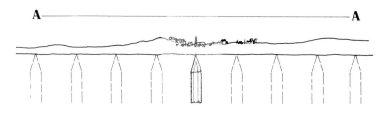

A-A = DISTANCE OFF

Distance off by pencil and eye method.

The hand used to measure angles.

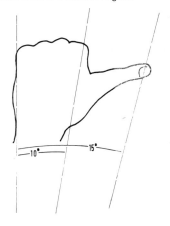

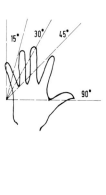

Distance by simple ruler method.

between 7 and 9, but this can be found by experimentation. The shoreline should also be as straight as possible, but it does at least tell you if you are 'far or near'.

Taking a ruler, attach a piece of string to it and make a knot at exactly 60 cm from it. Holding the knot against your nose and the ruler at full stretch, measure the apparent height of a prominent object of known height (say a lighthouse). The height of the object in feet divided by the apparent height in millimetres equals your distance off in cables (1 cable is approx. 200 yards). For example, a 60-ft tower apparent height 30 mm is 2 cables distant.

These are rough-and-ready methods but they are better than nothing and with practice they can become quite accurate.

Signs in the sea

Sailing by eye is rather like a detective game in which clues are scattered liberally about the place, but are mostly in code. To make matters more interesting, the code can be wildly misinterpreted if you do not have a pretty accurate idea of your whereabouts. The sea itself is full of such clues and a study of them is both fascinating and invaluable. If you do not know quite where you are, then every wave and ripple seems to indicate a shoal or submerged rock, but if you are sure of your position they may take on a completely different and happier meaning.

Wave form depends a great deal on the depth of water and the nature of the bottom they are passing over. There is a very distinct change in wave form when ocean swells cross the continental shelf, for instance. There is also a great deal of difference between waves in a deep-water channel and those over a shallow patch. The detective work is in deciding just what the water is telling you.

In shallow, muddy water where the water is perpetually discoloured it may appear to be just the same in 'texture' where the depth is a few fathoms as it does over a patch just a couple of feet deep. However, in rocky waters the colour changes from a dark blue in deep water to a pale green over shallows, with the odd rock marked by an almost black shadow.

The sea offers an indication of two things: deep-water channels and underwater obstructions. When the wind is against the tide, a nasty choppy sea can build up and this will be greater in a deep-water channel than it will be over the shallows. This is because the tide flows faster down the main channel and offers more resistance to the wind: like a cat, it does not like being stroked the wrong way. On a very calm day when the sea is glassy, the main channel is likely to be marked by slight rippling, again because the water there is moving faster than it does over the shallows. However, if the wind is with the tide (in the same direction as the tide) the channel will be smooth and the shallows will be rippled, since the stream in the channel is fast enough to reduce its resistance to the wind.

A bar at the entrance to a port is usually marked by some disturbance of the water and with an onshore wind there are often breakers. These signs tell the navigator quite clearly that there *is* a bar, but they can be deceptive about its precise location. With an onshore wind the seas will in fact pass over the bar and break a short distance inshore of it, so that from seaward you see the backs of the breakers *beyond* the bar. A point to remember: the same thing can happen with overfalls and tide rips where a rock or sharp rise in the seabed causes the tidal current to shoot up to the surface at some distance from the obstruction. Never sail too close to such disturbances unless the exact depth of water is known.

In areas of deep water and very fast tides you find 'tidal races'. When there is anything of a sea running these tide races are best avoided, for a passage through them can be frightening. On a calm day the sea seems to boil with huge smooths or slicks forming on the surface. I know that I have on many occasions found myself sailing into such areas and had to take a close look at the chart and echo sounder to reassure myself that there really was deep water there.

Just occasionally you come across a line of foam and debris on the water where two tidal streams meet, each bringing its own flotsam. Again these can be a disturbing sight if you do not recognize them for what they are.

Dirty weather

However carefully we listen to and take note of weather forecasts, there comes a time when we get caught out with a rising wind or fast

Look in the relevant pilot book and then watch out for harbour entry signals whenever approaching a strange port. If you carry VHF radio keep a listening watch on the local port control frequency and if you like radio-in to warn the local marina that you are looking for a berth.

Not a submarine's conning tower, just an unlit buoy in a very strong tidal stream. You certainly know which way the tide is running, but this is just the kind of thing you dread coming up against at night.

Yachts entering this harbour have to take great care to follow the tiny buoys in their sweep round the off-lying shoal patch. The right-hand yacht has just passed one buoy and there are two more astern of the nearer yacht. Notice that even in these calm conditions swells are breaking on the shoal. Think what it would he like in an onshore blow.

reducing visibility and at such times we have to make a snap decision on whether or not it is safe to make port. Even a moderate wind against a spring tide can kick up a nasty sea for a small boat and a heavy rain squall or a light sea mist can blot out the land, any of which may be a local phenomenon that could not be expected from an overall forecast.

I have tried to stress the importance of keeping a constant check on your position and progress along the coast, for it is when the weather turns dirty that you really need to know where you are. If you have been checking off buoys and landmarks conscientiously and can say with confidence 'the river mouth bears northeast from here and is distant two miles', you are in a strong position to decide your next move.

The questions you have to answer are threefold: is the weather going to worsen, are you safe to make a dash to the nearest refuge or should you stay at sea and ride it out? The idea of 'staying at sea and riding it out' may be highly romantic and may in the end make a good clubhouse yarn, but with your wife and children aboard it can be an extremely harrowing experience that should not be undertaken lightly – and yet it could be the safest course of action to take. If you have a safe anchorage close at hand with an easy approach and you think you have time to get in before the weather worsens, then you will probably decide to put in, even if it means scrabbling down a deep reef and motorsailing. If, on the other hand, there is a rocky, harbourless coast under your lee and you are not absolutely sure of your position, then you may have no choice but to claw your way to windward, get a good offing and stay there. We will look more closely at handling a small boat in heavy weather in Chapter 13.

You may find, of course, that as you approach your chosen port you are bucking a foul tide and making no progress. Here again a knowledge of your position could save you. It may be that the tide will turn fair in an hour or so, in which case you decide to plug on, or again it may be against you for ages and you will look to another anchorage for refuge. In the end it all comes down to the business of knowing the boat's position, which is what pilotage is all about; a probably unplotted but *known* position.

Depth of water

One of the most useful aids to inshore pilotage is an accurate measurement of the depth of water under the boat's keel. This is not simply to confirm that you are either afloat or aground, but to help you pinpoint your position. For example, if you are running in towards an as yet unsighted harbour (and assuming no radio direction finding aids), you may be able to fix your position with some accuracy by finding the depth of water. Say you look at the chart and find that at $1\frac{1}{2}$ miles off there is a 4-fathom (7 m) patch marked and at 1 mile a 2-fathom (3.6 m) line is shown. A watch on the depth will show when you pass over the patch and then the line, and combined with your compass course, this information will give a rough guide as to your position. This procedure is known as taking a chain of soundings and although fitting it to the depth pattern shown on the chart can usually only give a rough position guide it is another useful piece of information in times of need.

The commonest way of measuring the depth of water is by using an echosounder. This is an electronic instrument that sends out a sonic impulse from a transducer mounted on the hull underwater and times how long it takes to bounce back off the bottom, thus calculating the depth of water *below the transducer*. The display of this information can take the form of a flashing light on a dial, a needle pointer on a dial (an analogue display), digital readout, a graph or even a voice recording. Naturally there are points for and against each system, but they are all good in that they provide a continuous output of information, unlike the old leadline that had to be cast and hauled in and cast again. It must be remembered, however, that the echosounder only tells the depth of water beneath the transducer, taking no account of the depth of keel beneath it or its depth beneath the surface of the water. It may be possible to calibrate it for these errors, but do remember them.

A useful feature of some instruments is an audible depth alarm, which sounds if the depth either decreases below a set level (i.e. you are in danger of running aground) or if it increases beyond a set depth (i.e. you must veer more scope or there is sufficient depth to cross the bar or whatever).

The two other methods still in use, though certainly not as common as they used to be, are the handlead and the sounding pole. The handlead consists of a plaited line several fathoms long with a lead weight on the end, which is held coiled in one hand while the lead is swung and thrown clear (cast) ahead of the boat with the other, then when the line comes up straight, the depth is read from the markings on the line. Traditionally the line is 20 fathoms long, but for a small cruiser 10 fathoms should be enough. Again, traditionally, markings were not put on the line every fathom, but I would suggest doing so on the shorter line, perhaps like this:

1 fathom cord with 1 knotted tail
2 fathoms cord with 2 knotted tails
3 fathoms cord with 3 knotted tails
4 fathoms white rag
5 fathoms leather with hole in it
6 fathoms white rag with two tails
7 fathoms leather 1 tail
8 fathoms leather 2 tails
9 fathoms leather 3 tails
10 fathoms white rag knotted

The point about this marking system is that all of the markers can be identified by feel, making use at night much easier, but you may well prefer to work out your own markings. The lead itself has a hollow base which can be filled or 'armed' with tallow to bring up samples of the seabed. Such samples are of great value as further clues to your position and are something that an echo sounder cannot give you. Aside from being a cheap alternative to an echosounder, however, the use of a leadline or sounding pole is to determine the levelness or slope of the bottom where you will dry out as the tide falls. With either of these it is possible to sound all round the boat, whereas an echosounder is confined to displaying a reading of the depth straight below it.

A sounding pole is only really useful in very shallow water as it would otherwise have to be so long it could not readily be carried on board. The pole is marked in bands, usually alternate black and white, each being one foot in length, and one end of the pole is weighted to help it sink. All you do is lean over from the cockpit and take a sounding. The end can be armed like a lead and, being a rigid pole, the bottom can be 'felt'.

All of these methods are valid in their own right, but it must be watched that in each case the boat's draft is not taken into account by the instrument itself and you must make the appropriate allowance. Also they all tell you the depth of water you are in, not what you are approaching.

Harbour signals

Because harbours are sheltered and protected areas, their entrances tend to be narrow and where there is much commercial traffic, or where there is a blind corner, they usually have a system of signals to tell you when it is safe to enter or leave. Unfortunately these signals are not the same in every port. Publications such as the *Macmillan and Silk Cut Nautical Almanac* or *Reed's Nautical Almanac* provide details of the signals, with other navigational information on the port. Local sailing directions too will list them, but always take care and check the signal before going in or out.

Landfalls and accumulating errors

Although in the general course of coastal cruising you are not often out of sight of land for more than a few hours, it can be disturbing the first time, particularly if you stop to consider the possibility of not being able to recognize your landfall when you make it. On short coastal passages you are unlikely to be far out, but a headland viewed from only slightly different angles can be quite unrecognizable as the same place. Strong light throws up minor hills as stark mountains to eyes looking for low hummocks. A bay that appears large on the chart can mysteriously fade into the rest of the coastline and be invisible to the navigator until he is quite close inshore. Buoys can appear to be way out of position according to the chart, simply by being approached from an odd angle. All of these things are disturbing to say the least and the worry is increased if the navigator is not dead sure of the boat's position

Generally speaking, a large yacht is likely to make a better landfall than a small one, not only because the navigator can sit down at a proper chart table with all his instruments to hand rather than trying to perch with a piece of plywood on his knees, but also because the boat is moving faster (and is therefore out of sight of land for a shorter time) and the helmsman is able to hold a steadier course in the larger yacht. But, of course, it is the smaller boat with the tired crew that needs the good landfall.

We will take a closer look at some of the intricacies of navigation in Chapter 10, but it is as well to know some of the things that can contribute to error when undertaking coastal pilotage. Perhaps the biggest source of error, and usually the most embarrassing, is the helmsman who does not admit to steering anything other than the set course. You soon learn at sea that (in open waters) the navigator sets a course as a *guide*. If it can be steered accurately, so much the better, but otherwise, if he is any good he will not mind you steering a safe course on which either you or the boat is happier (within a few degrees of the set course), *provided that you tell him*. A one degree error over 60 miles only means a lateral error of one mile at the end, but a helmsman who steers 5 degrees off, without admitting it, and a navigator who says 'the tide's running at 2 and a bit knots, we need a touch of leeway as well' and so on, are combining to create a big mistake. Occasionally, of course, a mistake is made and another one happily cancels it out, but you can never rely on this to happen.

The other thing a navigator sometimes has to do is study the helmsman (without his knowing it) and see to which side of the course he is tending to steer. A tell-tale compass mounted at the chart table makes this quite simple. Going to windward some people steer free, others pinch up. Boats too have their foibles. Some carry a lot of weather helm and will tend to gripe the whole time. Running dead before the wind is the worst time. Start two boats off together on opposite gybes and you can guarantee that they will not stay parallel for long; they will either diverge or collide. Far better to set a safe course without fear of a gybe and tack downwind allowing the helmsman to steer a steady course down each leg.

Logs, too, can be a source of error by over or under reading. It must be remembered that they only tell you the distance run *through the water*. A boat making 4 knots against a 2-knot tide is only going to cover half the distance over the ground that she records through the water.

All of this really adds up to the old question of whether it is better to head for a point and try to calculate which side of it you are if you miss, or to put in a known error by aiming well to one side right from the start. The point is to realize that the landfall you make will not always *appear* to be the one you want. Be prepared for this and try not to panic, take it easy, even if you sight land at only 5 miles (8 km) off, you probably have over an hour in which to identify it before you have to worry too much – unless there are any offshore hazards. And do not forget that you can always heave to and think.

10

Coastal navigation

In Chapter 9, we dealt with pilotage or sailing by eye. Now we come to the more formal business of coastal navigation. Whole books have been written on this subject alone so I can only hope to introduce the bare bones of it here and to encourage you to make a separate and careful study of it. In order to navigate or pilot a boat we need charts, so we will start with them.

Charts and symbols

The main chart publishers in the U.K. are the Hydrographic Department, Ministry of Defence, Barnacle Marine, and Imray and Wilson, though there are a number of other concerns publishing large-scale harbour plans and localized charts. The MoD (Admiralty) charts are the basis for all the others and are generally recognized as being the best of the lot in a broad sense. The only drawback for the navigator on a small cruiser is their size, which can be anything up to 52 in × 28 in (132 cm × 71 cm) when opened out flat and about 28 in × 20 in (71 cm × 50 cm) when folded for stowage. The Barnacle Marine charts are not quite as large and fold down to book size, making stowage easy, and the Imray ones are small flat sheets or larger sheets that fold down like the Barnacle Marine ones.

Many chandlers stock charts, usually for their locality, but the Admiralty ones are best purchased from an Admiralty chart agent who will correct them up to the date of purchase. Which charts you choose is largely a matter of personal preference, but the Admiralty ones cover all areas and are recognized as being the mother and father of charts.

Charts provide the navigator with a fantastic amount of information in a small space by using a fairly simple series of symbols. Because the sea and seabed contain such a variety of things – shoals, wrecks, buoys etc. – the list of symbols is quite long and in fact the Admiralty publishes a complete booklet (BA No. 5011) to display them. Sometimes a magnifying glass will help in reading the small symbols close inshore on a small-scale chart.

Just one point to make clear: a *small-scale* chart shows a large area in less detail; a *large-scale* chart shows a small area in great detail.

Pilot books

When you hear talk of 'the pilot', as in *The North Sea Pilot* or *The Irish Coast Pilot*, it is the Admiralty pilot books that are being referred to. These volumes, although intended primarily for the use of ship's navigators, are valuable adjuncts to the Admiralty charts and, as with the charts, there are volumes to cover the whole world. All the facilities at each port or harbour are meticulously listed, from where

Navigator hard at work on the cabin table maintaining a careful DR plot on a cross-Channel passage. The cabin table, while not ideal, may be better than a foldaway chart table, being bigger and easier to sit at.

Many production boats fit a foldaway (or in this case slide-away) chart table. They are better than nothing but usually have serious drawbacks when compared with the luxury of a fixed table on a larger yacht. In this case the lower left corner of the table is completely unsupported, so cannot be leant on and the navigator must sit sideways to work at it. There should also be no one asleep in the quarter berth at the time. The bookshelf just above it is handy for navigation books, and the flexible chart light fitted on the bulkhead is handy too, but where do you stow the charts? One answer would be to keep them flat under the berth cushion or in a deckhead box. Whatever you do, don't roll them up like they do in the Hollywood movies. You will never be able to flatten them out for real navigation.

to anchor or obtain fuel to the nearest de-ratting point, but always with the emphasis on ship facilities. Approach channels, lights, buoys, beacons and sound signals are all detailed, together with very useful topographical information to aid you in making a landfall. In some of the pilots, drawings of 'views' are given to show the navigator, for example, what a particular headland looks like from two or three different angles. These again are of much help.

Apart from the Admiralty pilot books there are many published with the yachtsman in mind. Some yacht clubs produce local pilots, notably the Clyde Cruising Club and the Irish Cruising Club. There is also the Cruising Association Handbook covering the whole of the British Isles and near Continental waters. For the Solent and South Coast of England Adlard Coles' *South Coast Harbours and*

Anchorages (Faber 1982) is the standard work, while for the Thames Estuary and East Coast it is Jack Coote's *East Coast Rivers* (published by *Yachting Monthly*, 1983).

No book giving pilotage information can hope to stay up to date for very long (and may even be slightly out of date on publication because of the long preparation time) as marks, and in many cases shoals and bars, change quite rapidly, but if care is taken they may prove to be your salvation. While we should always carry charts showing every harbour along our planned passage, we may not always carry one of the largest scale for a particular entrance and that is when the pilot comes into its own.

The *Macmillan and Silk Cut Nautical Almanac/Reed's Nautical Almanac* have already been mentioned. If you want to know something about anything you will find it in one of these massive volumes $9\frac{1}{2}$ times out of 10. Published annually they are absorbing books of tide tables, light lists, weather, navigation, buoyage, radio work, distress procedures; you name it, it is there. All I can really say is that if you intend to go cruising you must have an up-to-date copy of one of them on board.

Navigation instruments

As with so many things in sailing today, the range of navigation instruments available to those with money to spend is all but limitless. There is certainly no problem in spending a couple of thousand pounds on electronic instruments alone. Few bits and pieces are truly *necessary*, but many are very practical and nice to have to hand as aids to simple, accurate position-keeping.

Among the *essential* items come a good steering compass, charts, echosounder (or leadline), radio capable of picking up shipping forecasts, watch or clock (with second hand) of known error, soft pencils, sharpener, rubber (eraser), parallel rules or Douglas protractor or Hurst plotter or one of their variants, dividers, almanac, local pilots, log book, notebooks and a distance log. These are not listed in any particular order of merit because they are all required. We will look more closely at the steering compass in the next section of this chapter; the charts, leadline and echosounder have already been discussed. Chapter 16 deals with weather forecasts, so we will omit that for now. Always use a soft pencil on charts; 2B is about the best as it can be rubbed out easily and does not leave deep trenches in the surface of the charts. HB pencils are fine for log

A small roller parallel ruler in use on a small boat chart table (actually a plywood board propped up on one bunk) carrying an open Admiralty chart. Such rulers are excellent where the chart can be opened flat like this, but on small chart tables they are impractical.

entries as these should not need to be rubbed out so often and the pencils stay sharp that much longer, though a sharpener is still needed.

Although they are beautiful instruments roller parallel rulers may be impractical on a small boat without a proper chart table where the more common 'walking' rulers are often the easier to use. The Hurst plotter (and one or two variants and imitations) consists of a gridded transparent plastic square with a circle of plastic marked in 360 degrees and a long arm mounted on top of it. The disc can be clamped to show magnetic variation and with the grid aligned to a meridian or parallel of latitude on the chart, the arm can be used to read or lay off a course. Its main advantage is that the arm is flexible and can therefore be used with a chart spread out on your knees in dire circumstances. The Douglas protractor is a gridded square of clear plastic with a 360-degrees notation round the sides. To lay off a course the centre hole is placed over the departure point, the grid is aligned with a meridian or parallel of latitude and a mark is made at

On most small boats 'walking' parallel rulers like these are quite effective. The hinges must not be too tight, or the rules twist as they are walked, but if too loose they can also cause problems.

the side next to the bearing of the destination (say 030 degrees). The departure point and this mark are then joined up using the edge of the protractor as a ruler.

There are several variants on these two types available, but most work in a similar way. Choose one that you understand and feel will be simple to use on your boat.

As to dividers, I would suggest that despite their extra cost, the one-handed type are infinitely preferable to the ordinary school geometry set type. But be sure to use them properly or your money will have been wasted. *Squeeze* the shoulders so that the arms cross and the points separate; *squeeze* the arms so that the points close up. Never pull the shoulders apart, that is a two-handed use.

The almanacs, *Reed's* and *Macmillan and Silk Cut* and the local pilot books have been discussed. A log book is necessary not only as a record of events but as an integral part of navigation of the vessel, but more of that later in this chapter. A notebook saves scribbling calculations on charts and easily lost scraps of paper. Distance logs fall into two categories: towing logs and through hull

160

logs. Towing logs may be mechanical, known as patent logs, or electronic. Both require a small rotator to be towed some distance astern, linked to a recording head that displays distance and, often, speed. Patent log rotators or 'fish' are towed on a long line which is twisted as the rotator spins and so turns cogs and wheels in the recording head to operate clock-like dials. The electronic type of towing log has the spinner towed on an electrical cable through which minute magnetic and electrical changes are sensed and shown on digital or analogue displays.

Hull logs have a small impeller projecting through the underside of the hull, which then acts like the towed electronic unit. Some impellers are retractable for weed clearing and they can be either like a propeller or like a paddlewheel. These electronic units can feed more than one display, so that, if required, there can be readouts for the helmsman and the navigator sitting at his chart table.

Towing logs should not be streamed until in clear and reasonably

This is a Sestrel plotter, much like the Hurst plotter. It has a fixed square base with a pivoted compass rose and a swinging ruler arm. The rose allows setting of variation and the square base is easily aligned with latitude or longitude lines, while the ruler arm is flexible and can therefore cope with an uneven surface. A good instrument on small boats.

deep water and should be handed before re-entering congested or shallow waters. To hand a patent log, unclip the line from the recorder and pay the line out into the water as you haul in the spinner, then coil it in from the spinner end. This way you avoid kinks and snarl-ups. By the way, if the patent log does not show speed, an idea of it can be obtained by watching the tenths of a mile scale over a 6-minute period (one tenth of an hour) and multiplying by 10. Thus 0.4 miles in 6 minutes equals 4 knots.

In addition to this list of essentials there are some items that could be classed as 'highly desirable'; handbearing compass, radio direction finder, binoculars and stopwatch. Not all steering compasses are sited so that it is easy to take a bearing of something directly from them unless that object is more or less dead ahead or astern and for this reason a handbearing compass is very useful. There are many types of handbearing compass on the market and as usual each has its merits, but for small boat use some of the best are ones that, by use of carefully designed optics, allow the bearing to be read with the eyes still focused on the object, thus making snap bearings both accurate and easy. Such compasses are the Mini Compass and the Suunto handbearing compass.

Radio direction finders are commonplace now as prices are not ridiculously high and their general acceptance and use is widespread. In principle a radio receiver picks up coded transmissions from a shore station, an in-built compass provides a bearing on the transmitter and this, crossed with one or two other such bearings, provides a fix. The individual transmitter identifies itself with a Morse code reference then emits a continuous tone for taking the bearing. The positions and call signs of these beacons are listed in the almanacs or on special charts.

Binoculars have such obvious uses as spotting buoys and landmarks, but do not go for a pair with too great a magnifying power as it will be difficult to hold an object within the narrow field of view. It is much better to buy a pair with lower magnifying power and larger object lenses (the big end ones) as they will be more manageable and will gather a lot of light, making them useful for nightwork as well. A pair of 7 or 8 × 50 glasses would be a good compromise.

Accurate timing of flash sequences is of the essence when trying to identify a light and to this end a stopwatch is an enormous help. It need not be expensive, but must be easily operated and read.

So we come to the luxuries in the navigator's list of equipment. In this, we include barometer, sextant, wind speed and direction

A conventional prism type handbearing compass. The object you want to take a bearing of is held in the Vee sight and the scribed line and pointer are aligned with the reflected black line which gives you the bearing from the compass card. In this case the bearing would be 038°.

instruments and other electronic instruments. A barometer provides a check on local pressure systems and can make interpretation of the weather forecasts much more accurate. It also gives the whole crew something to tap and shake their heads gloomily over when they want to stay in port an extra day.

A sextant, as we will see in Chapter 19, is not the mysterious instrument it is made out to be, nor is it one to be used solely for astro-navigation. It has a definite place aboard all coastal cruisers as well as those venturing out on longer voyages.

Sophisticated electronics in the form of Decca and Loran and satellite navigation systems, speedometers, wind speed and direction indicators, anemometers, course computers and what have you are the very last things to spend money on if you own a small cruiser. That is not to say they are not useful items, but they can well be managed without if the budget is tight.

Handheld calculators and programmable calculators with programmes for navigation all have a use on board but can well be done without. If you have one anyway, there is clearly no harm in using it on board, but I would hesitate to say it was worth buying one specially.

Compasses

Compasses are another quite expensive piece of equipment, but in their case it is worth spending some money as the whole business of guiding a well-found yacht from A to B is centred on the compass. There are three main types: the grid compass, the dome compass and the edge reading type.

Modern compasses have their cards marked in a simple 360-degrees notation, usually at 5-degree intervals or 2-degree intervals. Often, to simplify reading, some digits are missed off, thus 030 degrees might be marked 3 and 240 degrees would be 24.

The card in a grid compass floats beneath a plain glass top around which is a rotatable bezel marked with two parallel lines across the glass. In use, the course required, say 240 degrees, is set by rotating the bezel until the 240-degrees marker lines up with the ship's heading marker on the fore and aft centre line of the boat. All the helmsman then has to do is keep the north pointer on the compass card beneath the north mark between the two scribed lines. The advantage of this system is that it is easier to keep a needle between two marks than it is to align a single mark and a single line (as in the case of a dome compass) and that should the helmsman forget the course set, he has only to look at where the bezel is fixed. The drawback comes when the helmsman cannot lay the set course. He then has to keep on moving the bezel to check his average, but this is not too serious a matter after a little practice.

Dome compasses, as their name implies, have a simple floating card with 360-degrees notation surmounted by a transparent dome. In many of these compasses the card and lubber line (the heading marker) are both gimballed within the compass bowl thus avoiding the necessity of any external gimbals – unlike the grid types. The dome acts as a magnifying glass making it easier to read the card.

The third type, the edge reading compass, is more or less back to front. Usually mounted through the after cabin bulkhead, it is designed to be read at eye level, so the edge of the card is turned down and marked 180 degrees out from the figures on the surface of the card, i.e. the edge north mark is just below the south mark on the card's face. Also the lubber line, instead of being on the forward side of the compass, is on the after side, gimballed within the bowl. This all sounds more complicated than it is: the helmsman simply reads the markings and uses the lubber line near to him rather than the one away from him that he uses on the 'look down on' types of compasses.

Choice of compass is mainly dictated by where it is to be mounted and that place must be chosen with regard to two things: it must be where the helmsman can see it and where it is not going to be too close to any ferrous metals. The first point is obvious, but not always easy to comply with. Where a boat has wheel steering, the compass can usually be mounted on the steering pedestal and there is then no problem, but most small cruisers have tiller steering and that means mounting the compass at one end of the cockpit. If it is mounted under the tiller at the after end the helmsman is never looking where he is going – either he watches the compass and not the ship's head or vice versa. If it is mounted on a bracket on the after face of the bridgedeck the sheet hand may kick it and if it is mounted on a board across the companionway it will be stepped on by anyone going into or coming out of the cabin. Put it on one bulkhead and the helmsman can only truly see it from one side of the cockpit. Provided the cockpit is not too long, it can be recessed into the upper surface of the bridgedeck, but the crew must not sit on it. Really you have to look at your own boat and decide on the least objectionable place.

Then, of course, the compass must not be near any ferrous metals or permanent magnets otherwise it will be affected by deviation, which we will look at later. The helmsman must also be able to look fairly straight at it to avoid parallax errors in steering. Illumination too can cause problems. Luminous numbers are rarely enough and a light must be fitted, but it must not be a bright one which will ruin night vision. Red or green is best. All you need is a glow, but a light fitted with a rheostat is the ideal as each helmsman can adjust it to suit himself. The electric wires to the light should be twisted together to avoid any possibility of compass deviation being caused by the current in them.

Variation

Variation is the angular difference between True North and Magnetic North. Unfortunately this angle is not constant and in some parts of the world it is to the west of North and in others to the east. It must always be applied when converting from Magnetic to True or the other way from True to Magnetic.

In the middle of a compass rose on the chart you will find a note that says something like 'Variation 8° West (1976) decreasing 6' annually'. That is to say that in 1986 the magnetic variation will be 7° West. Occasionally small-scale charts print isogonic lines (lines of equal variation) instead of putting the variation on the compass rose because it changes several times in the area covered by the chart.

Applying variation is really quite simple. Say there is 8° Westerly variation in your area and you read a course off the chart as 095°T (True). The Magnetic course (deg M) will be 095 + 8 = 103°M. Had it been 8° Easterly variation, then the Magnetic course would have been 095 − 8 = 087°M.

Deviation

The close companion of variation is deviation and together they make up 'compass error'. While variation is the difference between Magnetic and True North, deviation is the difference between Magnetic North and Compass North. It is caused by ferrous metal – such as engines, radio loudspeakers, knives and so on – or electrical fields too close to the compass. Steel boats need a lot of careful attention but with a wooden or GRP boat the compass deviation should be very small and almost all of it correctable. Compass correcting is not a simple subject and if you find a large amount of deviation you should call upon expert advice from a compass adjuster. Of course, the best way to reduce deviation is to move the offending piece of metal or move the compass, but most boats carry a degree or two of deviation on some headings.

Compass swinging

The next question, logically, is how do you find out what deviation the compass carries? Here the idea is to compare compass bearings of a distant object with the known magnetic bearing while the boat is held on various headings. The difference between the compass reading and the known magnetic bearing is the deviation for that ship's heading. These discrepancies are noted and made up into either a deviation card or a deviation curve, which is used each time you want to convert a True course to Compass or a Compass bearing to a True one.

The procedure is to select a convenient buoy (preferably not a fairway buoy) and a conspicuous landmark about 5–6 miles from it. Read the True bearing of the mark from the buoy off the compass rose on the chart and apply variation to convert it to Magnetic. Next go out to the buoy, preferably at slack water, and get the helmsman to steer first north, then south, east, west, northeast, southwest, northwest, southeast, while staying very close to the buoy. As he steers each successive heading he should sing out 'on' when actually steering the required course and 'off' at other times. When he is settled on the course you take bearings of the distant object and note them, together with the boat's heading. These bearings are then compared with the known Magnetic bearing and the difference is the deviation on that heading. Thus, if the Magnetic bearing as measured from the chart is 175°M and the Compass bearing is 173°C on a heading of due East, the deviation on the heading is 2° East. If the bearing is 176°C on a heading of North, the deviation would be 1° West on that heading.

From all these readings a table can be drawn up, for example:

Compass heading	Deviation
N 0°C	1°E
NE 045°C	0°
E 090°C	3°W

Compass heading	Deviation
SE 135°C	4°W
S 180°C	3°W
SW 225°C	1°W
W 270°C	1°E
NW 315°C	2°E

This table can also be presented as a deviation curve, thus:

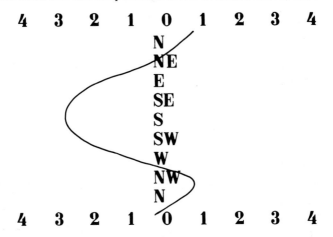

A rough-and-ready alternative is to trail someone astern in a dinghy with a handbearing compass and as the ship is put on various headings, the man in the dinghy notes the course on the handbearing compass. This method can be used at sea by holding the handbearing compass clear of all metal objects and sighting along the line of mast and forestay. Here it must be remembered that the deviation so found holds good only for that particular heading and another check will have to be made again as soon as the course is changed.

The application of variation and deviation is quite simple but must be remembered, whether converting from True courses and bearings to Compass or the other way round. So, a few examples:

1 Compass course 135°C, variation 6°W. What is the True course?
  Variation   6°W   from compass rose

Deviation	4°W	from deviation card
Error	10°W	
Compass course	135°C	
Error	10°W	
True course	125°T	

2 Compass course 045°C, variation 8°W, What is True course?

Variation	8°W	from compass rose
Deviation	6°E	from deviation card
Error	2°W	
Compass course	045°C	
Error	2°W	
True course	043°T	

3 Compass course, 240°C, variation 5°W, What is True course?

Variation	5°W
Deviation	7°E
Error	2°E
Compass course	240°C
Error	2°E
True course	242°T

4 True course 185°T, variation 6°W. What is the Compass course?

Variation	6°W
Deviation	5°E
Error	1°W
True course	185°T
Error	1°W
Compass course	186°C

5 True course 320°T, variation 20°W. What is the Compass course to steer?

True course	320°T
Variation	20°W
Magnetic course	340°M

Here the Magnetic course has been found first because the variation is large and the True and Magnetic courses are therefore rather different. The deviation is found for a Magnetic course of 340 degrees.

Magnetic course	340°M
Deviation	4°E
Compass course	336°C

Buoyage

In British and European waters a system of buoyage for navigation known as the International Association of Lighthouse Authorities (IALA) System A is used, while America and Canada use System B. Under IALA System A there are five different types of mark used:

1 Lateral marks, consisting of red and green buoys to mark, respectively, the port and starboard sides of a channel as approached in the direction of the flood tide.
2 Cardinal marks, indicating in which direction clear water lies, thus protecting a particular hazard.
3 Isolated danger marks, simply marking remote, small hazards, such as rocks or small shoals.
4 Safe water marks, used to show that there is clear water in that area.
5 Special marks, not intended for navigation but to show a particular area or feature, such as a dumping ground. In principle, colour and shape of topmark show their significance by day and a flashing light showing a particular sequence by night. Pictures of the system are widely publicized in the almanacs, official publications, navigation books, posters and also gummed labels for affixing in the cabin.

It is always important to identify positively any buoy seen, but once done so a look at the chart will usually clear up any uncertainty about its significance.

Course plotting

When we want to get from one port to the next we need a course to guide us, even if we can check landmarks and buoys on the way. First we need to know where we are starting from (our departure) and second where we want to arrive (or make our landfall). The easiest thing to do is choose a mark of some kind, outside each of the two ports, which is shown on the chart – say a buoy or beacon. The obvious thing then is to join the two points up, transfer that course to the compass rose, read off the True course, apply variation and deviation to give a Compass course and tell the helmsman to steer it. But if you are sailing in tidal waters there is always the tidal stream to be taken into account as it will invariably set you off course one way or another. This tidal set has to be allowed for.

North cardinal mark of the IALA system A buoyage convention. This indicates that there is clear water north of the buoy.

out of position or if you are close to it it may be at the limit of its riding scope. When you are running in on a coastline and getting slightly anxious, by all means take bearings on the looms of lights as a rough guide, but do not rely on them until the light itself dips up over the horizon and you can take a proper bearing of it. In such instances an RDF, Decca or Satnav set can be of great value. Anyway, you rarely need to panic as soon as you think, after all you will probably have to run another few miles before you are anywhere near the coast, and a few miles in a small cruiser means an hour or so, not minutes.

Having said that, I will repeat that all opportunities of checking your position should be taken and to this end it is as well to take a bearing on any identified object even if there is nothing to cross it with. By doing this you in fact have half a fix and if you then run on until a second bearing on some other object can be obtained you are almost there. Simply lay off your course and transfer the first position line along it for the distance you have sailed over the ground (i.e. the log reading corrected for the tide etc.) and find the point where the first bearing, now transferred, crosses the new bearing and that is your position.

Another method of using a single position line is to sail on until the

A running fix. First sight from right is YX; second sight is ZX. YX is then transferred along length of D to give position.

bearing of the object has changed substantially (40 degrees or so) and take a second bearing of the same object. Plot both bearings, then lay off your course and mark along it how far you have travelled over the ground. Move the first position line up until it passes through that point and your fix is where it cuts the second position line. This is called a running fix.

Very similar to the running fix is the method known as doubling the angle on the bow. For this you again need just one object. Take a bearing of it when it is, say, 30 degrees *off the bow*, a second when it is 60 degrees *off the bow*. This you will note is not the same as saying double the bearing. Calculate the distance made good over the ground and this is equal to your distance off the object along the second position line. Thus you have a position and a distance off in one go.

The great stumbling block with both of these methods is that you need to know accurately the distance made good over the ground and what with varying boat speed and unknown tidal streams this can be a bit of a tall order. It is in fact the essence of Dead Reckoning so I will say more about it later.

Some other points about bearings: it is often helpful when entering a strange harbour to work out 'safe bearings' on certain landmarks beforehand. For example, you may find that if a church is kept between 010°T and 355°T you have a clear passage between two rocks. On leaving harbour it is useful to check in the same way and also to obtain an idea of your leeway or the effect of a cross current or stream, by taking back bearings on a landmark to see how it compares with the reciprocal of your course. Lastly, take bearings on approaching ships. If the bearing stays the same (or nearly the same) you are on a collision course and will have to do something. If it changes substantially you should be clear, but keep checking.

Leeway

This is a rather awkward topic as its significance varies from boat to boat and according to conditions of wind and sea. When you are sailing hard on the wind a component of its force pushes the boat sideways and she makes leeway. But how much? In most cases it is not likely to be more than a few degrees and in rough going – when it is likely to be noticeable – the helmsman probably will not be steering to better than plus or minus 5 degrees anyway, so usually it is possible (on a reasonably short passage) to get away with ignoring it. A check should be made, however, by taking back bearings on shore objects or on the wake when sailing a fair course and comparing it to your course. If it is significantly different you will have to make due allowance.

Speed and distance made good

Whether you choose to fit a through hull log or buy a towing one, some sort of distance recorder is almost essential for coastal and offshore cruising. You can get away without one if it fails for any reason by keeping a careful check on boat speed through the water using guesswork, but this is not to be relied on for long. Better, if possible, is to time the run between two identifiable landmarks and work your speed out from that.

What must be remembered about any log is that it will only tell you the speed/distance run *through the water*. This is unlikely to be the same as the distance made good over the ground. If you make 4 knots for 3 hours you will travel 12 miles through the water, but if there is a 2-knot stream against you, you will only make good 6 miles over the ground. On the other hand, if you are being chased by a 2-knot stream then you will make good 18 miles over the ground. Always allow for this when working out how far you still have to go to the next mark.

Log book and DR

First let me clear up a little bit of terminology: Dead Reckoning (DR) is a calculation of the ship's position, with regard to course steered and distance run (through the water). Navigation by Estimated Position (EP) is also a computation of the ship's position, but in this case due allowance is made for the effects of tidal stream, current and leeway. Generally we are rather lax in our use of DR and EP as definitions and usually talk about Dead Reckoning navigation when we actually mean EP. A good DR plot (EP) is essential and is the basis of all navigation, including celestial navigation and it is wise to keep up such a plot at all times. In rough weather in a small cruiser this is not always possible, but the DR should be brought up to date as soon as conditions allow.

The process of keeping up a DR plot is made much simpler if you keep a comprehensive and well-planned log book. The best way I have found is to split it into two parts: the front (or one entire book if

DECK LOG

DATE TIME BST	LOG READING	COURSE REQUIRED	COURSE STEERED SINCE LAST ENTRY	WIND	BAROMETER	BOAT SPEED	REMARKS
1700	65.80	207°C	190°	nil	991	5½	A/c 215° Engine on
1800	71.20	215°C	215°	nil	991	5½	Forecast : NE 3-4, Fair, fog patches
1900	76.26	190°C	215°	nil	991	5¼	A/c 190°

NAVIGATORS LOG

DATE TIME BST	LOG READ'G	SINCE LAST PLOT	COURSE C°	DEV.° E W	VAR.° E W	T°	LEEWAY P S	WAKE COURSE T°	STREAM SET	RATE KNOTS	DRIFT MILES	PLOT POSITION LAT.	LONG.
1700	65.80	0.76	190°	+10E	-7½W	192½	0	192	080	2	1	50°04'N	01°38'W
1800	71.20	5.40	215°	+6E	-7½W	213½	0	213	085	3	3	49°59.5'N	01°38'W
1900	76.26	5.06	215	+6E	-7½W	213½	0	213	090	3½	3½	49°55.4'N	01°37'W

Examples of keeping log books on board.

you prefer) is the deck log and the back (or another book) is the navigator's log. The deck log must be filled in regularly and accurately by whoever is on watch, while the navigator's log is the sole responsibility of the navigator. Its format, together with typical entries, made on a cross-Channel passage are shown here. The deck log is pretty straightforward, except perhaps for the two sections 'course required' and 'course steered'. The first is the course the navigator would like to make (i.e. the one he has ordered) and the second is an *honest* account of the course that the helmsman actually manages to make between log entries. The importance of this was mentioned earlier. The navigator's section is a logical progression through the process of working out a plot, the whole point being that trying to think in a small cruiser in rough weather is not easy and if the system is laid out step by step you are less likely to make mistakes.

The process for plotting an EP is this. Enter the time in the first column, then take the log reading from the deck log and put it in the second. Subtract the previous reading from it and enter that distance in the third column. The course steered is again taken from the deck log. Deviation to be applied (plus or minus) is found from the deviation curve and variation is calculated from the error shown in the centre of the nearest compass rose on the chart. These errors are applied to the compass course and the true course (deg T) is entered in the seventh column. The degree of leeway to port or starboard is entered in the next column and is either added to or subtracted from the true course steered to give the true 'wake course' in column nine, though as I said earlier you may well decide that you can call leeway zero much of the time. Next catch your tidal atlas as it slips off the table and decide what the tide has done to you in the time since the last plot. Enter the average direction (deg T) in column 10, the rate in the next column and the drift over the last two hours or whatever time since the last plot in column 12. Now you are ready to plot the EP.

From your last EP or known position rule in the wake course (column 9) and mark off the 'since last plot' distance (column 3). From that point rule a line in the direction of the tidal set (column 10) and mark off the drift (column 12), using the latitude scale at the side of the chart as usual. (One minute of latitude equals one nautical mile.) Now you have plotted your EP. Believe it or not, this method works and after a few plots it comes very easily. The final column is just a note of your latitude and longitude in case someone accidentally rubs the plot off the chart or spills coffee on it.

11

Passage making

A truly well-found boat should be in a fit state to put to sea on a longish passage at any time, but in reality the family cruiser takes some preparation before she can really be called ready for a summer holiday cruise. All of her rigging, both standing and running, should be checked over; her sails looked at and restitched as necessary; fuel, water, food will all have to be taken on; the engine will probably have to be serviced – filters cleaned, oil changed/topped up, spark plugs cleaned and gaps checked, points' gaps checked; some sort of itinerary should be drawn up, no matter how rough, so that the relevant charts and pilots may be obtained and studied.

To decide which charts you need you first have to think about where you propose to go and how far you hope to get. A small cruiser with a young family crew can only really hope to make about 30–40 miles in daylight and even then if the wind is light or against them they may have to motorsail for a spell. Any passages of more than that distance will involve a rather long time at sea, possibly including some or all of the night, and if the crew is as described the skipper will probably choose to keep such passages down to a minimum – perhaps no more than two in a two- to three-week cruise. A crew that includes two or three strong, fit, well-experienced people may make several 24-hour passages if they choose and will be able to cover twice the ground that the family manages; that is their choice. The whole joy of cruising is that we can do as we please and go where we choose when we choose, changing our plans at the merest whim. When thinking about where to make for though, it is as well to bear the crew's limitations in mind. You must also consider the half-day or so wasted in getting underway at the beginning of the cruise; the two or three days' delay with bad weather; the three to four days spent in port sightseeing, shopping, showering, playing on the beach; the couple of days at the end 'just to be sure of getting back in time'. All of which leaves little time for actually going anywhere.

This is perhaps a rather pessimistic view of the average holiday pattern, but it is better to find that you have made better progress than expected and be able to visit another port or anchorage, than to set your heart on reaching a particular place and getting nowhere near it. To plan distances with any sense of reality you must have a chart in front of you, a pilot book in one hand and a pair of dividers in the other. The crew will need a day or so to settle down on the boat, but after that it is a good idea to get any long hops (or windward work) over and done with in the early part of the holiday while people are still fresh and eager.

For the purposes of planning a passage and, indeed, for much of the actual navigation, a small-scale chart showing the whole trip from departure to destination is an asset. You must also have large-scale charts of any ports along the way that you might put into if need be, or hope to put into anyway. These, together with relevant pilots and tide tables, should all be studied carefully during the planning stages with bearings, marks, lights, possible courses, distances and best times to arrive at headlands for a fair tide onwards all being worked out and noted.

Weather, of course, is a deciding factor in the cruising game. Several times I have had to curtail a summer holiday because of an overdose of rain. Gales, too, have taken their toll of days when we have had to lie up in some backwater waiting for it to blow over. If you have young children on board bad weather can be particularly frustrating, but there is nothing you can do about it, you just have to take account of it and alter your plans accordingly. Provided it is fine when there is a gale blowing out at sea and you are snugged down in a safe harbour there is no reason why you should not leave the boat safely moored and explore inland for a day; an ancient monument, a museum or simply a day building sand-castles on the beach. After all, sailing may be *your* fun, but it is a family holiday.

When planning a foreign cruise it now has to be remembered that the owner (or charterer) must inform HM Customs and Excise of the intended departure date and time on form C1328. The full details of this procedure are included in Customs Notice No. 8, copies of which can be obtained from Customs offices. Briefly, the scheme is as follows.

The proposed date of departure from the U.K. must be notified to

HM Customs and Excise as far in advance as possible using Part I of the form. Failure to make such notification is an offence. This Notice of Intended Departure should be posted or delivered to the Customs office nearest to the port of departure and is *only valid for 48 hours after the stated time of departure.* If, for any reason, your departure is delayed beyond that time Parts II and III marked 'voyage abandoned' must be despatched and a new Part I completed if you still intend going at some other time. It is a hassle and puts unreasonable pressure on you to stick to your plans – a pressure that must be strongly resisted for safety's sake if you feel the weather is changing or you are not ready – but it is the law.

If you have chartered the boat for your holiday you must ensure that the parts of the form relating to VAT payments on the boat have been filled in by the charter company owning the boat.

On returning to U.K. waters you must fly a Q flag (a plain yellow flag from the International Code) to indicate that you and your crew are healthy and require Customs clearance. At night the flag is supposed to be illuminated and again it is an offence not to fly this flag.

The nearest Customs office must be contacted and notified of your arrival within two hours, unless you arrive between 2300 hours and 0600 hours, when contact may be delayed until 0800 hours, assuming you have no animals on board. And here a quick reminder about animals and rabies. Do not take pets abroad and do not try to bring any back.

Notification of arrival can be made by either telephoning or actually going to the office and a list of Customs offices is provided in the booklet Notice No. 8. If you go to the office, or when the officer comes to the boat, have ready the completed Parts II and III of Form C1328. If no-one from HM Customs comes to see you within two hours' notification of arrival you are entitled to deliver Part II to the office or even post it, retaining Part III for the record.

All of this seems more of a nuisance than it really is and generally speaking yachtsmen have a good working relationship with HM Customs and Excise, which is well worth preserving, so do not do anything silly like trying to bring in too much drink or perfume without declaring it.

Finally, it is now required by the French authorities that any British vessel entering their territorial waters should carry full British ship's registry papers. A new, simpler registration procedure, run by the RYA, has been introduced, but again, do not try to avoid carrying these documents or you will land in serious trouble in France. This applies even if you are trailing your boat to the Continent for a holiday, not just when you arrive by sea.

Yacht and Boat Safety Scheme

This, or CG66, is the name given to a useful safety scheme run by Her Majesty's Coastguard. The CG66 refers to a form of that designation, which lists the details of your boat including her name, port of registry, home port, type, rig, hull and deck colours, sail colours and markings, engine capacity and all the other details that might possibly be of use if a search had to be made for you. Also on the form is the name and address of an 'agent', that is, someone who will get in touch with the Coastguard in the event of there being any concern about your safety or the boat's whereabouts.

The system is that you fill in the CG66 form, lodge it with the local Coastguard and then, if you are overdue on passage one day (for example), the listed agent calls the Coastguard and asks them to find out what has happened. Armed with so much detail about the boat, plu. information on the proposed passage, likely starting time, etc., the Coastguard can put out messages to all their stations along your route to see if anyone has spotted you or if you have been in touch by radio. Using Telex machines and all the modern facilities this check is very rapid indeed and speeds up the commencement of a full-scale Search and Rescue (SAR) operation should that prove necessary.

It takes little effort to fill the form in and have it put on file, but if the 'agent' plays his or her part, then the time spent could literally save your own and your crew's lives.

Departures (night and day)

The great thing about departures is to make them. If you have made up your mind to go, go. Do not dither about, it makes everyone nervous. However, do not make rash, ill-considered decisions and remember it is not fair on your crew to spring a night passage on them when they have been swimming or sightseeing all day and have just come back on board after a celebratory dinner. Heavy meals, particularly rich ones accompanied by alcohol, are not good stomach liners.

More often than not we make a final decision about a night

departure after listening to the evening shipping forecast and this allows time (assuming the tide is compliant) for a quick meal and the necessary preparations for departure before it actually gets dark (in the summer months). Try to leave in daylight so that the boat is already sailing, the navigator has sorted himself out, watches have been set and the crew is settled down when darkness comes. Obviously it is not always possible and if you will have to leave at night, try to get some sleep before you go.

Before setting off, either in daylight or at night, go over the whole boat checking all her gear. Show the crew where flares, fire extinguishers, lifebuoys, etc., are and how they work. Lash down any movable objects and point out to everyone how the dinghy (assuming it to be on deck) and the liferaft are fastened. The navigator should sort out his charts into the order he is going to need them and he should make a careful study of the pilots, because the next time he refers to them the boat will be unsteady, he is likely to be tired, under pressure and possibly feeling a bit rough. It will be easier then if he is already familiar with the information. He should also make notes of light sequences, buoys and possible courses, besides any available transits and safe bearings (or danger bearings). Each member of the crew should dig out his foul-weather gear and stow it to hand so that he can get it without disturbing anyone who is asleep. Extra warm clothing too should be handy if not actually put on. Thermos flasks can be filled with soup, coffee or anything warming. Sandwiches may be prepared and a box of 'goodies' should be put in an accessible place for hungry helmsmen. A waterproof torch near the helm is essential and all the navigation, steaming and compass lights should be checked.

If you are setting off on a long day or night passage, it is necessary to set watches as soon as possible, so that whoever is off watch can take his rest with a clear conscience. This is essential, otherwise, particularly when leaving in the evening, you end up in the potentially dangerous situation of everyone staying on deck getting weary together. I would suggest that if only one person is going to be on watch at a time, two hours is generally long enough, particularly at night when boredom and sleepiness are hard to fight. In daylight, unless the weather is extreme, he should be able to manage a three-hour trick. If there are three of you capable of taking watches, then two hours on and four off at night and three on and six off in the day gives each person a reasonable amount of time to sleep, eat, sunbathe or carry out running repairs.

When there are two of you, say a man and his wife, things are not quite so easy, especially if children have to be looked after as well. It should be no great hardship for a fit man to go without any sleep for one night, but he must be certain of having the chance to catch up on it the next day and he must be doubly careful in all decision-making or chartwork. Since it is never absolutely certain that he will be able to catch up it is a great help if his partner can take over for a couple of hours in the middle of the night and allow him to go below for a brew up and a nap. Many wives, of course, are just as competent to handle the boat as their husbands and in such cases a two-hours on and two off system works very well.

Landfalls (night and day)

In many ways making a landfall shortly before dawn is ideal. Lighthouses, lightbuoys and any other lit navigation marks are still plainly visible, yet by the time you close with the shore it will be daylight and you will be able to see well for any inshore pilotage. If you are going to have to make your landfall in the dark and make a harbour approach also in darkness, great care must be exercised. The end of a passage almost certainly brings a relaxing of vigilance on the part of the crew just when concentration is needed to keep clear of 'navigational hazards' – rocks, moored boats, etc. Indeed it may, on occasion, be more seamanlike to heave to offshore in a well-established, safe position, to await daylight for your harbour approach. Naturally this depends on circumstances of weather, crew and so on.

While it is much easier to pick up lit marks at night than in daylight when perhaps there is a light mist or the sun is in your eyes, it is more difficult to judge distances. Daylight shows clearly that you are still some way offshore, when at night you may think you are about to run up the beach. This also applies when you get into harbour. If you are going to anchor, take a good look round before choosing your place or you may fetch up in quite the wrong position, e.g. in the fairway, and have to move again. Do not forget too that you are required to hoist a riding light in the fore rigging besides displaying a yellow Q flag if entering a foreign port or returning from abroad. (In fact the Q flag should be hoisted on entering a country's territorial waters.) The riding light makes good sense in crowded or busy anchorages where boats are coming and going all the time. Make sure it burns all night if it is a paraffin lamp and that there is sufficient battery power to keep it going if it is an electric one.

Choosing a good, easily identifiable landfall is important. Some ports have what is called a landfall buoy in their offing. This is generally a large, lit mark some way offshore not marking any hazard, but simply telling you that you are in the right position to line up for the entrance. Where one of these is not available then a lighthouse or other mark possibly some little distance up or down the coast from your destination should be chosen. Though this may add time to your passage it ensures that you have a positive position to navigate from as you approach the confusion of shore lights. Trying to pick out a dim pierhead lamp from a mass of neon signs and street lights is no joke when you are tired.

RDF

The radio direction finder (RDF) set has become a widely used piece of navigational equipment on small cruisers as well as larger, generally better equipped, ones. Good sets need not cost enormous amounts of money and can be very useful position-finding aids. In essence DF sets are radio receivers with rotating aerials that provide a bearing of the station being received when related to either an integral compass or by angle relative to the ship's heading as shown by the main steering compass. The direction is found by rotating the aerial until a minimum or 'null' signal is received. The built-in compass then shows the direction of the station or a dial shows the angle relative to the ship's head. This bearing is plotted on the chart to provide a position line, requiring only one or two more PLs, either RDF ones or ones produced by handbearing compass readings, to cross and provide a position fix.

One thing to be very careful of, however, is the possibility of reading the reciprocal of the station's bearing. In other words, the navigator has to ensure against plotting a position line 180 degrees in error. Such a mistake is perfectly feasible as the same null would be read, but it could be a very dangerous error.

Radio beacons, as the transmitters are called, are arranged in groups for transmitting on the same wavelength. Each beacon goes through the same sequence lasting one minute: first the beacon's two-letter call sign in slow Morse repeated four times, then a continuous tone during which you rotate the aerial and take the bearing of the null and finally the call sign again, usually repeated a couple of times. The beacon is then silent for five minutes while the other beacons in the group go through their transmissions. Thus, in a six-minute cycle up to six beacons in a group can be heard.

Ranges of these beacons vary from about 5 to 200 miles, though they may be picked up outside their own range if atmospheric conditions are`right. If this is so, be wary of a fix using them. Strange effects can also be found at dusk and dawn and if there is land between you and the beacon. Frequencies and groupings of beacons are listed in the various pilots and both *Reed's* and the *Macmillan and Silk Cut* nautical almanacs.

Decca and Satnav

These sophisticated electronic navigation systems provide a very accurate, frequently (automatically) updated position and can give courses and distances to future 'way points'. They are expensive pieces of kit but are in increasing use and make the navigator's job infinitely easier. Satnav is the common abbreviation for satellite navigation.

Radio lighthouses

These are a new development utilizing VHF Channel 88. They are not widespread but are useful for those with a VHF set that has Channel 88 crystals fitted. These experimental stations are listed in the almanacs, together with an explanation of the counting of beats (sound signals) and the calculations required to provide a bearing of the station. The use of radio lighthouses may grow, but for the moment they are very limited.

Working the tides

Anyone new to cruising will quickly find out that far better progress is made with the tide under him than with the tide running against him. It is not always possible to sail with the tide, but when it is, progress is much swifter, smoother and on a long passage it can give many extra free miles. After all, a 4-knot boat and a 2-knot fair tide add up to 6 miles of progress over the ground per hour, while a 4-knot boat against a 2-knot tide makes good only 2 miles each hour.

Right back at the planning stage of a passage you must make a careful study of how tides are going to run. Notes should be made of likely arrival times at headlands, races, narrows or other 'tidal gates' and if, on looking up the tides, you find that you will be bucking the tide at one of these places, you may have to rethink your schedule. Should you in fact split the passage into two parts with a harbour in the middle? Or can you anchor under the lee of a headland and wait out the foul tide and be in a good position to take advantage of the full fair tide round and onwards?

Many ports and harbours have bars across their entrances and these must be approached only when the tide serves. So too with drying anchorages. It is all obvious perhaps, but you have to think about it beforehand; there is no fun in plunging off willy-nilly and bucking the tide for the first six hours, or taking it with you for a couple and then arriving to find you can not make port. The art of working the tides is to keep the effect of foul ones to a minimum.

Night sailing

The first and most obvious thing about night sailing is that you cannot see as much as you can by day. That is not quite such a fatuous statement as you may think. Being unable to see properly means that you have got to *know* where each halyard fall is, where each cleat is, where the torch is. While picking out marks that are lit is made easier, unlit ones are virtually invisible and judging the distance of lights is quite difficult. Shipping seems to multiply and approach at horrific speeds. Judgement of your boat speed is tricky without a speedo, you cannot see the sails properly to judge their trim and set and the wind often seems stronger at night. Also people are not used to being kicked out of their sleep in the middle of the night to be sent outside to sit and get cold for a couple of hours while steering a good course and keeping a sharp lookout.

Sailing at night can be a most exhilarating and rewarding experience; certainly some of my happiest memories come from night passages, but the first one should be undertaken only when you are sure of your (and your crew's) ability to handle your boat and when keeping track of your position is second nature. It is very easy to mix light sequences up as you rise and fall on the waves and consequently to become confused and panicky.

It is usually quite cold at night, even in high summer, and you may get wet with spray or dew, so a few thick sweaters or thermal underclothing with your oilskins are in order. A lifeharness clipped on to a strong point in the cockpit is sensible and if working up forward (say changing a headsail), then it should definitely be worn. A hot drink during the watch at some point is a great comfort and so

189

too is something to munch on. A nice practice is for the person going off watch to make a hot drink for the one coming on who is straight out of a warm bunk and probably needs waking up. It also means that for this transition period when night vision is being gained and the feel of the boat acquired, there are two people about. There is also the chance for a new watchkeeper to ask the previous one about any lights or instructions that he is not sure of.

Steering at night is very much a case of feeling the wind, the helm and the boat. Listening to the sails can also help. A flapping luff makes it pretty obvious when you have luffed up too close to the wind. Naturally a check must be kept on the compass, but staring at it the whole time is not necessary or a good thing. If you are in an eyes down position the whole time you are not keeping a lookout and that is a serious and dangerous crime. Usually you can lay the boat on her course, pick a star and steer on that, but remember stars move across the sky and your course must be checked regularly.

Of course, electronic sailing instruments are a great help at night,

A pramhood over the companionway provides useful shelter to keep spray out of the accommodation and on a windward leg to reduce the amount of spray being thrown back into the helmsman's face. Note, though, how vision through the spray covered window is greatly restricted. Because of this the helmsman or watchkeeper must emerge from its protection frequently to check for other shipping etc.

The sun goes down and it's going to be a long, cold watch. At times like this a set of good thermal underwear and waterproof oilskins are invaluable. Also a Thermos of hot soup or coffee won't go amiss in a couple of hours' time.

as is the cheaper Wind Hawk or Windex masthead wind direction indicator that has reflective patches on the underside that will often reflect a masthead tricolour navigation light, allowing the helmsman to see the wind direction. A burgee fails in this respect.

Compasses should be lit only sufficiently to facilitate easy reading, they should not be so bright that they leave the helmsman blind for several minutes after he looks up from it. A red bulb is quite easy on the eye, although some manufacturers now use green. Ideally a dimmer switch should be fitted to give complete control over the degree of illumination. Remember too if someone opens the hatch not to look below, or if someone uses a torch on deck, not to look at it. Similarly, anyone using a white light should warn the watchkeeper in advance so that he can avoid looking at it.

Watchkeeping

The first duty of the watchkeeper is to keep a good lookout for anything that might affect the safety of the boat and her crew, whether it is the approach of another vessel, flotsam, or a landfall. If he is the helmsman too he is responsible for steering a good, steady course, as close as possible to that set. If he is not able to lay it exactly he must note in the log the course actually steered and the times of any alterations. Certainly when you come off watch, but preferably every hour (or even half-hour), you should enter up the log. If a weather forecast comes up during your watch you must be sure not to miss it, either recording it yourself or getting someone else to.

When any situation arises where the watchkeeper is unsure of what to do – a ship coming in close, a rising wind – he must call the

Log streamed and 24½ miles clocked up. The cruise has begun.

Motoring in to a strange harbour is a difficult time with young children as the parents must pay attention to handling and docking the boat, but at the same time the children must be watched. These are sensibly clad in lifejackets, from youngest to oldest, and the deck is well 'fenced in' with netting on the guardrails to minimize the chances of anyone slipping overboard.

skipper. Do not be put off by the fact that he has turned in and fallen asleep after his own watch. It is for such occasions that he *is* the skipper.

On handing over the watch to the new person you must point out and identify all visible lights, if possible showing him your approximate position on the chart. For instance, you might say, 'That's Port Jovial over there, there's a ship going away from us there, but that light astern seems to be coming up. You'd better watch that.' You must also get him to repeat the course and any alterations that will be needed during his watch. When you first come up on a chilly night your mind is anything but active and if you do not go through this ritual you will find a few minutes later that you are staring at the compass with no idea of the correct course. What makes life easier is to have a slate in the cockpit to write courses and instructions on, such as '020°. Call navigator at 0330'.

As part of your lookout, do not look only at the horizon but also watch the sea between you and the horizon. This applies particularly in heavy seas when objects, even big ships, can be completely hidden from view in the trough of a wave. Remember also that a ship's lookout is watching primarily for the lights of other ships, i.e. high lights out on his horizon level. Your lights are below this and are arcing about, possibly seeming to flash, as the yacht rolls.

Lastly, move about quietly at night. The deck always creaks and even hushed voices are loud when you are trying to sleep. If you go foraging in the galley, do not drop the biscuit tin. Shield lights from the eyes of those off watch and when woken up for your own watch, get up immediately or you will fall asleep again and keep the person ending his watch on deck beyond his fair time.

Navigation lights

Under the terms of the International Regulations for Preventing Collisions at Sea – the rules of the road – sailing boats are required to carry a red light showing to port, a green light to starboard and a white light astern. In addition to these, a red light over a green one may be carried high on the forward face of the mast. On vessels of less than 65 ft (20 m) – which are the ones concerning us – the port and starboard lights may be combined in one lantern, but there must be an accurate cut off between sectors. In practice many people use tricolour masthead mounted units combining the red and green sidelights with a white stern light, thus using only one bulb and so reducing battery drain. All the lights must have a minimum range of 2 miles and should be displayed between the hours of sunset and sunrise when the vessel is at sea. There is one other thing to remember: no matter what sails may be set, as soon as you start your engine you become a power-driven vessel and must act accordingly. You must then also display a white steaming (masthead) light, with a 3-mile range, on the forward side of the mast, which shines through an arc of 225°, that is $112\frac{1}{2}°$ on either side of dead ahead. The all-round white masthead light often incorporated in tricolour lights is *not* a steaming light and should not be used as such. It is a riding light (and even so does not strictly conform to the rules as it should be displayed in the fore rigging).

Before putting to sea with the possibility of a night passage always check the functioning of the nav. lights and make sure there is enough charge in the batteries to keep them lit all night. If not, be prepared for charging periods. Do also be accurate about sunset and sunrise, do not just wait until it gets dark or say 'Oh well, it's light enough now we can switch off', for this could, in the event of an accident or collision, invalidate your insurance.

A thorough study of the regulations should be made (they are in the almanacs) not only to check up on what lights you are required to carry, but so that you can be fairly sure of recognizing another vessel and what she is doing by the lights displayed.

Meeting and avoiding shipping

Assuming that an oncoming ship does not make it plain that she has seen you by altering course to avoid you in good time, it is arguably safest to take it that she has not spotted you and take appropriate avoiding action. Should she alter course to avoid you then you must, of course, stand on, otherwise you will be creating a confusing and dangerous situation.

Even in quite deep water some of today's supertankers and container ships have very little room for manoeuvre because of their deep drafts and with their tight schedules for berthing and turning round in port they are understandably reluctant to alter course, slow or stop on the flimsy evidence of a lookout saying that he thought he saw a light. Also, with their great size and bulk there is an enormous blind area ahead of them, like a shadow cast by their bows. A yacht is particularly easily lost in that area.

We will discuss radar reflectors further in the section about Fog (see pages 228–31), but even though you display one – and it is very sensible to do so – there is no guarantee that you will be picked out amongst the 'sea clutter' and other random marks on a ship's radar display, especially in a busy area where the watchkeepers are having to keep their eyes on the movements of other large ships. It may still be best to assume they have not spotted you unless they alter course as required.

At best a yacht's navigation lights will be visible at the declared 2 miles, but even this is only so in good visibility and in a calm sea. If the weather is at all thick or if the boat is bouncing about a bit, this range will be cut drastically and the lights will show as flashes each time the boat rolls on a wave. When closehauled one light will spend most of its time colouring the sea, while the other flashes messages to the moon. But you must not take the attitude that if a ship cannot see you you need not carry lights. If people did that, how would two yachts see each other? Nor must you start swinging about altering course all over the place without giving time for any avoiding action taken by a ship to become apparent.

In various areas of congested shipping lanes separation zones and traffic flow systems have been set up. In effect these are like dual carriageways with traffic flowing in only one direction according to which side of the central reservation it is. It has considerably reduced the incidence of collision in these areas but has presented the yachtsman with a number of new problems. The main one is the requirement for a yacht crossing such a zone to do so at right angles to the flow of traffic and to do so as quickly as possible. This seems all right, but on many occasions it will mean motoring across to maintain course and manoeuvrability. If you enter a traffic scheme other than to cross it, you must obey it and follow the one-way system.

In these areas of heavy shipping it is essential to be alert, preferably with more than one person on watch, and to be in no doubt that the shipping has right of way. There may not be much room between succeeding vessels and you may have to wait for an opportunity to nip across the first lane, always remaining ready to 'slow her, stop her, go astern'.

Obviously a prime consideration when meeting any ship is to determine as early as possible whether you will collide if you both continue on the same courses at the same speeds. One way of doing this is to sight across the corner of the cabin top, a stanchion or other convenient object and, while maintaining a steady heading, see if the ship's bearing alters. If it does so significantly you will be clear, but if not someone will have to alter course or speed. A more sophisticated way is to take a bearing with a handbearing compass or by sighting across the steering compass and seeing how it alters. It should be pointed out though that this is fine in theory but not always easy in practice as the bearing may change only slightly over quite a period of time depending on circumstances.

Supposing that a ship is coming in at an angle across your bows, the best avoiding action to take is to head for her stern and follow it round until you are back on course. If she is coming up from astern you must swing well clear of her: in light weather do not be shy of starting the engine to give you greater speed to get clear. Although a ship (or any vessel) approaching from astern should keep clear, in restricted channels or separation schemes the onus is on you. Whatever you decide to do, make it a *positive, obvious movement* and *do it early*. Where the ship's lookout has seen you, there is nothing more confusing for him than to see a set of red and green dots swinging back and forth while you dither about.

Should someone come really close and for some reason you cannot get out of the way, then apart from shining a powerful torch steadily at the ship's bridge and occasionally on your own sails, the best thing to do is either call him up on VHF or light a *white* flare. Several of these should be carried with your other distress signals, for in a real emergency you may need more than one. A white flare is the recognized signal of a boat's presence not of her distress, so no-one will try to 'rescue' you. Conversely, do not use a red flare simply to signal your position, reserve them for when you are in trouble.

At night, a ship may tell you her direction of travel in the first instance by two white masthead lights, the forward one being lower than the after one. How far away she is poses another problem. The only positive thing is that in good visibility her side lights become visible at 3 miles (as opposed to the masthead lights' 6-miles range), but other than that there are very few clues. As she approaches the masthead lights and side lights become more clearly visible, the accommodation lights are seen, the dark shape of the hull may be made out and often the sea is lit up. Usually ships seem to be a long way away for a long time and then suddenly rush up on you. Really, as with so much of sailing, it is practice that tells you. Eventually you will be able to glance at a group of lights and say with some assurance that the vessel is passing clear. However, when you start doing that you must redouble your vigilance, never get blasé and always continue to watch a ship that has passed you until she has disappeared over the horizon, for it is only then that she has truly gone clear. Before that she may have to alter course to avoid another ship and so put the two of you back on a collision course.

One of the most confusing things to meet at night is a fishing fleet. Instantly you may think that the lights are those of a big ship far off; then you realize there are several small boats close to and you have got to avoid them. These boats are usually quite unable to take any avoiding action themselves – their gear just will not allow it – and so it is up to you. Tugs with tows and Naval craft on exercise may also need the same treatment and be extra careful if you meet another yacht.

Where you have to cross the mouth of a busy commercial port, do so as speedily as you can, even if it means going off course and beating back inshore. Cross as nearly as possible at right angles, since this keeps the danger distance down to a minimum.

Progress checking

Unless you take great care to *identify* each light you sight, it is horrifyingly easy to get confused about your position at night. One town's lights look just like another and it may only be by an offlying buoy or a lighthouse near the town that you can distinguish it from its neighbours. In fact all lights – buoys, lighthouses, light vessels, beacons, harbours lights – are identifiable by their characteristics: range, colour and sequence. A list of the characteristics of prominent lights along the coast should have been made before you set off, either from the chart or from pilots or the light lists in the almanacs, and this work now pays off with the list acting as a quick reference. The point is that each light must be accurately timed and so identified before you try to take a bearing on it and use it to get a fix. For timing lights there is nothing to beat a stopwatch, though with practice it is possible to become proficient in counting seconds, but this needs care – it is no good saying, 'One, whoops we're off course, two, no three' and so on.

Apart from the fact that you will be bobbing up and down on the waves and will consequently have to wait some time before you can be sure that you have seen the full sequence of a light, there should be no great problems involved with identifying individual lights, generally speaking. The difficult part is looking at the chart, where all the lights are neatly laid out, each one visible in relation to the others and interpreting this into what is actually seen. You have to allow for the angle at which you are seeing them – there may be a headland obscuring some or a buoy may appear to be on the wrong side of a shore light or you may not have noticed a seemingly prominent light has only got a range of a few miles, while another one can show up to 15 miles – it can all get very confusing if you let it. What you have to do is keep calm (an easy piece of advice to give), take each light in turn and determine its colour, group and timing, then find it on the chart. Remember you can heave to if you want to stay more or less in one place while you do all this. Once you have identified them you can take a useful bearing on them.

Actually, taking a bearing of a flashing light is none too easy because it always goes out just as you think you have it nicely lined up, but with patience it can be done. Remember, too, that buoys are notoriously hard to find in a seaway even in daylight, so try to use landmarks for making a landfall rather than a buoy. The shore lights will almost certainly have a greater range anyway, but can be hard to pick out from other non-navigational shore lights.

Once more, all this sounds a bit daunting, but really it is not that bad if you are careful. In fact, night sailing and picking out lights can be very exciting.

Dipping lights and looms

One of the more accurate ways of fixing your position is by a bearing of a mark and your distance off it. The bearing is laid off on the chart and your distance off marked along it. The problem at night is to find your distance off a light. Here the almanacs come to the rescue with tables of distances off lights dipping or rising. These are pre-computed tables that save you a fiddly calculation. First the difference must be understood between the loom of a light and a dipping light. The loom is quite simply the lightening of the sky that is observed while the light itself is still below the observer's horizon. A light is said to be dipping when it stands just clear of the horizon.

When the height of a light is given on the chart the process is dead easy; all you have to do is enter the table with the height of the light and the height of your eye above the water and read off the dipping distance. This, combined with a bearing of the light, provides your fix.

12

Engines and motorsailing

When you buy a secondhand boat you are more or less stuck with whatever motor is already installed, but if you are buying new, then you have a certain freedom of choice. Initially the decision must be between an inboard and an outboard engine. By virtue of the fact that it is a permanent installation, an inboard engine has the advantage of being ready for use at any time, while it is possible that an outboard will have to be heaved up out of a locker and mounted on a transom bracket before it can be used. This is all very well in harbour, but at sea it can be the devil of a job. On the other hand, once in position, the outboard takes up no room in the boat, while an inboard completely fills the space under the cockpit sole and may well intrude into the cabin as well. Again because it can be lifted clear of its mountings, an outboard is often easier to work on than an inboard and certainly clearing a fouled propeller is much simpler.

The propeller of an inboard engine is deeper and further forward than that of an outboard, which makes it much less likely to come out of the water in a seaway and gives it a better grip on the water. This has to be offset against the fact that because it is always in the water, you suffer considerable drag while sailing, which can be avoided by lifting or tilting an outboard clear of the water.

An outboard is usually cheaper than an equivalent inboard engine and you can, of course, take it ashore to an engineer if anything goes seriously wrong, while someone has to be persuaded to go out to the boat if you have a troublesome inboard. An outboard also bypasses the need for any sort of stern gear or through-hull skin fittings that are required by an inboard engine and are potential sources of leaks.

Whichever unit you choose there are bound to be drawbacks and perhaps the best idea is a compromise: an outboard mounted in a well at the after end of the cockpit. With such an installation you have the best of both worlds, particularly if there is a sliding hatch fitted under the well so that the motor can be tilted up into the boat and the hatch slid across to produce a smooth underwater hull when sailing.

Diesel or petrol

If you should decide to install an inboard engine, you are next faced with the problem of whether to have a diesel or petrol engine. By the way, strictly speaking a 'diesel' engine is a compression ignition engine, that is one whose fuel is ignited by heat generated when it is compressed violently. Both these types of engine have their advantages and you must weigh them all up and see which suits your purposes better.

Starting with money, diesels generally cost more initially than equivalent petrol engines, but their fuel is cheaper and tends to go further. Against this, petrol can be bought at any roadside garage while you might have to go looking for one that sells diesel (although most marinas have fuelling berths now which stock diesel). It should be remembered, however, that petrol is highly inflammable and represents a greater fire hazard than does the more docile diesel. It is no good, though, buying a diesel because it is 'safe' and then stowing a dinghy outboard with petrol dripping out of the carburettor or keeping a gas bottle with a leaking pressure valve: you have to be sensible about it. Diesel engines are much more susceptible to stoppage by dirty fuel than are petrol ones and great care must be taken to keep fuel filters clean.

Possibly the biggest argument in favour of petrol engines is that so many people are familiar with them from servicing their cars. Anyone who can tinker successfully with his car should be able to look after a marine petrol engine without too much difficulty and this may give him confidence in the motor. On the other hand, the workings of a diesel, particularly the fuel injection system, are rather complicated to unfamiliar eyes.

A marine engine of any kind has to work in a damp, corrosive atmosphere and from this point of view the diesel has the great advantage of needing no electrics to make it work. You may, of course, have an electric starter motor, but on the size of engine we are interested in it is (or should be) quite possible to hand start them.

This requires a hand-cranking system with room to swing the handle and a set of decompression levers within reach. These decompressors allow the engine to be turned over rapidly with reduced effort. Once the flywheel is turning rapidly, the levers are flipped over and the momentum of the flywheel (hopefully) starts the engine, a bit like bump-starting a car. When choosing a diesel make sure that hand-starting is available and that the decompression levers are within easy reach when cranking the motor, because there is not usually room enough for two people to work and anyway there may not always be a second person available to help.

A deciding factor in your choice of propulsion may be the weight of the engine. Because of the very high compression forces inside it, a diesel engine is a heavy brute very robustly built to withstand these strains. A petrol engine with its lower compression is a lighter motor altogether and may well take up less space, which is another serious consideration.

Applying the power

Most small auxiliaries in sailing cruisers drive straight through a gearbox, giving ahead, neutral and astern gears, with the engine final drive and the propeller shaft in more or less a straight line. Such a gearbox commonly reverses the rotational direction of the engine and at the same time reduces the speed of revolution, by say 2:1.

As we saw earlier, one of the problems with an inboard engine is that it takes up so much space in a small cruiser and for this reason it is now a common arrangement to have what is known as a Saildrive with the engine virtually on top of a through-hull drive leg. The whole unit is very compact and easy to install. Using pre-formed glass-fibre bearers, the boat builder only has to cut a hole through the hull, glass in the bearers and fit a flexible membrane round the drive leg. The Saildrive was made possible really by the fin and spade or skeg rudder being popularized and for such craft there seems to be no better way of installing an inboard.

The power output from the engine eventually ends up at the propeller and because this is ultimately what pushes the boat through the water it is important to choose the right prop. for the job. It is not an easy choice and much reliance must be put on the builder and engine manufacturer to advise you correctly. You start off by choosing a two- or three-bladed propeller, the two-bladed types being either fixed, folding or feathering. The fixed propeller stays as it is when sailing, the folding one claps its blades together like a butterfly folds its wings and the feathering one turns its blades so that they line up fore and aft to give the least resistance. A three-bladed propeller is usually fitted on bigger boats with slow revving diesels, often on work boats.

Propellers are described in terms of their diameter and pitch. The diameter is the diameter of a circle through the tips of the blades and the pitch is the distance the propeller would travel in a direction along its axis if it were turned through one revolution. This is a difficult one to imagine, but think of a propeller turning and cutting its way like a corkscrew through thick mud. It eats its way forward as it turns and the distance from its starting point to its finishing point after one revolution is a measure of its pitch.

Generally a fine pitch propeller (one that does not travel far) is used with a high revving engine pushing a heavy boat, while a coarse pitch propeller is used with a slower revving engine. There are innumerable ifs and buts about all this and it is worth listening to the advice of the manufacturer regarding the final choice of prop.

A real jack-of-all-trades is the feathering or variable pitch propeller, as this has rotating blades to give ahead, neutral and astern and feathered positions with infinite variations in between. Their advantage lies in not requiring a conventional gearbox and in the ability to vary the pitch according to the load and sea state.

Engine installations

From the point of view of the user, the most important things about an engine installation are that the engine should be completely accessible for working on; it should have an efficient cooling system; the engine box should have good acoustic insulation and the electrics must be well protected against corrosion. The actual mechanics of mounting and aligning the engine and arranging the electrics are best left to professionals or only undertaken after careful study of the problems.

Far too many engines can only be reached, even for routine oil checks, by crawling about on your stomach, contorting yourself round pillars and bulkheads. It should not be too difficult to arrange things so that by removing the companionway steps and a couple of panels the whole engine is revealed. In many cases you can remove various hatches, but this should not involve undoing a couple of dozen bolts – that is no good in a seaway when you are in a hurry.

The watertightness of access hatches is important as the engine and electrics quickly become corroded if saltwater is constantly dripping on them. I remember one boat where we made port after going through some rough weather and found the whole engine coated in salt; it looked like a log in a snowstorm. It also did not work properly.

Obviously an engine needs an efficient cooling system, whether it is air cooled or water cooled. In the latter case, each of the through-hull skin fittings must have a seacock (a screw-down valve), so that it can be shut off, and the intake must have a strainer on it. All of these seacocks and strainers must, of course, be within easy reach.

Lastly, it only makes sense that the engine should be made as quiet as possible and this means covering the inside of the engine space with an acoustic insulating material. Living with a noisy motor is unpleasant and unnecessary as there is good insulation material on the market.

Troubleshooting

The two occasions when an engine tells you most blatantly that there is something wrong with it are when it refuses to start and when it stops before you intend it to. So let us begin with starting troubles, the symptoms of which are pretty obvious. If the engine does not even turn over you may have a flat battery or one whose leads have corroded or come adrift, some other loose electrical connection or the starter motor may have jammed. First make a visual check of the electrics and if anything is clearly amiss there put it right, otherwise try starting the engine by hand.

A jammed starter motor can usually be wound back with a spanner, but check in the owner's handbook. When the engine turns over but still will not start there are a host of things to check: fuel level in the tank; blocked fuel lines; flooded carburettor; choked fuel pump; injectors blocked; dirt or water in fuel; dirty filters; damp electrics; oily, dirty or damaged spark plugs; incorrect ignition timing. The first of these can be remedied quite easily if you carry a spare can of fuel, but with a diesel engine any fiddling about with injectors or fuel system means that you have to bleed the system when you have finished and that is not the world's most wonderful job. Blocked fuel lines can usually be cleared right through stage by stage, but it is a messy job. The flooded carburettor will have to be drained and the excess fuel allowed to evaporate. Injectors are surprisingly delicate things and care must be taken not to damage

Outboard motors have their uses, but it's difficult to know what to do with them when they are not in use. Here the mounting bracket slides to the top of its tracks and the engine tilts so that the prop. is well clear of the water; at least it is clear in calm water, but in a rough sea it will be pitching in and out of each wave, putting great strain on the mountings. However to lift it aboard and have to remount it when required is also an unsatisfactory situation.

them if they are unscrewed; should they be faulty they will have to be dealt with by an expert and may need replacement. When you suspect contaminated fuel, empty the sludge trap, drain the water trap if one is fitted, clear the filters and fuel lines and hope that does the trick, otherwise you will have to empty the tank and clean it before refilling. Dry the electrics and spray them with an aerosol damp retardant. Clean or replace spark plugs, checking gaps at the same time. You will have to follow the owner's handbook to deal with ignition timing.

When an engine that has been running quite happily suddenly cuts out there is an overpowering silence, in which a crew tends to stand still, listening, as if expecting the engine to start up again. It will not; you have got to make it. Almost certainly it will be electrical trouble if an engine cuts out without any sort of warning, so check connections, dry everything and try starting again. With luck that should solve the problem, but if not then look at the distributor and

Good engine access is of great importance but is often not provided on stock boats. This is an example of one of the better installations where removable panels have left the engine all but freestanding.

Birth of a production boat. The very fact that the engine and stern gear have been installed at such an early stage leads one to wonder if access for maintenance is going to be any good. Certainly it looks as though a complete engine removal will mean a major restructuring job on the accommodation.

Good engine access. Removing the panel on the far side will allow almost all parts of the engine to be reached with ease.

see that all is well there – it could have water in or the capacitor could be damaged or faulty.

On most occasions an engine falters and coughs a bit before giving up the ghost and in this case there are several possibilities. First and foremost, lack of fuel; fuel lines blocked or broken; fuel pump choked; injectors blocked or damaged; air lock; air vent in outboard motor filler cap closed; contaminated fuel; filters choked; water inlet fouled. Check the level in the fuel tank even if you 'know it's full' – leaks can occur without being noticed. Inspect fuel lines for damage and clear or repair if necessary. Clean fuel pump if blocked. Remember to treat injectors with caution and preferably leave them alone until all other possibilities have been exhausted. An air lock will mean bleeding the system. Leaving the air vent closed on the outboard's fuel tank is a common failing (the other trick being to leave it open as you carry the outboard from the dinghy to the car, letting fuel pour out everywhere) and you might do well to make a surreptitious check that the fuel tap is actually turned on. Deal with contaminated fuel as before. Clean filters – petrol or diesel are good cleansers – and remember to close the seacock before removing the seawater strainer.

Those are the two basic exigencies with which we are concerned, but close to them comes the discovery that nothing happens when you try to put the engine in gear. The simplest explanation is disconnected gear controls; alternatives are a seized gearbox or a broken prop. shaft with the possibility of a rope or net wound tightly round the prop. preventing its turning. Assuming a quick look over the side does not reveal a large net or rope in tow, follow the control lines right through to see if they are damaged or disconnected. Failing that, try revolving the prop. shaft by hand. If you cannot turn it, try a cautious hand on the gearbox to see if it is overhot – lack of oil is the usual cause of seizure. With a broken prop. shaft it is usually possible to engage gear, but then there is a terrible graunching noise as you open the throttle – make a visual check of the shaft. If there is still nothing obviously wrong it may be necessary to make an underwater inspection of the prop., but try everything else first. When you do have to go over the side, do so with a lifeharness attached to the boat, if possible wear a wet suit (or better still a dry suit) and a pair of diving goggles. Take great care to protect your head as the rising and falling of the stern on even a slight swell can give you a serious crack over the head.

An overheating engine is generally the result of lack of oil or a fault in the cooling system, often occasioned by the water intake valve not being turned on or its being blocked. Alternatively the circulating pumps could be in trouble and you may have to replace an impeller. The fuel mixture may be wrong in a two-stroke and the injectors may be faulty in a diesel. It is also worth checking that there is water in the freshwater cooling system if one is fitted.

Rough running must be caused by something to do with the electrics, the fuel supply, the air intake or the timing. Excess vibration may be caused by loose mountings, a damaged propeller blade or a fouled propeller. Go over the electrics as described before and look at the distributor cap to see if it is cracked and therefore shorting. The same applies to the fuel and air supplies. Check timing according to instructions in the engine manual. Check fuel and air supplies. Once the problem is sorted out, make a note that a general overhaul might be a good thing.

Excessive blue exhaust smoke at normal running temperatures indicates burning of lubricating oil either by its being drawn into the induction manifold from an overfull air filter, or more seriously by its leaking past the pistons due to a mechanical fault there. On the other hand black smoke indicates poor fuel combustion, possibly caused by a faulty choke mechanism or incorrectly adjusted fuel injectors.

Clearly this is only the briefest possible summary of engine troubles, but it is a start. A happy engine is extremely useful, while an unhappy one is a misery to all, so look after your boat's engine and do not curse it; it might decide to sulk just when you need it.

Fuel consumption

Whereas it is easy enough with a car to talk in terms of miles per gallon this is clearly not possible with boats. For a marine engine we express fuel consumption in terms of gallons used per hour (or litres per hour), e.g. $\frac{3}{4}$ gallon (3.5 litres) per hour. Occasionally brochures do say that a boat carries so many gallons of fuel to give a range of X miles, but be wary of this figure as it is dependent upon engine revs, sea conditions and accuracy of course steered. Just as a car may not meet its advertised m.p.g. if you sit in several traffic jams, so too a rough sea will raise a marine engine's fuel consumption. It is, however, wise to carry out trials to determine the approximate fuel consumption at cruising revs for your engine, as you will then have some idea of how long you can motor on passage.

Maintenance

A well-maintained engine is far more likely to work than a neglected one, but many cruiser owners completely ignore the auxiliary until it goes wrong. The owner's handbook will detail the maintenance schedule for the engine and this should be followed, but if you are a 'better to leave well alone if it's running' person, the least you should do is to check the oil levels and if you do much motoring on a passage, remember to grease the stern gland regularly. At the same time the water in the batteries should be checked and topped up if low, otherwise the batteries will boil.

Some engine manufacturers, notably Perkins Diesels, run maintenance courses for people who own their make of engine. While they certainly do not promise to turn you into a mechanical genius overnight, such a course will equip you to look after your boat's engine far more efficiently and give you more confidence to cope with a breakdown. There are also car maintenance courses run by many evening institutes and although these are not entirely applicable to marine situations – I would love to see a boat fitted with disc brakes – they do offer a good grounding in mechanics.

Motorsailing

The first thing to remember is that as soon as you start the engine you are immediately bound by the rules of the road for motor vessels and by night are required to display a white steaming light. By day, if motorsailing, you must display a black south cone (point downwards) in the fore rigging.

There are any number of reasons for motorsailing – punching a foul tide round a headland, making a hard passage to windward easier, trying to beat the tide home. In each case your prime object is to reach your destination faster and possibly more comfortably than you would under sail alone. When you are on a long coastal passage you might decide to motorsail if the boat's speed falls below a certain point in order to save a tide; in other words, you are trying to keep the average speed up.

One other situation when motorsailing usually becomes necessary is when you have to cross a shipping separation zone.

The sailing cruiser on the left of this picture is motorsailing with just her mainsail set and, like the motorcruiser on the right, is thus bound by the International Regulations for Preventing Collisions at Sea as pertaining to powered vessels. She is correctly displaying a black south cone in her rigging to indicate that she is under power. The cone should actually be in the fore rigging rather than at the crosstrees, but we won't argue the point. In such hazy conditions as these it is particularly important that other vessels know exactly what you are and how you are going to behave.

Assuming it is blowing hard, the sea is rough and you want to weather a headland without putting in another tack, you have three options – to motorsail with just the jib set, just the main set or, if conditions allow, with both set. The choice between these is made in the light of your knowledge of the boat and how she handles under a variety of rigs and in the conditions prevailing. A boat on which it is usual to reef the mainsail before changing to a smaller headsail will probably drive better under engine and a headsail, whereas one with a small foresail/large mainsail configuration may do better under a well-reefed mainsail (which is more manageable anyway than a headsail) and engine. Of course if you can you will make the best progress with both main and jib set. This is something that needs experimentation to discover the best arrangement for your boat. In any case the sheets will have to be hardened right in to keep the sails flat and driving, as the apparent wind will be from further forward than when under sail alone.

Off the wind your increased boat speed will reduce the strength of the apparent wind and indeed in a light wind you may find it impossible to keep the headsail filled in the lee of the mainsail. It is better then to dowse it and use the main alone with the boom run off and a preventer rigged from the outboard end down to the deck well forward. This is set up hard against the pull of the mainsheet to stop the boom banging about and it helps too to keep the sail full.

Many people seem to think that if they have got to beat the tide home on a Sunday night, or if the wind is dead down a narrow channel, the thing to do is motor. This may not always be the case – motorsailing may well be the quicker and more comfortable way. If the sea is at all rough, butting into it under power means that you will be pitching up and down feeling miserable, while a boat motor sailing will be steadier and have extra drive to push through the seas. Sheet in hard and use the sails for steadying (plus some drive) and the engine to give the main drive.

13

Rough weather

Go into the bar of any yacht club and listen to the conversation. As soon as the beer begins to flow you will hear somebody starting to swing the lantern a bit. 'So there we were, you see, nothing up but a close-reefed burgee and still we were surfing at 10 knots. . . .' Do not worry, even if you know it was not blowing above Force 6 that day. He is enjoying himself and he may well have been scared stiff at the time. For a small cruiser, particularly one with a couple of youngsters on board, a Force 5 or 6 over a spring tide can easily seem like a full-blown hurricane.

It must also be realized that there is a tremendous difference between sailing in a full gale in the sheltered waters of an estuary or river mouth and sailing in the same wind several miles offshore. In an estuary with the shores only half a mile or so on either hand the sea gets choppy and covered with white horses, but with just a scrap of sail set many boats will still make progress to windward. Take these same boats offshore though and they will be in a most unhappy situation.

When we talk about small boats in gales we are talking about being in a situation that we will have done our utmost to avoid. We *can* fail in our attempts to escape though and if you are caught out at sea with your pants down and a gale rising, you have not only to prepare the boat for the battering she is going to take, but also the crew.

One point I should make is that the advice in this chapter – and indeed in Chapter 15 on distress – is entirely general. You must think about it all and adapt it to your own boat and circumstances: one just cannot be dogmatic about the sea.

Emergency reefing and steering

There will probably be many times during an average season when you have to reef, but on most occasions it will be a case of changing down the jib and taking a slab out of the main. Nothing drastic. However, once in a while we have to take in the deepest reef possible and then there are often some nasty surprises. Many boats sail with reefing lines rove for the first two reefs but not the third. Yet, when the third is required, the weather will already be bad and it is definitely not the time you want to be worrying about reeving off lines and pennants. I feel quite strongly that the last reef is arguably the most important and the lack of a permanently situated pennant is a serious omission on a family cruiser.

In similar fashion with roller-reefing mainsails, surprisingly large numbers of yachtsmen never try rolling down 10 or 12 rolls to see how the sail will set until it becomes necessary. Then, horror of horrors, they find the boom end droops so far that it fouls everything and makes tacking pretty dangerous. A little forethought and a trial run would have revealed this problem in time to remedy it either by tapering the boom to take up the bunt of the sail or by putting in a single, very deep row of reef points to be used when the roller system has gone as far as it practically can.

The same sort of thinking and forward planning applies to headsails. If you have a roller-reefing headsail, practice setting it as a pocket handkerchief to see if it will still be useable and whether or not sheet lead blocks have to be moved. If you have a simple series of progressively smaller headsails, is the smallest so-called storm jib really going to be small enough? Should you have a row of reef points put into it so that it can be reefed down *in extremis*?

Rough weather does not just affect sails, it takes its toll of equipment and one of the more alarming items that can suffer is the tiller. A spare should be carried, although it may prove very hard to fit it in bad weather, and if you can it is worth sparing a thought as to how you would devise a jury system. Where wheel steering is normally used there should be provision for fitting a tiller on the rudder head and do make sure that the boat can actually be steered using this tiller. It is not unknown for it to be totally impractical, being placed in a confined space, below decks, out of sight of the compass or the surrounding sea. Do not let the first time you try it out be in a real gale.

There are many stories of people with damaged steering gear

constructing jury rudders out of spinnaker poles and floorboards. None of them has found it easy in practice, but devising a system (and even trying it out) does make it easier in the mind-numbing conditions of a rough sea and steering gear failure.

Makeshift trysail

Once all yachts carried trysails. Then they went almost completely out of fashion. Then offshore racers got into trouble and they were compulsorily reintroduced for some offshore races. Still many cruising yachtsmen do not bother with them. So be it, modern mainsails are almost as tough as a trysail, which in any case is not an easy sail to handle, but it may be better than a deeply reefed, badly setting mainsail. Failing the presence of a trysail there are situations when it could be necessary to improvise one.

A trysail is a loose-footed triangular sail set on the mast in place of the mainsail. It can be set when the mainsail cannot be reefed any further or if by mischance it is torn or otherwise damaged. It should not require the use of the boom.

If a trysail is not carried, for whatever reason, it is possible to improvise one using a small headsail. A line from the foot of the mast is rove through the tack cringle, the sail is hoisted on the main halyard and is sheeted to the quarters. If you can do it, the sail will set better if it is bent on to the mast with a line running through the hanks. Do not sheet the sail to the boom end (even if it is undamaged), for although you then have the mainsheet as a purchase, it means that the boom will still be swinging about dangerously while setting the sail and while tacking or gybing. A better plan is to lead the sheets through quarter blocks and then forward to sheet winches (assuming some are fitted), but watch for the weather sheet chafing the stowed mainsail and do not omit to lash the boom down securely.

Jury rig

While we tend to think of dismasting as something that happens to some other poor bloke out in the middle of an ocean, a mast can break or bend in only moderate conditions just outside harbour. If you are only 2 or 3 miles offshore in reasonable weather, the chances are that you will be able to make port under power, but what if the engine packs up? Obviously you can send up flares and

Gale Force 9 in the Bay of Biscay. Not the kind of weather any of us wants to be out in. These are survival conditions for any yacht, but such pictures serve to take away any romantic notions about staying at sea in bad weather.

Tail end of a Force 9 gale – Atlantic Ocean, seen from the tanker *Gulf Briton*.

A 32 ft cruiser reaching up the Solent before a gale. As she is reaching rather than beating she can carry a reasonably large headsail with her deeply reefed main. On the wind it would be quite another story with tiny spitfire jib being the rig of the day and the crew taking a real soaking. Note radar reflector and the dinghy outboard stowed in the pushpit. Also the sensible use of cockpit dodgers to display the boat's name clearly and at the same time give the crew some measure of shelter.

say 'help' loudly on the radio, but first of all you must try to help yourself.

The commonest breaking points for an alloy mast are just above, just below and actually at the crosstrees. Many masts have not only the crosstree roots riveted on at that point, but also a tang bolted on each side to take the lower shrouds. In other words, it is a very high-stress area. The other likely breaking point is down at the mast step or at the partners where the mast passes through the deck. However, a break there is likely to be the result of a break higher up, you are most unlikely to have a mast go by the board in one piece. Wooden spars have the extra possibility of breaking at a scarf, though modern glues have lessened the likelihood.

When the whole mast or part of the mast goes it is left either in a tangled mess alongside in the water or as a tangled mess hanging down on deck. Either way you have got to clear that mess away before it damages the boat or crew. If you can save the broken part

217

and recover it aboard so much the better, but if it is trying to puncture the hull and seems likely to succeed before you can get it on deck, then you will have to cut it clear and let it go. An axe used to be a standard piece of equipment on boats, but now you would do better to carry a hacksaw with a number of spare blades and a large pair of boltcroppers or wire cutters.

Once the immediate mess has been cleared you can start thinking about how best to set up some sort of jury rig. It is pretty well impossible to give specific advice here as there are too many parameters and ingenuity will be the watchword, but there are one or two fundamental ideas to consider. Clearly the idea is to set up a mast on which you can set sufficient sail to give the boat a chance of making port, even if it is only downwind. The cartoon raft with two bearded, shipwrecked figures on board usually has an oar set up as a mast with a cross piece and a shirt spread on it. We hope to do a little better than that, but they have obviously improvised with available materials and that is the best anyone can do.

If the mast has gone near the crosstrees, but left the lower part standing, then you are well off. 'All' you have to do is rig up some shrouds and set a jib whose luff wire acts as a forestay and whose halyard will do for a backstay. Three things that will help in any situation are spare blocks, a supply of bulldog clips and the ability to apply a range of knots. The bulldog clips are used for holding two pieces of wire together (usually forming an eye) instead of splicing them and the knots for attaching shrouds to the mast and other lashings.

Apart from the section of mast left standing, you can improvise a mast with the boom, oars from the dinghy in the form of a low bipod or a longer pole by fishing them together, a piece of broken mast or a spinnaker pole or a combination of some of these spars. In any case you are not likely to be able to set much sail, but it should allow you to close the coast. With luck and care – you should check all rigging and mast fittings at least once during the season – none of this will happen to you, but it is worth sitting down and thinking about it on a cold winter evening when there is not much on television. That thinking could get you out of a nasty situation.

Seasickness

Most people are attacked at some time or other by seasickness, though there are a few annoyingly lucky souls who seem to be immune to it. Those who are not affected, please make a point of not scoffing or laughing at those who are, because I can assure you they are going through hell and you never know, it might be your turn one day. For the sufferers, do not be ashamed or embarrassed, good skippers and crew members will be sympathetic and will do what they can for you, but it is mainly up to you and do not expect anyone to clear up after you. Few people are actually incapacitated by seasickness and one of the quickest ways of getting over it that I have found is to carry on as normally as possible with your watches and other chores. On many occasions I have arrived on watch grizzly faced, clutching a bucket and with an icy sweat breaking out all over. In the beginning you think you are going to die; then you hope you are going to die; finally, and worst of all, you realize that you are not going to die. After that you start to get better.

Individuals have to find their own formula for recovery. There are numerous anti-seasickness drugs available, some of them with drowsiness as a side effect, besides various other methods like hypnosis, wrist pressure bands and a new idea of a pad stuck on to the skin behind one ear that releases a drug slowly into the body. For many people, myself included, a drug marketed under the trade name of Stugeron is the best available. For some it is a true wonder drug completely transforming their sailing activities and removing the possibility of seasickness completely. All you can really do is try various treatments and find which suits you best.

I think the sufferer should try to eat as soon as possible and drink plenty too, while some people will say that this is quite wrong and that you should force yourself to eat before you feel like it – let them, I say. Again, some people advocate eating dry biscuits and such things – I do not fancy that idea because vomiting hard, undigested items is very painful indeed. Bland things such as bananas, orange juice, well chewed apples (peeled), Marmite, Bovril; these are the things I start with but, as I said, it is very much an individual thing. However, drinking is essential to avoid dehydration.

When someone takes his trick at the helm and is being sick, insist that he wears a lifeharness clipped on to the windward side, so that he can be sick to leeward, but cannot go overboard. (Actually it is safer and easier if he uses a bucket rather than retching over the side.) Down below, give him a bucket, make sure he is kept securely in his bunk or is wedged upright if he is sitting. If he wants to sleep he will, but keep him warm. Do call him for his watch and only stop him doing it if he is really bad, but if you are in a shipping lane someone must stick their head outside every so often to make sure all is well. The point here is that a sick man has slow reactions, low concentration and his eyesight may be affected. I scared myself stupid once when I looked up from contemplating the bottom of a bucket and found a ship lying athwart our course about half a mile ahead. I swear it was not there a couple of minutes earlier.

At the risk of sounding patronizing, should your wife become sick you must steel yourself not to mollycoddle her as this is the sure way of having her collapse on you completely – and anyway, you can be quite sure she would not do the same for you. Women are far less fragile than we sometimes like to think and while I do not suggest you drive her on deck with a rope's end, you should try to keep her going. Children are often less prone to seasickness than their parents and will often simply go to sleep if it is rough – or else laugh at you being sick. However, there are drugs for children and it may be as well to dose them with one of these before putting to sea, at least until you know whether or not they suffer.

Food

Cooking at sea in rough weather is not at all easy, but it is necessary on a long passage because lack of food, combined with loss of body heat, will quickly make you weak, tired and careless.

For things like soup, really deep saucepans are needed to stop the liquid slopping out, while for stews and so on a completely closed pressure cooker is ideal. Not only is a pressure cooker fast, spillage is nearly impossible. However, in either case and indeed with any cooking, great care must be taken to avoid scalds and burns by falling on to hot pans or having them spill on to you.

The best plan before the onset of any predicted rough weather is to make up Thermos flasks of hot drinks such as soup and coffee plus a pressure cooker of something like stew with all the meat and vegetables thrown in together. Aside from that make up packs of sandwiches, put out lots of chocolate, raisins, fruit and anything else which will provide a snack.

Clothing

Just as important as food in the battle against cold is good protective clothing. Nowadays the market is full of good thermal underclothing and really waterproof oilskins, although none of it is cheap. It all has to keep you warm and dry without being so cumbersome that your movements are restricted and, most importantly, they must not be tight otherwise they will restrict blood circulation.

Oilskins need to have chest-high trousers, not waist-high ones, and should be fitted with storm cuffs plus a close-fitting hood with a drawstring to pull it in round the face. Better (and more expensive oilskins) have linings to reduce condensation and built-in life-harnesses and/or buoyancy aids. The harnesses and buoyancy aids are excellent ideas as you then automatically put them on whenever you don the oilskins.

A very considerable proportion of body heat lost is through the head, so use woolly hats under windproof oilskin hoods and keep the back of your neck warm and dry by wrapping a towelling scarf round it.

Hands too suffer from the cold but it is very hard to find a pair of gloves that keep your hands warm while allowing you to cleat a rope or winch in a sheet without winding the fingers in too. Any gloves are better than nothing on a cold watch, but if they are not close fitting they must be removed before working on fiddly jobs or ones involving gear or ropes under load. They are rather clumsy, but I have found woollen gloves inside heavy duty PVC gardening gloves to be a warm, dry combination.

Several layers of thin woollen clothing under oilskins will keep you nice and warm, but the modern thing is to use synthetic fibre pile thermal suits. These are mostly very good indeed, but they are not windproof or waterproof, so, like ordinary clothing, they must be worn under wind- and waterproof oilskins for maximum benefit. One other item of clothing worth considering instead of oilskins are the lightweight survival suits developed for workers on the offshore oilrigs. These are highly flexible for working, yet waterproof and contain sufficient buoyancy to keep you afloat. Not cheap, but real life savers.

Tactics

The obvious way to get prior warning of impending bad weather is to listen to the radio forecasts, in particular the shipping forecasts, which we will look at in detail in Chapter 16. The action you take after hearing a forecast of bad weather is governed by your position and circumstances, together with the imminence or otherwise of the approaching rough and tumble.

Reefed down and tramping along, this 25-footer shows how the modern cruiser can perform well in rough going. Her mainsail is roller reefed and sets very nicely with little boom droop. To weather she will give her crew a bouncy ride, but will look after them. Working on deck will need great care.

In the first place you must bring your dead reckoning plot up to date so that you know fairly accurately where you are. Assuming that the forecast gives you a few hours' grace, you can look around from your plotted position for somewhere that will give you shelter from the coming blow. This may be a harbour or an anchorage in the lee of a headland, but the two requirements are that it should be reachable well within the forecast time limit and that it should have as simple and clear an approach as possible, taking into consideration the direction from which the wind will be rising. It is just possible that there will be two equally well sheltered places within reasonable sailing time, one upwind of your position and one downwind. In that case you have to try to picture what the conditions will be like by the time you reach one of them. The downwind harbour or refuge may be reached sooner, but if it is on a lee shore the waves will tend to pile up in the shallowing water and it does not take much of this to turn an otherwise simple entrance into a very dodgy affair. On the other hand, the upwind harbour may take

A 22 ft cruiser reefed down and hammering along. The neatly tied-in reef was put in in harbour and the spitfire jib too was rigged there so that there was no need, once out in open water, to heave to and set everything up. Forethought and planning paying off.

longer to reach and also mean a slog to windward, but the nearer you get the more likely you are to find quieter water and the longer the entrance will remain passable.

You must also work out whether there is any possibility of having to enter in darkness and if there will be sufficient water at the state of tide when you will arrive. Where there are plenty of leading lights or a well-marked channel an entry after dark should not pose too many problems, but entering an unlit port in a rising wind may be very unwise. Particularly, one should be wary of crossing any offlying bar if the sea is kicking up. In order to make port in reasonable time or to get round a headland before the tide turns foul it is worth motorsailing, but do not leave yourself out of fuel when you finally get in.

When the forecast gives warning of a *fast* approaching blow, the questions to be asked remain the same, but the problem becomes that much more acute. In these circumstances it can literally be a case of 'any port in a storm'. A forecast blow 'in the next 12 hours' when you are already at sea very often allows you to press on for your planned destination, but an 'imminent' forecast means a drastic re-think. It might mean turning tail and running back whence you came. It will usually mean going into a place that for some reason you would not normally use and this is the time when all the charts you carry 'just in case' come into their own. So too does the homework you did (you did, didn't you?) before the trip, which should have included studying all these charts together with the pilots, to find out which harbours would be useable on such occasions. All time so spent will be tremendously valuable now, since in an emergency you will be nervous and worried, and familiarity with what you are reading and looking at will make absorbing its detail that much simpler.

Clearly the last place you want to be in a high wind is hard by a lee shore. A crack ocean racer may be able to claw her way to windward into the teeth of a gale, but a small, dumpy family cruiser certainly cannot. As soon as it looks like blowing up into an onshore gale (or even strong wind) you must try to find a safe retreat and, failing that, you must gain sea room. This will probably entail motorsailing to windward until you are well offshore and in a position to think again about a harbour or even about the possibility of heaving to and staying at sea. A well-maintained engine now pays dividends and it must be done as quickly as possible. Trying to gain an offing by beating into the wind against steep, short, sometimes breaking, shallow-water seas is just not on for most average family boats.

You may, of course, be too far from a port to be able to get in before it is blowing hard. Then you have two choices: to stay at sea and ride it out (assuming that you have or can gain sufficient sea room) or to make port in rough weather. The former is notionally romantic but in truth is miserable – it will be uncomfortable, noisy and frightening, but it could be safer than trying to get in. A narrow harbour entrance in an onshore gale becomes a place of heavily breaking seas which can easily drive a small boat on to the piers. Entering through such a mess can be far more hairy than staying out. The best hope is to crab across the rising wind and find shelter under a headland if you can, but in any case, think carefully and then act quickly.

14

Fog

When visibility is reduced to between 2200 yards (2000 m) and 1100 yards (1000 m) we use the term mist and when it is further reduced to less than 1100 yards (1000 m) we say that it is foggy. Waking up in a nice quiet anchorage and finding the world reduced to a few yards all round the boat and enclosed by cotton wool makes the decision to stay put very easy, but fog is a nasty sneaky thing that will unhesitatingly creep up on you at sea. With its approach come special navigational problems, the obvious one being how to see and avoid shipping. Leaving aside sound for a minute, the first intimation of the approach of a ship may be a darkening of the fog in an irregularly shaped patch. This is followed by a defining of the shape and a whitening of an area low down on the shape – the bow wave. If this is dead centre the ship is coming straight down on you and you will have to take avoiding action immediately. When it is at one end of a long dark shape, the ship is crossing your line of sight and should go clear. In between these two extremes you may see a short side and a long side to the white, showing that the vessel is crossing at an angle, with the long part on the side nearer to you, indicating her angle of approach.

Fog produces strange effects with sound: telling from what direction sound is coming can be very hard, compounded by the existence of what are called lanes of silence. These cut out sound completely, making it impossible to hear an approaching ship or the warning signal of a lighthouse. When a ship emerges from the silent lane its siren is heard with alarming clarity and intensity. For some reason in fog it is very common only to hear a ship's engines when she is *down*wind from you and not to hear them when she is upwind. When you try to listen for a faint sound it is a help if two of you listen. There is then less chance of imagined hearings and also some hope of getting the direction of the sound right. It looks a bit odd, but to aid

FOG. Thick fog at that and a hard-to-see ship crossing from right to left. The barely seen bow wave shows her speed and her general attitude shows that she will indeed pass clear, but alerts the crew to the need for absolute vigilance on watch.

concentration you can cup a hand behind each ear and close your eyes – but remember to *tell someone to be lookout*, for you would feel a right fool (apart from anything else) if you hit something while the whole crew had their eyes shut.

Going back to vision in fog, it is hard to judge distances of visibility, so a frequent check should be made, for instance by dropping a screwed up piece of paper overboard and watching it out of sight. At night paraffin-soaked rags or crumpled paper can be lit and used. Remembering that on most occasions a ship will be travelling faster through the water than you will be, even if the paper shows the visibility to be about 400 yards (350 m), you are going to have to think and act very fast indeed if a ship does loom up. Some people automatically start the engine when fog is about, but this destroys all chance of hearing a ship. However, if you want to get inshore to shallow water clear of shipping lanes, you may be well advised to motorsail.

While you may feel somewhat helpless in fog because there is very little wind and you are perhaps cagey about using the motor, be thankful that we do not normally meet fog and a strong wind together. Such conditions can be very frightening. In any case you must keep as accurate an account of your position as possible, but in fog and wind you have to be doubly careful.

If you are underway in fog, vigilance is the keyword and from a safety point of view, make the crew wear lifejackets not harnesses. Unlikely though the chance may seem, it would be a sad thing if someone were attached to a sinking vessel unable to unclip their harness.

Foghorns

Foghorns come in all shapes and sizes: trumpets that the operator blows through, plunger operated ones, electric car horns, aerosol horns, klaxons and many others. Most small boats carry either a mouth-operated trumpet or an aerosol horn, with car horns sometimes seen. I did know one chap who had a plunger-operated horn taken from a tug; it was about the size of his boat and a fantastic ship-scarer.

Tests carried out by a British yachting magazine showed that of these commonly used types of foghorn, the aerosol one gave the loudest and most nearly omnidirectional blast, while the mouth trumpet was weaker and very directional. The car horns were weaker still.

The aerosol horns emit a continuous note for as long as the operating button is depressed, but it is common for the diaphragm to 'freeze'. The gas (usually Freon) freezes droplets of water in the foggy atmosphere and the ice so formed prevents vibration of the diaphragm, so that no sound at all can be obtained until it has melted. Clearly this could prove dangerous and a reserve mouth horn should be carried.

The mouth-operated trumpet, though not as loud as the aerosol horn over short distances, has better carrying power over longer distances, where the shape of the trumpet projects the sound rather better than the splayed-out aerosol horn. Its advantages are that it emits a continuous note for as long as the operator can blow; it requires no mechanical or electrical aid for operation and it is robust and reliable. It is also relatively cheap and does not need replacement gas canisters.

Radar reflectors

While the hoisting of a radar reflector certainly does not make a boat magically immune to being run down by a ship, it does give a greatly increased chance of being recognized on a ship's radar display. Its presence in the rigging though must not allow the lookout's vigilance to relax. As its name implies, it is a passive instrument, only reflecting the beam of an already operating scanner and its reflection will only be noted if the radar operator is watching the screen. It is possible also for the reflector on a small boat – or one that is displayed too low down – to fall below the radar beam if it is close to the ship when the radar is scanning on long range. For instance, the echo of a boat about half a mile away may not show on the radar display if the 12-mile range scale is in use.

Without going into details of how they work, the larger the reflecting area the better and the higher it is hoisted the better as this improves its chances of standing clear above large seas in heavy weather when visibility is poor. Do not waste your time with metal jerrycans or any other substitutes as these are useless. When

Octahedral radar reflector correctly hoisted in the 'catch rain' attitude with a 'hole' uppermost. This neat hoisting and staying arrangement allows the reflector to slide up and down the backstay and be held firmly in the right attitude. These are the commonest pattern of radar reflector and are good if properly displayed and do not have bent or damaged plates.

A Firth radar reflector. This reflector houses a number of baby octahedral reflectors within the glass-fibre housing and with its easy, right-way-up hanging or mounting system it provides a very good, large, reflecting surface. Also the smooth glass-fibre case will not tear sails.

a metal plate octahedral reflector is used, make sure it is hoisted to display the correct aspect: which way this 'catch rain' position is can be found quite simply by putting the reflector down on a flat surface and letting go. It will take up the only possible stable position with a 'hole' at the top (to 'catch rain') and that is how it should be displayed.

Hoisting a reflector in the rigging creates problems of chafe, although such types as the Firdel and Lensref have completely smooth glass-fibre cases that reduce the problem greatly. Bowsing down the reflector halyard helps to stop it swinging about, but with an octahedral reflector take care the metal plates do not cut through their own halyard. Arguably the ideal is to mount the reflector on the masthead and an increasing number of cruising people take this sensible course.

Radar detectors

Whereas a radar reflector is completely passive, only telling the ship's radar operator you are there, a radar detector tells you that a ship nearby is using a radar set. It gives you an approximate bearing of the operating radar, thus giving you a chance to take avoiding action if you think the ship has not detected your presence. It cannot, however, tell you if there is a ship about to hit you that is *not* using her radar.

Fog signals

The International Regulations for Preventing Collisions at Sea lay down precisely the sound signals that vessels shall make in conditions of restricted visibility and although it is only required of vessels over 39 ft (12 m) to make these signals, it is as well for the owner of small boats to be able to recognize them and use them if necessary.

Power-driven vessels underway and making way through the water (including motorsailers) blow a prolonged blast at intervals of not more than 2 minutes.

Power-driven vessels underway but not making way sound two prolonged blasts with an interval of about 2 seconds between them every 2 minutes.

Sailing vessels, vessels not under command, those restricted in their ability to manoeuvre and those constrained by draft, fishing, towing or pushing, sound at intervals of not more than 2 minutes a prolonged blast followed by two short ones (morse code D).

Anchored vessels ring a bell rapidly for about 5 seconds every minute.

A full list of these signals is to be found in one of the almanacs and is well worth studying so that you can use the right signal and recognize what a signal heard means.

When you look at the chart you will find that many lighthouses, buoys and lightvessels make aural fog signals with various devices, such as: diaphone, siren, reed, explosive, bell, gong and whistle. Their purpose is to warn people away from danger and each has its own peculiar sound, thus:

Diaphone – low note ending in a grunt

Siren – medium-powered high or low note (or both together, though it is possible that only one will be heard due to one of fog's many strange effects on sound)

Reed – high note from a horn

Explosive – signals explode in mid-air

Bell – mostly wave-activated fitted to buoys

Gong – self-explanatory

Whistle – usually found on isolated buoys

In conditions of fog always have the foghorn ready to hand and be prepared to make the correct signal describing your boat and her movements. Realize also that unless a ship sees you on her radar and is able to avoid you, the onus of collision avoidance will be entirely on you, the relatively more manoeuvrable vessel.

Working inshore

The obvious first course of action on finding yourself in a shipping lane as fog sets in is to get out of it quickly and the best place to make for – assuming calm conditions – is shallow water. A big ship cannot follow you there and you can anchor until conditions improve if you wish. But navigating towards the coast in poor visibility is rather like inching towards the head of a flight of stairs when the lights fail – one step too many and you are in real trouble.

It is under these conditions that an RDF set and an echosounder show their worth, though a Decca or Satnav would be even better. If fog closes in quickly and you are not too sure of your position, a DF fix can give you an adequate departure for working out your course inshore. Obviously if the DF fix is greatly at variance with your DR plot one or both will have to be reworked, but unreliable bearings may be obtained at dusk, dawn or when very close to the coast with the signal from the beacon making a small angle to the coastline. Once you have fixed your position you can lay off a course to take you clear of the shipping lane as quickly as possible. The odds are very much against a harbour entrance lying directly along that course, so the coast (or at least shallow water) must be found and then a new course steered to a port (unless you decide to anchor off).

The situation you do not want to be in is the one where you have run your calculated distance, nothing has been sighted, until suddenly land appears looming out of the fog high above you and a rapid about-turn has to be executed. To avoid this a chain of soundings is taken on the run in and is compared with the chart. It will be seen that along the course line the seabed rises and falls or rises slowly with a sharp upward trend close inshore, or shelves steeply the whole way, but whatever it does it follows a recognizable pattern. Thus, if while you sail in you take a series of soundings, correct them for tide etc. to reduce them to chart datum, plot them on a piece of tracing paper and fit that plot over the chart, an accurate check can be kept on your progress. With a leadline it is probably only practical to take soundings about every $\frac{1}{4}$ mile, but with an echosounder a continuous reading can be taken.

Once you have reached shallow water out of the danger of shipping you can start thinking about either anchoring or making for a nearby harbour. When choosing an anchorage the normal rules apply with regard to what the bottom is like for holding, whether there is shelter from prevailing or expected winds, if there is a clear escape route and what depth there will be at low water. Though you are unlikely to persuade any of your crew to keep a full anchor watch, do pop your head out every so often to see that all is well and to make a check on the visibility.

Should you decide to make for port once you are out of immediate danger from shipping, you must either use the methods discussed in the next section or work your way in on a series of DF bearings. Where the harbour itself has a radio beacon at the entrance you may be able to home in on that (provided it does not lead you over a shoal or other obstruction), by checking that it is dead ahead each time it transmits, but great care must still be taken to ensure that you do not run foul of any dangers, particularly if a cross tide is running. A careful check needs to be kept on distance run so that you do not pile up on the breakwater or shore.

Creek crawling

Groping along a coast and into a harbour mouth or up a creek consists of a series of buoy-to-buoy hops, interspersed with intervals of worry as to where or when the next mark will appear. Success depends on being able to estimate speed over the ground and for this we use a ground log, which is a lead attached to about 150 ft (45 m) of line with a knot about 40 ft (12 m) from the lead, another 100 ft (30 m) further on and a tail of 10 ft (3 m) to attach it to the boat. Then, working on the basis that 1 knot = 100 ft (30 m) per minute, you drop the lead over the side, start a stopwatch when the first knot runs out through your fingers and stop it when the second one runs out. Hence the boat's speed over the ground can be determined from the table below:

100 ft (30 m) in 2 minutes = $\frac{1}{2}$ knot
100 ft (30 m) in 1 minute = 1 knot
100 ft (30 m) in $\frac{1}{2}$ minute = 2 knots
100 ft (30 m) in 20 seconds = 3 knots
100 ft (30 m) in 15 seconds = 4 knots
100 ft (30 m) in 12 seconds = 5 knots
100 ft (30 m) in 10 seconds = 6 knots

To determine the strength of current or stream, the boat is anchored and the lead is replaced with a bucket or funnel drag log. The bucket is thrown over on the end of the same line and its time and direction of running out are noted, then the table given above is used to find the rate of current or stream flowing. Incidentally, do not try to run this line out from a coil, it will foul up. Either have it on a reel or flake the whole lot down in a plastic washing-up bowl or push it higgledy-piggledy into a bucket. It is then contained but should run freely.

Now we have the rate and direction of the current or stream and with our speed over the ground we can calculate the course between two buoys allowing for set and so work out the time it should take to make the passage. From the point of view of keeping up a constant speed, you might consider it worthwhile using the motor, otherwise frequent speed checks will have to be made. Fine then, we run our distance (time) and no buoy appears, what now? The immediate reaction is to 'play a hunch' and shoot off to where we think the buoy might be. This is fatal. If the buoy is not there, then you are truly lost. The only thing to do is work out and follow a search pattern. How would you conduct such a search?

First, it is important to determine the visibility in the thickest patches of fog. This can be achieved by throwing overboard a balled up piece of newspaper and timing it out of sight. Then by reference to the table given before and knowing the current rate, the visibility can be found.

Secondly, an effort must be made to determine in which direction the buoy lies. If the tide is foul it is reasonable to assume that you have undershot and vice versa with a fair stream. The other possibility is lateral error caused by poor compass course steering or a cross-setting current.

With, say, 50 yards (45 m) visibility you can already scan a band 100 yards (90 m) across your track besides seeing 50 yards (45 m) ahead. Thus, in fact, you are not likely to have to go far to find the buoy, assuming you have undershot. Put on a 90 degree turn to one side for about half a minute, followed by a 180 degree turn and a track time of one minute to take you back across your original track. Then turn again and so on back and forth.

Following a depth contour with the echosounder is a perfectly good way of keeping track of your progress, but is not always as easy as it sounds. Unless the edge of a bank is well defined it is hard to tell exactly when you are sailing along it. A gradually shelving bottom may take 100 yards (90 m) to rise a significant amount and even a rapidly changing contour is hard to find if approached at a narrow angle. If you do want a position check, approach the chosen contour as nearly at right angles as possible.

Sometimes it is necessary to be certain that you are going to leave a buoy or danger mark on one particular hand. In such situations you need to introduce a known error. Where the buoy lies on the downtide side of a danger the tidal allowance must be worked out accurately and deliberately under countered. In that way you will be sure that the tide is pushing you away from the buoy and so keeping you clear of the danger. On the other hand, if the buoy lies on the uptide side of the danger, allowance for set must be deliberately over done. It is likely, of course, by doing this that you will miss seeing the buoy at all, but you can be fairly certain that it is clear on the safe side.

Throughout your dealings with navigation in fog, keep up a very careful DR plot and when an expected mark does not appear on time, do not go off following a hunch trying to find it. Organize a search pattern and follow it, plotting as you go. Even when all seems lost, keep plotting as it is likely that a depth reading or the chance sight of a landmark will suddenly make everything fit like a jigsaw and you will be sure of yourself again. The following table of speed against distance resulting in time in minutes is useful when buoy-hopping.

Of course, if you have a Decca or similar navigation system fitted you are in a much stronger position for navigating safely in these conditions. The trouble is that they do cost a lot and you certainly can manage without, even if it is more difficult.

Distance in cables	Speed in knots								
	1	2	3	4	5	6	7	8	9
1	6	3	2	$1\frac{1}{2}$	$1\frac{1}{4}$	1	$\frac{3}{4}$	$\frac{3}{4}$	$\frac{3}{4}$
2	12	6	4	3	$2\frac{1}{2}$	2	$1\frac{3}{4}$	$1\frac{1}{2}$	$1\frac{1}{4}$
3	18	9	6	$4\frac{1}{2}$	$3\frac{1}{2}$	3	$2\frac{1}{2}$	$2\frac{1}{4}$	2
4	24	12	8	6	$4\frac{3}{4}$	4	$3\frac{1}{2}$	3	$2\frac{3}{4}$
5	30	15	10	$7\frac{1}{2}$	6	5	$4\frac{1}{4}$	$3\frac{3}{4}$	$3\frac{1}{4}$
6	36	18	12	9	$7\frac{1}{4}$	6	$5\frac{1}{4}$	$4\frac{1}{2}$	4
7	42	21	14	$10\frac{1}{2}$	$8\frac{1}{2}$	7	6	$5\frac{1}{4}$	$4\frac{3}{4}$
8	48	24	16	12	$9\frac{1}{2}$	8	$6\frac{3}{4}$	6	$5\frac{1}{4}$
9	54	27	18	$13\frac{1}{2}$	$10\frac{3}{4}$	9	$7\frac{3}{4}$	$6\frac{3}{4}$	6
10	60	30	20	15	12	10	$8\frac{1}{2}$	$7\frac{1}{2}$	$6\frac{3}{4}$

15

Distress

When you go to sea you take on the responsibility not only for the safety of your vessel, but also for the lives of your crew. In Britain there is a volunteer lifeboat service, the RNLI, financed by public contribution, that undertakes hundreds of rescue operations each year, many of them involving small boats. Other countries such as the United States and Germany have government-sponsored organizations to deal with rescue operations. The existence of any such service is a great comfort, but if you stop to think about it, there is no reason at all why the lifeboat crews should put their own lives at risk to help complete strangers who have got themselves into trouble. Your intention should always be to avoid trouble, but equally importantly you must cultivate the ability to get yourself out of all but the very worst scrapes.

Whether it is a matter of a fouled anchor or a broken mast, the onus is on you and the key is usually improvisation. Good seamanship naturally plays a big part and indeed on many occasions it is poor seamanship that gets people into trouble in the first place. Some people are gifted with the ability to make something out of nothing and others have to carry as much in the way of spare parts, tools and bits of wood as they can.

In all this I am certainly not suggesting that if help is forthcoming it should be turned down. If there is something wrong with your engine and the man on the next boat is an engineer you would be daft to say no to an offer of a helping hand. What you must not do is *expect* assistance as a right.

Flares

The time when you need flares (pyrotechnics, distress signals, call them what you will) is when you have done your utmost to get out of a

237

disaster situation and failed. They are your last resort and should therefore be reserved for true emergency situations. Running out of petrol on a nice day with a light breeze blowing is no time to call out the lifeboat, but being aground on an exposed lee shore with a rising gale forecast may well be. Do not leave calling for help too late; dithering about saying 'shall I, shan't I?' could cost a life.

Four main types of distress signals are available which are suitable for use by yachtsmen. Rockets (often called parachute flares) propelling a red star to a height of more than 1000 ft (300 m), where it is ejected and then falls over a period of about 40 seconds suspended from a small parachute. These are designed for use when out of sight of land or immediate assistance and are visible up to 35 miles on a clear night or some 6–7 miles in daylight. They are of limited value, however, in low cloud as they may spend most of their time in the cloud.

With help in sight a red star flare is recommended and the most common form of this is a two-star signal which projects a star to a height of 150–200 ft (45–60 m), followed after a few seconds by a second one. The stars have a burning time of 6–7 seconds. When you have been sighted and help is on the way, or when you can see a potential rescuer, a red hand flare should be used at night or an orange smoke flare by day.

There are now several types of 'personal' flare available that consist of a tiny launcher and star capsules. These, carried in an oilskin pocket can literally be lifesavers if someone goes overboard or the crew has to take to the liferaft.

Finally, white flares should also be carried as these are used to warn ships of your presence. They are not distress signals, but if a ship is bearing down on you at night and you cannot get out of the way, a white flare certainly helps to get you noticed.

Everyone on board must know where the flares are kept – they must be in a very easily accessible place – and they must know how to use them without having to read the instructions first. Each flare is marked with an expiry date and you are advised not to rely on the signal after that date. They are not cheap to renew and many people hold on to them after the expiry date, but this really does not make sense except to keep them as extras. The danger is that in an emergency they may malfunction leaving you without that means of summoning assistance. Always check the condition and dating of flares at the beginning of the season and again several times during the season or before any coastwise passage. Flares that show any signs of having been wetted or of cracking along the casing must be treated with suspicion and not relied on. Small dents in metal casings or caps may not be important, but if they are badly damaged they can be dangerous.

Despite being kept in polythene containers it is still possible for damp to affect flares and a bag of silica gel or some other drying agent can be usefully included to absorb some of the moisture. Once lit, a flare will continue to burn even though soused in water and in fact one of the standard tests for flares is that they should still work immediately after being soaked for a minute with the caps off.

For the kind of coastwise cruising we are contemplating it should be sufficient to carry a couple of parachute flares, four hand flares, two smoke flares and some white ones. Manufacturers do produce packs of flares for various types of small craft and one of these should be suitable with the addition of a few extra white flares, for example.

It should perhaps be made clear that if you see a distress signal while at sea you *must* render what assistance you can. That is an obligation on all vessels.

VHF

Many family cruisers now carry VHF radios and these are generally excellent for putting out distress signals as the rescue services or another vessel cannot only be alerted to your plight, but can also converse with you, discover the exact nature of your trouble and confirm your position.

Channel 16 is the distress channel, but it is also the 'calling' channel on which initial radio contact is made between two stations before they transfer to a 'working' channel. This means that it is very busy most of the time and so any distress call is prefixed by the words 'Mayday, Mayday, Mayday' (from the French for 'Help me'). The yacht's name is then given three times. 'Mayday' is repeated, followed by the yacht's name and her position. The nature of the trouble is then given briefly, together with the kind of help needed. Finally the radio operator says 'Over', releases his transmit button and listens for a reply.

Once contact has been established more details can be given, but if no-one hears the first call it must be transmitted again in the same format: 'Mayday, Mayday, Mayday. This is yacht Seagull, Seagull, Seagull. Mayday Seagull, Point Erskine lighthouse bearing

A mast can, unfortunately, fail anywhere, anytime. On this boat it broke in a river, not two miles from their home mooring, failure being at the crosstree root. All eyes concentrate on the tow rope snaking out towards them from a motor boat offering some friendly help.

065, 2 miles. Dismasted with fouled propeller, require tow and medical help for injured crewman. Over.'

Like any other form of distress signal, a VHF set is not infallible – for example, flat or flooded batteries put it out of action immediately – but it is a marvellous lifeline and is a piece of kit worthy of serious consideration if any longer cruises are to be undertaken. You must, however, obtain a proper operator's licence together with a registered call sign and so learn the proper use of the set. Stick to the correct procedures, do not babble endlessly, especially on 16, and the radio will become a useful ally; you can book marina berths, seek weather information and report progress along your coastal passage to Coastguard stations.

Fire extinguishers

Whether it is the result of fuel spilled when topping up tanks or a leaky gas bottle or a lighted match dropped in a rubbish bin or a flare-up in the galley, a fire on a boat is devastating unless tackled instantly with adequate extinguishers. Many people placate their consciences by hanging a solitary aerosol extinguisher on the bulkhead, but this is hardly enough for even the smallest of fires. I know it is always easy to tell people to spend money, but with fire extinguishers you really do have to and economy is not achieved by buying small, cheap appliances. Look for a maker's date stamp when buying and make sure that the extinguisher is still well within the guaranteed life.

Care is needed not to damage extinguishers as any loss of stored pressure will result in a loss of efficiency and even possibly failure to operate at all. Always store an extinguisher in proper mounting

Dismasted on a rough day in the Firth of Forth. Her mast, broken in two places, poses a threat to the hull, but quick work on the part of the crew allowed it to be recovered aboard without damage to the boat. In such circumstances a quick decision may have to be made to cut the whole lot away and lose it in order to save the boat from holing. Each crew member is sensibly wearing a lifejacket, but with the boat's unpredictable motion without the steadying influence of her rig, lifeharnesses for working on deck might be a good idea. The problem would be in keeping the safety line from tangling in the broken spars and rigging. With the boat lying dead in the water, anyone falling over the side while trying to recover the rig (which acts like a sea anchor or drogue) would at least not drift further away and could either swim back or be within reach of a heaving line.

The rig has been safely recovered after a dismasting offshore and with insufficient fuel to get home under engine a tow is gratefully accepted. It is tricky collecting the tow rope in a rough sea and the crew concentrates hard. They haven't thought yet of the rough ride to come. . . .

brackets to ensure that the firing pin cannot be knocked, thus partially releasing the pressure.

Denting indicates a loss of stored pressure and excess corrosion also warns of possible damage, but in any case you are advised to have appliances serviced about every three years.

Do ensure that you and all of the crew know how to use the extinguisher, because in a real situation there will be no time to fiddle about trying to read faded instructions. Remember too that total discharge takes only a few seconds, which is why controllable discharge extinguishers may be preferred, and a good aim is essential. Fight the fire from the point nearest to you as you will then be able to get in closer to the real seat of the fire. Use a sweeping motion from side to side low down and as close as you can safely get to the flames.

It is recommended that boats up to 30 ft (9 m) or so carry at least two 3 lb (1.4 kilos) or equivalent extinguishers of either the dry powder or controllable discharge BCF type. Ensure that they are readily accessible at all times. It is absolutely useless to have to waste precious time hunting in lockers for them. Additionally, a fire blanket is ideal for most galley fires as it smothers them, yet is reusable and makes no mess.

First aid

Unless you are prepared to complete a course in first aid it is wise to buy and study a simple book such as those produced by the RYA or the St John Ambulance Brigade to prepare yourself to deal with minor injuries. The almanacs also offer useful advice for quick reference.

You cannot really expect to deal with very serious injuries unless you study first aid in depth, but a basic 'repair' kit must be carried that includes the following: assorted dressings, bandages, adhesive tape, cotton wool, sterilized lint, scissors (sharp), safety pins, antiseptic cream, splinter forceps, indigestion pills, anti-seasickness

With the tow rope well secured the tow home begins and even at a very sedate speed the seas are such that waves constantly break against the boat sending sheets of spray across her to drench the crew and provide a thoroughly miserable time, especially for the helmsman who has to steer very carefully astern of the towing boat.

pills, mild laxatives, aspirin or similar, sunburn ointment or calamine lotion, thermometer.

With a kit like this you can treat minor ailments, but you must be prepared to seek proper medical help for serious injuries or illnesses. It must also be realized that first aid is only what its name implies, which is immediate initial treatment, enough to suffice until qualified aid can be sought.

Hull damage

While holing is, thankfully, a rare occurrence, some thought should be given to the possibility of hull damage and underwater damage in particular. The convex shape of a boat's hull gives immense impact resistance and this strength in combination with the inherent toughness of modern materials means that a very severe blow will be needed to puncture the hull. What may happen though is damage to or even the loss of a skin fitting, which can lead to water coming in faster than you can easily pump it out.

With a glass-fibre boat it may be possible to use an underwater setting epoxy paste, but otherwise the best course is to plug a hole or crack with softwood plugs. These need to be tapered and wrapped in rag before being driven in and secured with shores to strong points. On a wooden hull it may be possible to nail well-greased canvas or plywood or copper tingles over the damage, preferably from the outside.

Should you get a hole underwater, either by pounding on rocks or hitting some floating wreckage, try immediately to raise the hole above the waterline. This will probably require the boat to be laid on whichever tack puts the damage to windward. You may have to heave to and in rough weather shorten sail to reduce the strain on the hull and stop it opening up further. Where such serious damage has occurred the crew must be prepared to put up distress signals, put out a 'Mayday' on the radio and even to abandon ship, either by using the liferaft or dinghy or, in an extreme situation, beaching the boat and wading ashore. However, a boat usually floats longer than expected and while abandoning should not be left until it is too late, the crew should stay with the boat as long as they can, particularly if help is known to be on the way.

Cushions, mattresses, oilskins, towels, clothing, anything like that can be used to stuff into a hole, but it will be more effective if an oilskin or a sail is wrapped around the clothing first. Once something has been pushed into the hole, it must be wedged there as tightly as possible. Lashing a sail or an oilskin over the outside of the damage will also help, but it is difficult to do so effectively because ropes will have to be passed under the hull.

Unless a boat is very badly holed a long way from land it should be possible to control the inflow of water sufficiently to allow her to reach port or to await help, even if the pumps have to be manned constantly.

Salvage

Yachtsmen have always done their level best to help each other out of difficulty with no thought of reward and long may they continue to do so, but it is possible that you will one day find yourself in a salvageable situation and it is then that you will need to know how to keep a salvage claim down to a minimum or, better, to avoid it altogether.

Salvage is the act of saving or helping to save a vessel or cargo of any sort when in danger. It is not claimable by the vessel's crew or by a pilot and is not payable when life only is saved.

If it seems at all possible that your helpers are going to consider themselves rescuers and make a salvage claim, do not accept a tow until agreement has been reached about price and destination, then, if you can avoid it, do not allow anyone from the towing vessel to come aboard your boat (we are not talking about RNLI or other lifeboat services). Also, if possible, always pass your own rope for the tow rather than accept one from the rescuer. If the would-be rescuer starts demanding salvage before doing anything to help you, try to reach a witnessed (and preferably written) agreement. You can use the form provided in *The Macmillan and Silk Cut Nautical Almanac*, for example. This makes provision for a set price or for a price to be settled by a Lloyd's appointed arbitrator. This will, at least, ensure a fair deal, but do write in the log the main points of the conversation and any reference to specific monetary sums.

Remember that for a salvage claim to hold good, danger must be proved to have existed and the rescue attempt must have been successful; no cure, no pay. You must inform your insurance company as soon as possible and when a claim is made against you you will have to provide a chart showing your vessel's position and your log book to help to establish the prevailing weather and other conditions.

A friendly offer of a pluck off a mudbank when you have grounded on a falling tide should not be turned down out of hand, but be sure to point out that you are in no danger and are only accepting the kind offer as a convenience. Finally, never disclose the value of your boat or whether or not she is insured.

Insurance

Considering the high replacement cost of boats and their gear the premiums asked for insuring them are not excessive. Do be sure when insuring not to undervalue the boat or you will be well out of pocket if you have to make a claim. It is also particularly important to get a high third party cover as courts these days make substantial awards for injuries, and repair costs for damage to other craft may be pretty hefty.

As with anything else, it is worth obtaining two or three quotes for insurance and do *read* the details of the cover being offered, particularly the lists of exclusions and excesses.

Several companies now offer tailor-made yacht policies providing for 12 months use so that if a boat is laid up afloat in her marina berth there is no problem in going out for a sail on a nice winter day. You do not have to make special insurance arrangements. It is usual to have to state your normal cruising limits, such as 'Brest to the Elbe' or 'U.K. coastal and inland', and having stated them you must be sure to inform the insurers if you intend cruising beyond them. If you are forced outside by stress of weather then you should be held covered automatically. If you intend doing any racing you will need a policy that covers you for racing risks and the other point to remember is that you may have to make special arrangements if you intend doing any singlehanded cruising.

Code flags

While it is most unlikely that the family cruiser will carry a complete set of International Code flags, I suggested back in Chapter 4 that it was 'highly desirable' to carry the flags U,G,H,N,C,V. According to the International Code of Signals all the letters of the alphabet, bar letter R, have individual meanings, thus U means 'You are standing into danger', G means 'I require a pilot' and is replaced with H meaning 'I have a pilot on board' as soon as that gentleman comes aboard. The letters N,C hoisted together (N over C) mean 'I am in distress and require immediate assistance'. V means 'I require assistance' without anything about being in distress. Each of these signals can equally well be flashed by light at night with the same meanings using Morse Code.

16

Weather forecasts

Of prime importance to the cruising yachtsman is the question of what wind strength and direction he may expect during a proposed passage. Given a fair wind of moderate force he can sail in rain, hail or shine, but with either no wind at all or far too much he is not going to get anywhere. When describing wind we talk about the *direction from which it comes* and its strength as indicated by the Beaufort Scale of forces or its actual speed in knots. I have emphasized the direction from which it comes as we talk of tides and currents in terms of the direction in which they are flowing or setting, thus an east-going stream and an easterly wind will be in opposition to each other.

The Beaufort Scale is normally used from Force 0 (calm) to Force 12 (hurricane), each Force being defined by lower and upper wind speeds measured in knots. In open waters the wind strength can be judged by sea conditions, but in inshore waters this is more difficult. Electronic wind instruments refer to wind speed and may be in either knots or miles per hour, with knots being preferred.

Beaufort Wind Scale

Beaufort No.	Limits of wind speed in knots	Descriptive term	Sea criterion
0	Less than 1	Calm	Sea like a mirror
1	1–3	Light air	Ripples like scales
2	4–6	Light breeze	Pronounced wavelets, glassy tops
3	7–10	Gentle breeze	Large wavelets, crests begin to foam
4	11–16	Moderate breeze	Small waves, lengthening; whitehorses

5	17–21	Fresh breeze	Moderate waves, pronounced long form; many whitehorses, possibly some spray
6	22–27	Strong breeze	Large waves; extensive foaming crests, probably some spray
7	28–33	Near gale	Heaped seas, foam begins to blow in streaks downwind
8	34–40	Gale	Moderately high waves of greater length; pronounced streaks of spindrift

Do not worry too much about the higher Forces (9 and upwards), it gets too nasty, but if you want to frighten yourself, they are listed up to 12 in the almanacs. The wind speeds are measured at a height of 33 ft (10 m) above sea level and will be somewhat less close to the surface of the water. The sea criteria listed for each force refer to open sea well away from land effects, but they will be similar inshore, though the seas will be shorter and steeper.

There is more to it than saying 'We won't put to sea if a Force so-and-so is forecast' because much depends on the duration of the proposed passage, the direction of the forecast wind and exactly when the wind is forecast to blow at that strength. We can all take a certain amount of spray and slog to windward, but we sail primarily for pleasure and while our boats may be able to batter their way into a 5 or 6, why should we have to endure the associated discomfort if we do not have to? On the other hand, if there is a Force 4–5 forecast which will be from abaft the beam, we may well have a fast and exhilarating sail. It is a case of knowing the boat's and the crew's capabilities and judging accordingly whether to put to sea or stay in port.

Sea areas

The shipping forecasts, which are the ones most relevant for us, are broadcast for a number of individual sea areas round the British Isles and adjacent waters. In several of the sea areas there are weather reporting stations that provide information about conditions existing at specified times and these reports are included at the end of the shipping forecasts.

Obtaining and interpreting forecasts

Where does the yachtsman get a weather forecast from? First and foremost he listens to the shipping forecasts broadcast by the BBC on Radio 4, 1500 metres (200 kHz). These reports, which we will look at in detail later are broadcast four times daily. In addition to the shipping forecasts, the BBC also transmits forecasts for inshore waters around the country. The times of such forecasts may be found in current almanacs and official publications.

Many local radio stations also put out forecasts for their own area, so that between all of these the yachtsman has a good forecast service on the radio. These can be supplemented further by VHF radio calls to Coastguard stations on passage or telephoning a local met. office.

As well as the sea areas covered by the shipping forecasts, there is a list of weather stations from which reports are received of current weather conditions. Each of the shipping forecasts starts off with a summary of gale warnings in force. This is followed by the general synopsis, the area forecasts for the next 24 hours and at the end any reports from coastal stations. To make all this a bit clearer, the following is a typically nasty late season report:

> And now on 1500 metres the shipping forecast issued by the Met. Office at two three three oh on 28 September. There are warnings of gales in Viking, Forties, Cromarty, Forth, Tyne, Dogger, North and South Utsire, Fisher, German Bight, Humber, Lundy, Fastnet, Irish Sea, Shannon, Rockall, Malin, Hebrides, Bailey, Fair Isle, Faeroes and South-East Iceland
>
> The general synopsis at one nine double oh: Low 976 just west of Shetlands now filling slowly and soon moving north-east 15 knots to west Norwegian coast with secondary low 994 forming in Skaggerak by midnight. Anticyclone 1029 Azores stationary with ridge to Denmark Strait, moving steadily east.
>
> Now the area forecasts for the next 24 hours.
> North and South Utsire, Viking, Forties, Cromarty. SW to W 7 to severe gale 9 veering NW and becoming cyclonic 5 near Norwegian coast later. Showers, good.

Forth, Tyne, Dogger. SW slowly veering west to NW 6 to gale 8. Squally showers, good.

Fisher. SW veering NW 7 to severe gale 9. Becoming cyclonic 6 in E later. Showers, good.

German Bight, Humber. SW veering W to NW 6 to gale 8. Occasional showers, good.

Thames, Dover, Wight, Portland, Plymouth. W to NW 5 to 7. Scattered showers, good.

Biscay, Finisterre. NW 5 to 6 in N, 3 in S. Scattered showers, good.

Sole. NW 5-7 moderating slowly later. Showers, good.

Lundy, Fastnet, Irish Sea, Shannon. W becoming NW 5-7 locally gale 8 moderating later. Occasional showers, good.

Rockall, Malin, Hebrides, Bailey. NW 6 to gale 8 locally severe gale 9, moderating slowly from W later. Squally showers, good.

Fair Isle. Cyclonic becoming N 7 to severe gale 9. Rain at first, moderate or good.

Faeroes, South-East Iceland. NE to N 7 to severe gale 9. Squally showers, good. Icing nil.

Now the reports from coastal stations for 2300 BST on Friday.

Dowsing. WSW 7, lightning, 5 miles 999.

Royal Sovereign. WSW 6, rain showers in past hour. 11 miles, 1006 falling slowly.

Channel light vessel. W 6, 13 miles, 1006 falling slowly.

Scilly. W by N 5, 13 miles, 1008 falling slowly.

Valentia. W by N 4, rain showers in past hour, 13 miles, 1007 steady.

Ronaldsway. WSW 4, 27 miles, 999 steady.

Tiree. W by N 6, rain showers in past hour, 19 miles, 992, steady.

And a report at 2200 BST from Bell Rock. WSW 6, 16 miles, 989 falling more slowly. And for the same time, 2200, Varne, W 5, 11 miles, 1005.

The above is a complete shipping forecast, lasting in this case some $5\frac{1}{2}$ minutes. I have quoted it in full here so that an idea of the sequence of events can be obtained, but what does it all mean? Why do they make such seemingly silly comments as 'showers, good'?

The general synopsis is pretty well self-explanatory, but it is useful to know the terms used to describe the expected movements of highs and lows across the forecast areas. A system is said to be moving slowly if it is progressing at less than 15 knots, steadily at

15–25 knots, rather quickly between 25 and 35 knots, rapidly at 35–45 knots and very rapidly when it is making more than 45 knots. The importance of knowing how fast a weather system is moving lies in the fact that it is the highs, lows, ridges and troughs that determine our winds and weather, thus if we know where a particular system will be at a particular time (approximately), we can make a reasonable forecast of the conditions that will then prevail.

Next, the sea area forecasts 'for the next 24 hours'. Because of the limited air time allowed for shipping forecasts, sea areas are often grouped together and an average wind strength given, but usually this is quite acceptable for the weekend yachtsman. For each area or group of areas the information is given in a set sequence and that is: wind direction and strength followed by any alterations to either; whether or not there will be rain, snow, thunder, hail, fog etc.; visibility; an icing report for SE Iceland.

In these forecasts, visibility is described as being good (more than 5 miles), moderate (2–5 miles), poor (1100 yards to 2 miles) and fog (less than 1100 yards). In the coastal station reports a further term, mist or haze is used when visibility is between 1100 and 2200 yards. So then, when you hear 'showers, good', the announcer is not a keen gardener, he is saying that there will be showers but visibility will generally be more than 5 miles.

The reports from coastal stations, normally timed much later than the general synopsis, give a good indication of what is happening at the moment and of how far the weather system has moved since the synopsis time. They too stick to a pattern of information with wind direction and strength first, then a report of any rain, fog etc. and visibility, the barometric pressure in millibars and finally a comment on whether the barometer is steady, rising or falling and how fast it is doing so. The reports often speak of 'precipitation in sight', which simply means that they can see rain, sleet, hail etc. but it is not actually falling on them.

Often the forecaster says that the wind is going to do something (ease, increase, veer) 'later', 'soon' or 'imminently'. These terms are defined as follows: Imminent, within 6 hours; soon, in 6–12 hours' time; later, in more than 12 hours' time.

Using forecasts

It is not sufficient just to listen to a forecast for your particular area, you must at the very least listen to those for the areas either side of you and to the weather reports from the nearest coastal stations. The experienced yachtsman listens to the whole forecast and builds up a picture of the current and expected weather patterns, thus enabling him to hazard a pretty good guess as to what will happen in his particular locale. Since individual sea areas are so large and as they are often grouped together, it is quite likely that the weather just a few miles offshore will be quite different from that forecast for the general area, although that forecast may still be accurate as an overall picture. To decide exactly what is going to happen locally needs an understanding of pressure systems and their effects but it is made easier by the construction of a weather map from the forecasts. Pads of charts are available and with practice it is possible to draw a map by using the synopsis given at the beginning of the forecast, individual area forecasts and the reports from coastal stations, though it must be remembered that these are given at a different time from the synopsis.

Taking down a forecast is not always easy as the announcer has to rush to fit the whole lot into the allotted time, so a system of shorthand or a tape recorder must be used. The latter is useful as you can replay the tape at any time – perhaps when you are fully awake –

Mare's tails, usually harbingers of wind or at least a change in the weather.

Many yacht clubs, such as this one, display a storm cone when winds are forecast to be Force 6 or above. This is a south cone (point downwards) and indicates that strong winds are expected from somewhere in the southerly sector. A check with the local met. information service should be made before putting to sea.

The storm passes and the sky brightens with fast moving clouds. There are still rain showers and squalls about though.

and is not subject to errors. Whatever happens though do not rely on memory alone. Few people remember accurately after breakfast what they heard sleepily before dawn.

Before setting off even for a weekend afloat it is well worth studying the weather maps printed in some of the daily newspapers and shown on TV for several days in advance, particularly the Atlantic charts. By doing so you build up a full picture of how the pressure systems are moving, deepening, filling and so on. You can also make a surer judgement, in the light of this wider knowledge, of current forecasts. A regular study of these weather maps helps to familiarize the newcomer with conditions associated with various pressure patterns. This knowledge will be invaluable at sea in predicting windshifts and changes in strength, particularly the speed with which these things will happen.

DIY forecasting

Apart from weather maps and forecasts, an idea of approaching weather changes can be obtained from watching the sky, a barometer and the sea. Meteorology is far from being a simple subject and the following notes are necessarily rather broad generalizations, but they serve to show how useful a closer study of the subject can be for the yachtsman.

Cirrus clouds, the rather fibrous clouds often referred to as mares' tails, very often precede a period of bad weather. If they are seen moving in from the N or NW and thickening into a sheet of cirrostratus, through which the sun shows surrounded by a halo, then a backing and freshening wind can be expected, especially if the barometer falls sharply. The development of altostratus (a level sheet of grey cloud) following cirrostratus produces what is commonly called a watery sky and does indeed herald rain and general deterioration.

Small happy-type cumulus clouds like bits of cottonwool are signs of fair weather, while larger, towering cumulus with dark patches in them indicate showers and squalls.

Rapidly moving clouds in the upper layers are signs of unstable conditions, but do not give a definite indication of approaching bad weather, although you should be wary of squalls and showers. Cumulonimbus often produces severe squalls from quite unexpected directions. Altocumulus, thin middle cloud formed in regular layers and waves, with castellated edges indicates widespread thunderstorms.

Should the wind veer to the NW after the passage of a cold front, then a short spell of fair weather can be expected, but if the barometer subsequently starts to fall and the wind backs to SW, then bad weather is fast approaching. Generally speaking, whenever clouds get lower you should be on the lookout for bad weather.

Cold and warm fronts: typical of 'unsettled' weather.

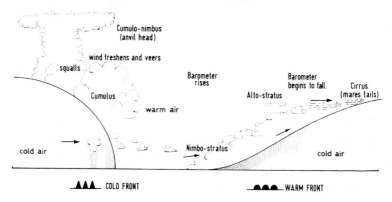

A couple of relevant rhymes to be accepted with caution:

If clouds are gathering thick and fast,
Keep sharp lookout for sail and mast,
But if they slowly onward crawl,
Shoot your lines, nets and trawl.

When rain comes before the wind,
Halyards, sheets and braces mind,
But when the wind comes before the rain,
Soon you may make sail again.

The barometer too gives an indication of weather trends, but it is often rather ambiguous. For example, a gale can be heralded by a falling barometer and backing wind as well as it can by a rising glass and a veering wind, but both barometer and wind usually give significant indications if anything serious is going to happen. Gales blowing with a falling barometer are generally less squally than those with a rising glass.

A steady rise in pressure during the summer usually indicates a period of fairly settled weather. During a period of unsettled weather a rapid rise is often followed by a fall, but a general improvement of conditions can be expected if the rise reaches a reasonably high level.

Another couple of relevant rhymes, also to be accepted with caution:

When the glass falls low
Prepare for a blow;
When it slowly rises high,
Lofty canvas you may fly.

Long foretold, long last,
Short notice, soon past,
Quick rise after low,
Sure sign of stronger blow.

Sea state changes with the strength of the prevailing wind and in fact there is a description of the sea for each of the Beaufort Forces (see table on page 248). This is fine for judging the strength of present wind, though it is not as easy in coastal waters as it is well offshore, but the descriptions in no way forecast coming winds. About the only indication is when the sea becomes leaden and a swell builds up. This may well presage a rising wind, but a swell can also be the result of a dying gale far away.

17

Trailing

Trailing small cruisers home to lay up in a backyard can save a lot of money in winter storage charges and trailing them to a new cruising area for your summer holiday – trailer sailing – can greatly extend your cruising scope without subjecting the family to ridiculously long coastal passages that take up most of the holiday time. However, it cannot be undertaken lightly as a considerable amount of planning is required.

Insurance

This is a prime requirement since the normal boat insurance policies are unlikely to include cover while on the road. You may also have to arrange extra cover through the car's insurers. It should not be a particularly high expense, but insurance is vital and plenty of notice must be given to the insurers of your intention to trail.

Trailers

When a boat is actually sold or marketed as a 'trailer sailer' there will be a purpose-designed trailer available for her, but in other cases you will have to buy a ready-made trailer of stock design or have one tailor-made for your boat. In both cases it is essential that the trailer is not only man enough for the job, but that it fits the boat properly. In the water a boat is supported all over her hull with the weight evenly distributed, but on a trailer her weight is concentrated on the keel and various support arms. If any of these is located in the wrong place or is not fitted snugly up to the hull a great deal of stress can be put on weak areas as the trailer/boat combination bounces along on the road. The springing of the trailer is important too as it determines just how much the boat will bounce up and down on these supports.

Trailers are destined for a rough, tough life as they are almost always left out of doors the whole time in all weathers and will often be subjected if not to total immersion in salt water, then to a corrosive salt atmosphere. Under such conditions it is unlikely that even the best paintwork will last very long and it pays off in the long run to have the trailer galvanized before it is painted.

The other parts of the trailer most likely to give trouble are the brakes and wheel bearings. The former seize up very easily with the least bit of salt-induced rusting, while the immersion in cold seawater of hot wheel bearings causes the water to be sucked in doing untold harm. So-called sealed bearings on trailer wheels are, in most cases, only resistant to the ingress of salt and sand; they are not actually proof against it and once any does enter the water seals are quickly destroyed. The problem is eased and the bearings are given a greater life expectancy if plenty of medium heavy grease is pumped into them immediately before and after immersion. Do not use underwater grease as this is unsuitable for road running temperatures. Remember too that it is best whenever possible to let the hubs cool right down before immersing them, as quenching the hot hub in cold water creates an internal vacuum that draws the water in.

Some of the trailers purpose-designed for trailer sailers avoid some of the problems of immersion by using a 'piggyback' cradle. With this arrangement the boat sits in a four-wheeled cradle that in turn sits on the trailer. Come launching time the cradle and boat are rolled off the trailer on dry hard standing and the cradle is wheeled into the water. Admittedly its wheel bearings suffer, but not in the same way or to the same extent that the road trailer ones would. The drawback to these piggyback systems is that the relatively small wheels of the cradle require hard ground or a concrete slipway to run easily without bogging down.

An alternative to the piggyback is the broken-back trailer that has a hinge about halfway along its spine. This allows the boat to be slipped off (or on) without the trailer having to be put so far into the water as it would if it had a rigid back. However, this arrangement is generally only suited to small, light displacement cruisers.

Once separated from the towing vehicle a trailer needs a jockey wheel at the coupling to allow it to be manoeuvred. This is a permanently attached wheel on a wind-down leg that revolves like a castor and allows the trailer to be pushed round rather than having to be lifted and manhandled. The jockey wheel is wound down before uncoupling from the car and must be lifted right up again well clear of the ground before towing commences.

A heavy-duty winch mounted on the trailer is a great help when recovering a boat and can, with smaller craft, turn it into a one man operation. It does require the boat to have a ring set into her stem for the winch wire (rope) to clip on to, but with proper rollers on the support arms it certainly makes things easier and keeps the trailer less deeply immersed. In an emergency the winch can be used, once the boat is loaded on to the trailer, to haul both boat and trailer up a soft slope to the towing vehicle parked on hard standing. This requires the wire to be unhooked from the stem eye and instead attached to the ball towing hitch on the car. Piggyback trailers have to have a winch to pull the cradle up and the boat does not need an eye set in her stem as the winch wire hooks directly on to the cradle itself.

In addition to having rollers on the support arms, it also makes handling on and off the trailer easier if there are rollers let into the keel channel. These would normally be made of heavy duty rubber or nylon.

Finally, when you have a towing hitch fitted to the car you will have to have an electrical take-off socket fitted by the hitch and wired up to the car's electrics so that a trailer lighting board can be used. The traffic indicator flashing unit normally fitted to the car will have to be replaced with a heavy-duty type to cope with the extra flashers on the trailer and somehow you must ensure that the lighting board is removed from the trailer before it goes anywhere near the water and that it is put back on again and connected up before driving off down the road.

Loading and securing

There is always going to be a certain amount of gear on board a boat when she is being trailed, but particularly when taking her away on a summer holiday when all sorts of gear will be thrown aboard as a convenient storage place – and this in addition to her normal cruising inventory. Such a lot of weight, if badly distributed, can lead to steering and handling problems for the towing vehicle.

Keep all the heavy items as low down in the hull as possible to avoid raising the centre of gravity unduly and try to concentrate the weight in the middle of the boat, even on top of the keel so that it is borne by the keel not an imperfectly supported area of hull. Wedge any heavy gear so that it cannot slide about and pack bedding in lockers to stop food and other stuff flying about on corners. Treat the whole process as you would preparation for putting to sea.

The total weight should be so distributed that the towing hitch has roughly 10 per cent bearing down on it, though front-wheel-drive cars may require slightly less to ensure proper traction. If the trailer

The waggoner's or trucker's hitch gives useful purchase without the use of blocks. The diagram makes its formation clear and here it is being used to haul a dinghy up onto a seawall, but it might also be used for bowsing down a dinghy stowed on deck or a boat on a trailer.

is 'heavy on' it affects steering and could cause front wheel skids, while if it is 'light on' it can cause snaking.

Once the weight has been sorted out you have to lash the boat herself down properly. The first problem here is that any knot in any rope is going to settle and allow the lashing to slacken, so regular checks will have to be made in the early stages of the drive. An alternative to rope is synthetic fibre webbing straps (like car seat belts), with special tensioning and locking fittings on the ends. These webbing straps do not suffer the same stretch problems as rope and should maintain their tension throughout the journey.

The principal aim when securing a boat on her trailer is to prevent her sliding either backwards or forwards on hills and under heavy braking. Starting at the keel, hammer wooden wedges in firmly under the heel and toe to stop backwards or forwards movement and between the keel and the sides of the channel (on both sides) to stop lateral movement. If the trailer does not have them built in, then supports must be placed under stem and stern so that lashings at these points will not hog the boat when they are bowsed down hard. Pass these lashings right across the deck at both bow and stern, using the mooring cleats to stop them slipping off, but not relying on them to take any strain. Lash down to the frame of the trailer not to any support arms and bowse the lashings down really firmly using something like a lorry driver's or waggoner's hitch to provide a purchase.

The waggoner's hitch.

Diagonal 'springs' from each bow down to the trailer at the stern and from the quarters to the trailer at the bows will prevent movement backwards and forwards. Pads of foam rubber will stop these ropes chafing the hull and they can be used to good effect on other lashings too.

If the mast is carried on deck it must be well supported and wrapped in carpet or thick rags or foam rubber to prevent chafe wherever it touches the deck or rails. It must be lashed securely to pushpit and pulpit and perhaps at a midway point to a grabrail to reduce flexing on bumpy roads.

Finally, check the tyre pressures on both car and trailer. The owner's handbook for the car should give an indication of the correct pressures and the trailer manufacturer should do the same for the trailer, otherwise enquire at a tyre dealer. Generally rear tyres on the car should be pumped up another 2–4 lb over the normal pressure.

Route planning

A few evenings spent with some Ordnance Survey maps planning out your route (much as you would a sea passage) can save a lot of trouble once you start your actual journey. Finding yourself stuck halfway over a narrow humpback bridge is only funny to onlookers. Obviously you must try to avoid very steep gradients and very narrow or twisting lanes, but try also to keep out of big towns at peak hours or when everyone is doing their Saturday shopping. Any information about fuel stations and cafes should be noted, but beware when pulling into a garage that the canopy does not hit the top of the boat. Look carefully for any marked obstructions or hazards such as low bridges and make out a route card giving the road numbers and towns, with alternatives if possible.

Trailing

If you are unused to driving with a trailer it is wise to do a little practice without the boat on the trailer. Make sure you can estimate the width of the tow and that you can back the trailer into gateways or parking spaces. Even with quite a small boat, manoeuvring a trailer round by hand is not light work and it is well worth learning to do everything with the car coupled up.

Immediately you get underway with a loaded trailer you will

A 20 ft trailer sailer using a piggyback trailer and trolley system. It's a well-thought-out combination with a properly designed trailer and trolley. The trolley, sensibly, has elongated guide arms to make sure it can be found when docking the boat on it and that the boat is guided into place correctly.

discover how much it affects the towing vehicle. Acceleration seems to disappear and your brakes seem to have gone on strike. Get used to using each gear to its maximum torque and do not be afraid to change down. Accelerate gently and brake smoothly, thinking ahead as much as possible.

When passing a parked car or some other obstruction do not be too hasty about pulling back in – remember the trailer. Also allow yourself very much more time to overtake than you would normally.

You will, of course, have to swing much wider round corners than you are used to. A bit like an articulated lorry, if you cut round close, the trailer will mount the curb or you will wipe out a central reservation bollard, which will not endear you to the local police force.

After you have been on the road a short while, pull off into a layby and check all the lashings on the boat as they may have slackened off. On busy roads the occasional halt to check everything also allows cars to get by you safely. A long line of vehicles behind you is not what you want.

When going downhill always use a low gear rather than ride the foot brake as that can overheat and give trouble. If you have to park on a hill, either going up or down, set the handbrake with the car in gear and put chocks under the trailer wheels, especially if going uphill, as the over-ride brakes on the trailer do not work then.

Trailer snaking is a danger to be watched for. It is usually indicated by a sudden lightening of the steering and is caused by bumps in the road, gusts of wind, unbalanced wheels or incorrectly inflated tyres. Or going too fast. If you do find the trailer is snaking, *do not brake*, but ease off on the accelerator until it is controlled again.

When backing the trailer it is often easiest to think of steering the towing hitch. That is to say, turn the steering wheel the way you want the hitch end of the trailer to go, remembering to stop and pull forward to straighten up before trying again if there is any sign of the trailer jack-knifing.

Launching and recovery

Though launching and recovering a boat with a trailer need not be a difficult job, it is not always straightforward. Any softness of the 'hard'

and the car sinks in; any chop on the water and the boat surges about damaging herself on the trailer; any cross wind and it is hard to line up boat and trailer. In fact the initial consideration must be to select a hard or slipway that has a firm surface extending well off below the water's edge and, if possible, select a site sheltered from the prevailing wind.

Take care not to run the car so far into the water that the exhaust goes under. To avoid this, or when there is any doubt about the solidity of the hard, set the car on firm ground and run a tackle between the towing hitch and the trailer, using the jockey wheel and possibly the trailer winch to run the trailer down to the water. The same system can be used to recover the boat and trailer, but also you can secure the tackle (or use a simple rope) then drive the car forwards, thus drawing the trailer up the slope. Do mind that the jockey wheel does not bed itself in and get bent though.

With a piggyback trailer a soft surface is perhaps even more of a problem since the cradle's wheels are so much smaller than those on the trailer (except for the jockey wheel). However, as there are no worries about putting the cradle in the water, it can, if necessary, be left for a rising tide to lift the boat off. On hauling out, though, the problem can be severe and care must be exercised. If you do leave the cradle on a rising tide, run a line to something secure so that it can be pulled out when the boat floats off. Always move the car and trailer to a parking place well above high-tide mark once the boat is afloat.

If you are not going to be on board when the boat lifts off the trailer, make sure there is a line ashore so that she does not drift or blow away out of reach.

A trailer immersed and waiting for a boat to be floated on to it is a trailer lost, so secure marking poles to it that will guide you on to it as you pilot the boat back for hauling out. If there is a cross current or wind you will have to work quickly to pull the trailer up so that the boat settles squarely on the trailer without drifting off. Even if you plan to use a trailer winch to haul the boat on to the trailer it will still be necessary to keep the boat approximately aligned.

Do not forget when the trailer has been immersed to regrease the hubs before motoring home. Also always check tyre pressures before setting off.

18

Maintenance

Maintaining a boat in good order is wise in that it protects your inevitably heavy investment, but it also goes a long way towards ensuring the crew's safety and enjoyment. The work can be split into three main phases: fitting out at the beginning of the season; 'in commission' maintenance and laying up.

Fitting out

This is the time when it is easiest to put right anything to do with the hull or the more remote parts of the boat such as masthead fittings. Any major work that the boatyard will have to tackle should be put in hand early, preferably in fact at laying-up time so that they have the whole winter to do it. Too many owners leave everything to the last minute and yards and sailmakers are swamped.

Before the hull is antifouled it must be inspected carefully for any signs of damage, osmosis or corrosion of skin fittings. Any minor chips or blemishes can be filled with a gelcoat filler and rubbed down to fair them in once the filler has set. Replace spent sacrificial anodes that have wasted more than about 75 per cent. Chip rust from cast iron keels and repaint with antirust treatment. Inspect propeller for damage and look too at the shaft support bracket or rubber sealing gaiter round a Saildrive leg.

On deck, reseat any fittings or windows that leaked during last season. Check the fit and fastenings of all hatches and test the security of stanchions, pushpit and pulpit. Make sure sheet tracks are tightly fastened down as they suffer a lot of working during the season. Clear cockpit drains, scuppers and any drain holes on ventilators or other fittings.

The accommodation should be washed down, dried out and aired, paying particular attention to bilges and toilet compartments.

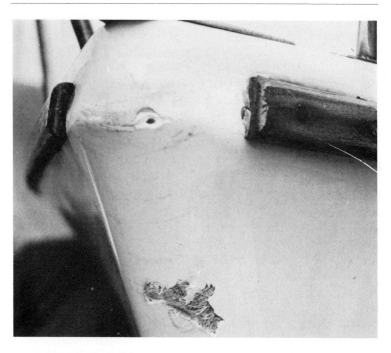

A chip out of the stem of a glass-fibre cruiser. A swinging anchor, a collision with a marina pontoon? Easily done and fairly easily repaired, but it must be repaired quickly to prevent more serious damage.

Alloy spars and stainless steel rigging require little maintenance, but a lot of checking and close inspection for hairline cracks or broken strands. Any such symptoms should be treated most seriously, calling on expert advice if necessary.

Halyards should be inspected for chafe and sheave boxes on masts for wear or damage. Overhaul all halyard winches following the maker's recommendations, particularly regarding cleaning and lubrication.

Remove tape from rigging screws, check them for bends, damaged threads, locking pins and so on then re-tape them to prevent damage to sails.

Sails should have all their stitching carefully checked and all broken threads and chafed or torn areas repaired. This is best done by a sailmaker, many of whom offer a sail valetting service. Batten pockets and hank fastenings are particularly vulnerable to chafe, so check them.

268

The engine needs a good general service including an oil change and probably a new set of plugs and points in the case of a petrol motor. Check fuel lines for damage and clear fuel filters. Make sure the engine mountings are secure and clean any corrosion off the electrics, particularly the battery terminals. It may be as well to put the battery on trickle charge for a day or two to make sure it is topped up. Clean out water intake strainers. Check engine control cables for wear.

Navigational

With so much in the way of electronic navaids being carried these days it is essential to make a special check of all such instruments and their wiring. Any faults in the instruments themselves will probably have to be dealt with by specialist service engineers, so get on to them in good time.

Renew out-of-date charts, almanacs and tide tables just before launching, remembering that popular charts may be sold out and need ordering. Make sure compass lights work and return the compass to its maker if any bubbles have appeared during the winter.

There must be a thousand other jobs to be done at fitting out time including having the liferaft serviced, re-marking anchor cables, painting dinghies and renewing flares. There are certainly too many to list them all here, but let it be said that much sailing time can be lost through skimping on fitting out time, so be warned.

In commission maintenance

This is very much like preventive medicine, where you are trying to stop trouble happening rather than waiting to have to cure it after it has happened. Everything needs maintenance throughout the season, largely because of chafe. This is the worst enemy of any gear on a boat. The constant movement invariably means one thing rubbing against another and if it goes unchecked something must give. This applies to sails and their stitching, ropes, fenders, clothing in lockers, tins of food rubbing on pipes and so on. Constant vigilance is needed.

Winches should be stripped down, cleaned of salt and lubricated regularly. Engine control cables must be greased and seacocks opened and closed regularly to ensure proper working and to make

Running repairs are often necessary no matter how careful your pre-voyage check. Maintenance is a full-time job and it helps to reduce the number of these emergency repairs that have to be made at sea.

sure they have not seized in one position. Batteries in torches and lifebuoy lights should be renewed periodically. Remember to buy new flares if they go out of date during the season. The occasional compass check is sensible to find any unexpected errors that may have crept in unnoticed. The engine, of course, needs regular servicing and batteries must be kept topped up.

The list again goes on and on, right down to cleaning out bilge pump strumboxes, limber holes and scuppers, laundering bedding and refastening loosened hanks and shackle pins. Keeping your boat up to scratch is time consuming but can be enjoyable and certainly promotes safety in parallel with peace of mind.

Laying up

If you do not let the boatyard remove weed and barnacles from the bottom of your boat with a high-pressure spray when they haul her out you are going to have to scrub and scrape hard, immediately, before the fouling has a chance to dry. Let it dry and you need a sander, it becomes a terrible job and one note of caution: never, never, dry sand antifouling, the dust is poisonous, always wet sand it – and that means by hand.

Drain off water tanks and leave seacocks open – assuming you are laying up ashore! – so that frost does not cause problems during the winter. Remove all food and perishables. Take off bunk cushions and bedding, charts, instruments, radios and electronic instruments that would attract thieves. Follow the makers' instructions for laying up the engine. Undress the mast, inspect all the rigging, grease the bottlescrews. Examine sails and put repairs in hand straightaway to save any last minute hitches in the spring.

The aim of laying up time is to reduce the amount of work needed early the following year to recommission the yacht. Thus time spent in 'winterizing' things, even in putting a quick coat of paint or varnish on wood that has rubbed bare, is time well spent. You will be in a much better position in the often poor spring weather to get back afloat on time with a fully prepared boat ready to go cruising again.

There are several books available on boat maintenance and fitting out that can be read for detailed advice in addition to the many articles published by yachting magazines. The guide, though, is to protect. Coat GRP topsides with a layer of polish, cover the boat with a good, waterproof cover leaving plenty of through ventilation but trying to guard against driving rain and snow. Coat electrical terminals with Vaseline (petroleum jelly), strip and grease seacocks, lubricate winches. In other words do all you can to prevent weathering or other damage that will require time to be spent putting it right in the spring.

19

Cruising further afield

After a couple of seasons spent cruising coastwise, getting to know your boat and learning your own capabilities, it is more than likely you will begin to yearn for broader horizons. A foreign trip. A day and night at sea. Two days and nights at sea. Really going offshore out of sight of land.

Initially it is only wise to limit yourself to short passages to reach foreign parts as there will be problems enough with strange ports and customs without having too many anxious hours wondering if your·navigation is going to provide you with the landfall you want. It is possible that you will have to find a larger boat in order to make cruises beyond your normal limits, but even if this is the case, provided that you have learnt and practised the arts of coastal cruising you should have few real problems in 'going foreign' for the first time.

RYA Yachtmaster tickets

The RYA runs a series of examinations to provide yachtsmen with 'tickets', proving they have reached various standards or levels of competence including crewing, sailing dayboats and, ultimately, the Yachtmaster Offshore and Yachtmaster Ocean. It is the Offshore certificate that is of particular relevance to family coastal cruising skippers as it should give them sufficient confidence in their abilities to make prudent cruises around the U.K. and European coastlines.

Gaining the certificate is broken into four stages: (a) the shore-based course; (b) the practical course; (c) seatime; (d) the final examination.

The shore-based course is most often completed by attending a series of evening classes at any of a large number of further education establishments. The practical course requires attendance at a recognized sailing school running the appropriate courses. Seatime is recorded in a special RYA log book as it is built up. Each entry must be signed by the skipper of the boat you are on and which, ironically, may be yourself. A substantial number of hours is required including both day and night sailing. Finally there is the main examination that includes an oral section given by an RYA approved examiner. After that you receive your Certificate and by then you will have earned it.

Details of the Yachtmaster syllabus are available from the Royal Yachting Association, Victoria Way, Woking, Surrey. It is a daunting syllabus but well worth pursuing in order to make sure you learn the essentials to go to sea safely and confidently.

Husband and wife outward bound on a 900 miles passage with their big catamaran. Such duos form the basis of many, many cruising crews and with good understanding between them they seem to handle almost all situations admirably. An able spouse can provide welcome relief at the helm during a long night allowing the 'other half' to catch up on navigation, cook a meal or get some rest.

Six and a half knots under reefed mainsail and small jib on a cold, close fetch in the Baltic. Note the stove pipe leading from a charcoal stove that barely managed to keep the temperature in the cabin above freezing. The deck remained almost permanently covered in ice for upwards of a week. All this was in the spring, so what autumn cruising in a cold climate would be like I hate to think; at least the harbours we visited were quiet. This was actually a small delivery trip of a new 34 ft cruiser from England to the east coast of Denmark and there was still some work needed on equipping the boat. Hence the use of a laboriously threaded lacing through the reef cringles. A proper set of slab reefing pennants would have made the job ten times easier.

Papers and regulations

When cruising in foreign waters or returning from abroad there are certain rules and regulations to comply with. In general, cruising yachts are subject to very few restrictions and are left pretty much alone by the authorities and this is exactly why you must be quite sure to comply with what regulations there are, otherwise governments will clamp down and spoil everyone's fun and freedom.

The basic papers you need to carry are: ship's papers, log book and passports for each member of the crew. The ship's papers are intended to prove ownership of the boat and are usually either a Certificate of Registry or an International Certificate of Pleasure Navigation, but in some cases a Customs form C1328 may suffice.

Besides these papers you will need to carry currency or traveller's cheques, a Q flag and the appropriate courtesy flag. The

274

Q flag (a yellow square) is flown in each country visited before customs are cleared. The courtesy flag for the country in whose waters you are sailing is flown throughout the period you are in those waters. It is a small version of the country's maritime ensign.

Before leaving your home port for a foreign cruise you fill in a Customs form C1328 as described in Chapter 11 and this, in addition to making re-entry to the U.K. easier, will help as additional proof of ownership while abroad.

On entering a country's territorial waters the appropriate courtesy ensign is hoisted (plus of course the Red Ensign) and also the Q flag, then once in port you wait until the Customs officials arrive to clear your vessel. In some small ports you may have to notify them by phone, but this should be mentioned in pilot books. Always make first for a recognized port of entry.

When returning home again you must also fly the Q flag on entry to U.K. territorial waters and until cleared by Customs.

One last word of warning – do not try to smuggle, and that includes animals, for rabies is a very real danger. You probably will not get away with smuggling attempts and any trouble will spoil the yachtsman's current good relationship with the Customs and Excise men. If you play fair with them they will play fair with you and that is the way to keep it.

Sextants and coastal navigation

The sextant, far from being the mystical beast it is usually portrayed as, is really a very simple instrument and is just as useful in coastal navigation as in offshore work. All it does is measure angles. So far as coastal navigation is concerned it can be used vertically or horizontally to measure the angular height of an object or the angular distance between two objects.

If you measure the angular height of a charted object and refer to a table in the almanac it is very simple to determine how far you are away from the object, i.e. your distance off. This distance, combined with a careful bearing will give a good position fix. Where there are three charted objects available a horizontal sextant angle fix may be made. This is one of the most accurate fixes possible and is often used by cartographers.

Knowing your distance off an object can be vitally important if, for instance, you need to be outside an offlying shoal that is unmarked

A sextant in use for measuring a vertical angle. There has always been an aura of mystery surrounding sextants but in reality they are simple measurers of angles and in this role they are very useful to the coastal navigator.

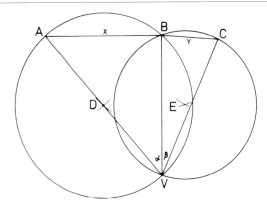

A horizontal fix with a sextant using three terrestrial objects.

or the other way round if you want to pass inshore of a submerged rock. In practice all that you do is measure the angular height of the object above sea level (or more accurately high water mark), note its charted height and refer to a table of distances off. When using a lighthouse as the object it should be remembered that you use the centre of the lantern not the actual top of the lighthouse, as the charted height is that of the light not the tower.

A horizontal fix is more complicated. The diagram above shows the set up with A, B and C as the charted objects and x and y as the distances between them. Angles alpha (α) and beta (β) are measured with the sextant, then they are used in conjunction with their associated distances x and y to find (from a table in the almanac again) the radii of the two circles. With compasses centred alternately on A and B (then B and C with the second radius) small arcs are drawn to intersect at D and E. Where these circles intersect – in this case at V – is the vessel's position. As I said, it is complicated, but it can be extremely accurate.

A simpler, though possibly less accurate, method is to construct the angles alpha and beta on a piece of tracing paper with a protractor and move this around on the chart until the lines pass through the objects marked on the chart.

In my opinion the ability to find distance off quickly and accurately is reason enough for carrying a sextant on board the family cruiser. Add to that the precision possible with a horizontal angle fix and no one can deny its usefulness.

Index